CW01500825

ACKNOWLEDG

This work would not exist but for the years of patient help and guidance from my *tres amigas*. Karen Syed rescued me from the slush pile once upon a time. Teresa Basile taught me, still teaches me this craft, and Hanley Kanar will never let me quit.

PHILIPPINES MAP

*The fictional village of Apostol

RUNNING WITH CANNIBALS

A Novel of the Philippine-American War

ROBERT W. SMITH

First Published: February 2022

ISBN: 9798273184602 Paperback

Cover design by Janet B. Taylor
Front cover image: "Filipino landscape with Nipa hut (1905)" Fabian de la Rosa (1869 -1937) with Filipino Peasant with salacot & rooster Tipos del Pais (1841) by Justiniano Asuncion
Back cover image: "Vista Del Rio De Patero" by Jose Honorato Lozano, 1821
Book layout and design by C and J Taylor

Published in the United States of America.

.

AUTHOR'S NOTE

With the exceptions of some public figures, including William Howard Taft, Arthur MacArthur, Emilio Aguinaldo, Frank Betron, and the U.S. Army defector, David Fagen (24th U.S. Colored Infantry Regiment), the characters in this work are fictional. The story itself is based on actual events from the Philippine-American War (1899-1902); specifically, the Balangiga Massacre. Filipinos generally refer to it as the Battle of Balangiga (09/28/1901). The protagonist in this novel was inspired by the life and experiences of Sgt. Frank Betron, 9th Infantry Regiment, a survivor and key actor in the battle.

PROLOGUE

Late fall, 1900, somewhere in Pittsburgh, Pennsylvania

The young man with no name peered nervously into the street from his window above the Broken Dagger Saloon. Atop the spartan, steel cot beside him lay the morning newspaper. It proclaimed his impending doom in bold letters for every soul brave enough to endure the brutal freeze in search of a newsstand: *Two in Custody, City-wide Hunt for Third Gettysburg Bridge Suspect.* The short walk for a paper had chilled him to the bone but was not without purpose. If any unwanted followers had spotted him, at least one would still be outside keeping an eye on the boarding house.

The frozen urban street below pulsated with life, commerce, and horseshit, even as a fouling, ashen cloud, fed by trails of filthy black smoke, shrouded the city with the stench of prosperity. As a general rule, freezing temperatures would keep the smell down, but not today, he thought. He could see no sign of police or Pinkertons among the throngs of horse-drawn carts, wagons, urchin peddlers, and street vendors crowding the cobblestone. Morning was as good a time as any to fade anonymously into the grit and poverty and greed of the wretched city he had never warmed to. But where to fade and how had suddenly become life-altering questions.

A determined knock on the door drew his attention from the window. "Who is it?" He regretted betraying a sense of urgency, but better that than panic.

"Mrs. Hubbel," came his landlady's voice. "I'd like a minute, Mr. Johnson."

Johnson. Was that the name he'd given her the other night? He would have to start thinking like a fugitive, and quickly, or it would be jail food for dinner. Easier said than done, he thought, for someone with no experience at evading police. The man grabbed his saddle bags from the bed, already loaded with his meager belongings, the sum total of his young life, and stuffed them under the cot lest she start asking questions. *If only I had a horse to carry them*, he thought.

He cracked open the door and the rail-skinny old lady eased through in a well-practiced move. She might have slid under the door at will, he thought. "I'll require the next three nights' rent in advance,

Mr. Johnson," she announced, all the while scanning the room. He was an average height at 5'6", but the woman was so short that her presence created the illusion of distance between them. Still, she was at least a full-blown busybody and at worst a dangerous threat. Either way, he'd worn out his welcome.

The man saw no point in broadcasting his plan, or lack of a plan, as her ignorance might buy him a day or so. Even a few hours head start on his journey could make a difference. He was down to his last six dollars, not counting an allotment for train fare, just in case, but reached into his pocket for some change. "I'll tell you what, Ma'am," he began, trying to recall the woman's name. "I'm picking up past due wages tonight from my old employer. How about I give you the eighty cents for tonight and we settle up in the morning?"

She started recounting the money in her palm and said, "Very well. It will be another three nights due tomorrow evening, Mr. Johnson." Her eyes began scanning again and landed on the cot, in the direction of the open newspaper. The headline stared up from the old mattress like a danger sign. "Good day, Mr...Johnson," she added, turning to leave.

The man eased the lock into place behind her and put his ear to the door, needing to hear her fading footsteps. Something about the way she said, *Mister... Johnson.* Yes, he'd stayed too long in this vile place with no purpose, no plan, hiding hopelessly in fear as the rats circled. Fear is not a plan, he thought, and panic is only slow death. *No more.*

Sitting on the cot, he tried to relax and collect his thoughts. The newspaper story, he knew, had decreased his chances of escaping the city. His former name and description would be everywhere by noon. They might as well have published his portrait with the story...*age twenty-four, long chestnut colored hair and deep blue eyes with a naked lady tattooed on each forearm.* The description was better than a photograph. Until a few days ago, the damn tattoos had been just an annoying reminder of his lost weekend. As long as he kept his coat on, he might be all right. The police would move on to more current pursuits eventually, he figured, but the Pinkertons would never stop coming, not so long as the world's wealthiest man had a nickel to keep them on the trail. *Damn him.*

From the cot, he watched as a beefy cockroach popped out from underneath a warped floorboard and settled defiantly between the man's feet, perfectly framed within a ray of light from the small window. The scenario looked oddly like a formal challenge, cockroach to man, executed in the dramatic style of a stage play or a public duel.

The challenger was defying this young man to crush him before the roach could disappear again behind the wall some eight feet away over an open floor. The young man sprang to his feet, launching an attack with the sole of his left shoe, but the roach only mocked his feeble effort, exploding across the floor like a fired musket ball. The courageous bug was safe inside the wall silently mocking him before the young man could even land a right sole to the floor.

Sometimes the simplest, most obvious plan is the best, he thought. The man with no name had to escape the city today by whatever means possible while he still had a trace of space and time left. He could figure out a better plan later from someplace safer, hopefully.

The police would have been to his real boarding house by now, the one he lived in on the other side of town, back when he answered to the old name. They wouldn't find anything because he didn't own anything. They wouldn't learn anything because no one knew anything about him. His few friends from work knew only that he came from rural Western Pennsylvania and had no family. *What else was there to know?* He thought.

Did he leave something there, perhaps? A clue, however small? *No, nothing. Impossible.* Three days ago, he had a name. Now he didn't. End of story. He'd chosen this hovel of a boarding house randomly. His only possession was a photograph, one damn likeness from his whole life, and it never left his person. Besides, the image pictured him as an eight-year-old boy standing with his father. He'd recovered it from the rubble of the fire so many years ago. As long as he had the picture, his father lived.

Pop stood tall in the faded old portrait; tall as old wounds would allow a proud, time-worn soldier to stand. The old man and the old Union uniform, both faded by time and trials but bonded by honor and courage. Thank God Pop was not around to witness this nightmare. He reached for his billfold seeking assurance. There it was, safe and wrapped in brown paper, a loving hand on the boy's shoulder as the youngster stubbornly cradled a cumbersome, old cavalry sword.

He grabbed the saddlebags from under the cot, but something drew him back to the window where at once he spotted the hat across the street in front of the freight office. He'd seen that hat at the newsstand this morning but dismissed it, a black fiddler's cap, popular among Eastern Europeans and seafaring types, but seldom seen in the urban crush of big cities. The bearded man with broad shoulders was leaning against a canopy post, struggling to light a cigar in the cold wind with no obvious reason for lingering. The heavy woolen greatcoat, complete with a long cape-style collar marked him as ex-military, as former soldiers were known to dye the popular garment black for transition to civilian wear.

A sick feeling churned in his stomach, like that of a man who'd blindly taken his first step over a cliff in the dark. The unfortunate soul could almost feel the soft blades of grass drooping teasingly over the ledge, only inches from his outstretched hand as he mourned a fatal mistake, but in that moment, the inevitability of his fate cruelly mocked the effort.

With his coat buttoned up and the saddlebags over his shoulder, the man reached for the old newsboy hat on the table before leaving. The wavy, chestnut hair would be a dead giveaway for anyone searching by description, and he tucked it in the best he could under the cap. In the same instant, the flimsy door to his room imploded from its hinges as a parade of uniformed police poured in behind it, and the man with no name faced his rendezvous with destiny. With two friends surely facing a hangman's noose, surrender equaled slow suicide. In a split second, he chose the cliff over the noose. Just maybe, he thought, he could fly.

The window was barely large enough to accommodate his slender frame, and he proved it the hard way, headfirst through shattering glass. Like the man grasping in vain for the ledge, he reached instinctively back for the window, knowing this was his last mistake and praying only for instant death.

The canopy withstood his impact long enough to break the fall and drop his twisted form almost gingerly onto the plank walkway, complete with his saddlebags and cap. He'd forgotten it was there. Struggling to untangle himself from the Broken Dagger canopy, he could see the man in the hat, drawn pistol, charging from across the street as a crowd began to gather. A noticeable limp did not seem to slow him down. More importantly, the man could see him, clearly.

4

Leaping to his feet, he sprinted into the bitter cold wind like a frightened deer from the hunter. A strange feeling overtook him, like this had happened before, like he had lived the same nightmare. Yes. He was running from the fire again, and it was just as real, just as terrifying. A shot! Then another. Down one street, up another, finally along the Monongahela River toward the point where the rivers meet to form the Ohio. Housing and shops gave way to enormous industrial facilities across the river. On and on, he ran through the morning, avoiding major streets and attractions.

The city was largely a mystery to him but, nearing the start of The Ohio, he finally seized on a point of reference. A familiar sight appeared on the opposite bank of the Allegheny. Exposition Park stood on the river's north bank, encircling the only plot of open ground in an ocean of small factories and mills. He remembered going to the Pirates game there two years ago with a group from the job. He liked the Pirates and followed them faithfully in the newspaper. The train allowed an easy commute from his boarding house, but twelve hours at the mill six days a week always seemed to drain him of the energy to socialize, maybe meet a girl, and find a place to feel at home. No matter now.

The man came to a bridge with a trace of shelter beneath massive, weathered Oak beams, snow free, but with neither warmth nor peace. He could burrow and hide like a rat, waiting for darkness to set him loose. But a rat has a plan, he thought, forage and store and dig and flourish. *Try to sleep for a few hours,* he told himself. *You will think of something.*

AS STREETLAMPS BEGAN TO BATTLE THE COMING DARKNESS ONE by one, he stood near the intersection of the three rivers, where water blocked his escape from the city. The man turned right, back along the Allegheny into an area of shops and hotels, wandering in a haze of fading hope.

How did all this happen? And why to him? Turning himself in to the police seemed like the best option now. He wasn't brave enough for actual suicide. Dejection and pain made the noose seem more palatable and prolonging this torturous fox hunt would only elongate his suffering. Hanging seemed a merciful death now, based on everything he'd seen and heard, as long as they did it right, with a real hangman and gallows and such. Not like in all those photographs he'd seen of Negroes lifted off the ground and swinging by crushed necks from trees with bulging eyes and disjointed heads peeling from shoulders like spoiled fruit from a branch.

Witnessing a live hanging was not among his modest life experiences as a simple farm boy and worker, but pictures and stories were enough to show him there were worse ways to be executed, allowing for proper protocols, of course.

Shivering from the sweat-soaked clothing under his coat, bruised and exhausted from the ordeal, he spotted the huge vertical sign for the Union Hotel. It would be his oasis in this hour of need, for better or worse, the place where his fate would be decided, for he could no longer run.

With darkness closing in, the temperature was sure to keep dropping and, in this condition, death would find him before morning. A ravishing thirst plagued him, challenging every step. He knew he must be hungry but felt nothing from his gut. His last meal was yesterday. A small diner occupied a part of the brick building's street-front facade. The diner was well lit in the descending nightfall, but his failing senses could discern only outlines of blurry human forms inside.

A big coal wagon behind two gigantic horses rumbled by slowly to block his view. Just ahead of him, a merchant appeared from a bookstore. While locking his door, the old man turned a curious gaze directly on the man with no name, who suddenly realized he was standing beneath a glimmering gas lamp. He was attracting attention now, he knew, and his hand was called. The man had seen his face. Time to show his cards.

With a sense of resignation, even relief, he passed behind the coal wagon, across the cobblestone to the front of the café. He could see a well-dressed couple seated at the counter, hotel workers maybe, and a uniformed man enjoying a late meal at one of the tables along the wall, an electric trolley operator, he thought. A man in a white chef's hat stood behind the counter with his back to the window. Like it or not, he thought, the Hanover Café would be his refuge in this storm.

He stumbled into the place and settled at the counter, near a rear door and apart from the other customers. The warmth of the room nearly robbed him of consciousness. *I must look like a disaster,* he thought. Someone was talking to him, the chef hat. If he could just warm up for a minute more, catch his breath. Everything around him slowed down. People and things began to move in all directions. Women, two, he thought…or…

"WE RECKONED YOU MIGHT SLEEP CLEAR THROUGH SUNDAY," said the female voice from above. It was a quiet, no-nonsense voice, the perfect voice, he thought, for the roundish face and big brown eyes coming into focus. She held a cup of something. "Try to sit up if you're able, young man. We'll get some tea into you. When you feel better, I'll give you a nice breakfast." These were orders, not questions. He knew the difference.

The man suddenly realized he was in someone's living quarters, naked under a blanket with bandages around his right shoulder. He said, "Where are my clothes?"

"My daughter is washing them," the woman replied. "The shirt is trashed with blood, but the bullet just grazed you. I cleaned it up nicely. We'll give you one of my husband's shirts."

"Why are you helping me?" the young man asked, struggling to sit up as the woman adjusted the pillows.

His answer came from a deep male voice across the room. A slender teenaged girl stood beside the man, holding his trousers. The old man from the café had lost the white hat and wore a sparkling clean white linen shirt beneath clear brown eyes. He sported a scar across his left cheek and was thumping toward the bed on a peg leg. Despite being short of stature with a missing limb, he walked with authority. "It's what Jesus would do," said the old man, "Besides, I just happened to see the photograph in your waistcoat. I served in the 83d Regiment, U.S. Colored Troops in The War," he announced proudly. "Might have even been in a scuffle or two aside your daddy. I saw from the photograph he was 62d Pennsylvania."

The Negro was a distinguished looking gentleman, the young man thought, and carried himself proudly, still a dangerous thing, even in Pennsylvania. He was old, at least fifty-five, but impeccably groomed with fine-looking round, silver-rimmed spectacles and a perfectly trimmed mustache that just turned the corners of a wide, natural smile. "Yes. I'm beholden to you, Sir…and your wife," the young man said.

The old man waved him off. "Nonsense. Might have been with your daddy at The Battle of Hanover as well." Then the old soldier held up his palm. "The cause that bound us in that terrible and holy time outweighed our many differences. But don't tell me. Don't say his name because I don't want to know yours...although I'm pretty sure I know it already. Didn't need to see the tattoos."

The youngster already knew that he knew but the knowledge stirred no anxiety. Somehow, he had landed in the hands of a good man. "I don't have a name anymore," he said.

The old fellow sat beside him on the bed, nodded a couple of times approvingly, and said, "I think that's just as well, Boy. If I recognized you from the papers, it's a sure bet others have as well. At some point the coppers and the Pinkerton's will be swarming around here. By the way," he added, holding out his hand, "My name is Jimmy Jeffries. This is my wife, Sarah. We both work here for the Union Hotel. My old colonel is the hotel manager. We run this little café. I cook and my ladies do the waitressin' and cleanin' and such. We live here."

Before the young man could respond, the door opened, and Sarah entered from the restaurant. "Got a man out in the café askin' questions about the white boy," she announced. "I told him wait for mah boss."

The man sat up and pulled the blanket off his chest before remembering he was naked. Reaching for the trousers, he said, "I got to..."

Jimmy clamped onto the kid's shoulder, holding an index finger to his perfect mustache. Authoritative brown eyes said, *Don't move or speak. I will deal with this.*

The man had lived with the fear for three solid days, since learning of the charges, but those next few minutes were the most terrifying because now his fate was completely in the hands of others. With no windows to breech, no means to fight back, the man was completely impotent. And what if he did somehow manage to escape into the street? He would be like a treed coon awaiting a merciful bullet.

But the old Negro came back through the door alone, promptly flashing a magnetic smile. It was unique in some unidentifiable way, the fugitive thought. "I think he believed me," Jimmy announced. "Told him you was here but I threw you out. I tried to find out what they knew, but the man wasn't about to answer my questions, and I didn't want him getting suspicious."

"Police?" the young man asked. "What did he look like?"

"Pinkerton, around forty, funny cap and a beard."

It was a bad omen, thought the young fugitive, trying to pull up his breeches under the blanket. "Well, I'd better leave you folks be," he said. "If you could direct me to the B & O station, I'll try to catch their train to Chicago. Maybe I can figure something out when I get there."

The old man shook his head, then laughed. "Boy, you'll never get as far as that station, let alone ride off in a fancy passenger train, even if Jesus hisself buys you a train ticket. Pinkertons will be all over that station now. I got me a better idea."

NATURE GRACIOUSLY PROVIDED THEIR COVER WITH A MOONLESS night as the two men slipped out of the Union Hotel into the street just after midnight. Making their way circuitously through the alleys and back streets on foot, they crossed the Monongahela River over one of the countless bridges into a massive and chaotic complex of railroad yards. They stopped beside an old storage shack only a few feet from rails, and the old man pointed to a tower at the bottom of an enormous man-made hill. "That's where they make up the outgoing trains," he said. "All the P & LE freight trains go north to Lake Erie. They always deadhead a couple of dozen flat cars and box cars for freight from the inbound ships. I'll get you close, then you on your own. Now, let me hear you explain your plan, Boy."

The fugitive, delighted to finally have a real plan, ticked off the major points like the star student he never was. "I duck into one of the box cars and stay out of sight until we hit Lake Erie. Then, I sign onto an outbound freighter to Chicago."

"Yes. Yes. They always looking for healthy boys to shovel that coal on the ships. That gets you to Chicago. Then what?"

The young man reached for the letter in his coat pocket, to make certain it was there mostly. "Then I find your son in Chicago at this address and give him this letter. He will get me a new job out of the country."

Jeffries nodded. "Right, but you need a new name first. Remember! Nothing flashy or fancy pants. Some normal, maybe a white trash name like Buck or Billy Bob. And don't tell me what name you choose. I don't want to know."

Suddenly, the old man raised his index finger for silence and pointed to the right of the tower, where an armed guard was patrolling along the track. Whispering, he said, "We have to be careful about the guards. You'll need to cross an open area to board the car."

"One question," said the fugitive. "Why won't you tell me where your son works?"

Jeffries looked annoyed for the first time, but in a schoolmaster kind of way. "Damn, Boy," he whispered. "I told you he works for the government. It don't matter a hog's holler what he does. You just give him that envelope with my letter. The address is on there, clear as day. He will do the rest."

When they were within fifty yards and clear of the guards, the old man offered his hand. "Good luck to you, Boy," he said.

The man in search of a name could not resist one last question. "Why are you doing this for me, Mr. Jeffries?"

"Let's just say it's my leg, Boy."

The young man looked at the peg leg and, almost casually, asked, "Where did you lose the leg?" expecting to hear the name of some famous battle, but the answer confused him.

Jeffries smiled. Because his natural mouth looked like a smile, it was a powerful thing to see the smile when assembled with effort, as the corners of the mustache lifted like little angel wings. "Same place you lost your innocence," he said. "God forgive me, but I have no love for that man, the way he treat folks."

He knew instantly that Mr. Jeffries once worked at the steel mill and had lost his leg somehow in that toxic and oppressive working environment. The old man's sympathies were solidly with the labor organizations. In that moment, the whole picture became as clear as the young man's good fortune—up to this point anyway. "Goodbye, Mr. Jeffries," he said. "Thank you."

Jeffries grabbed the young man's arm, and the brown eyes narrowed. A second or two passed before he spoke. "You have good in you, Boy. I can see that. It's wild and buried deep like rich virgin soil under a sea of grass. But if you manage to live long enough, listen to it, and let it guide you. Over time, it will show you who you are. Until then, remember, the wealthier the man, the longer the reach.

It could be many years before he forgets about you. Could be you'll have to wait til he dies."

Then Jimmy pressed a few paper notes into the young man's hand and wrapped his fingers tightly around them. "You'll need a few dollars," he said. "If one of the guards catch you, likely he'll look the other way for a dollar."

The young man had to think for a few seconds but couldn't make heads or tails out of the *virgin soil* part, not yet anyway. Jimmy Jeffries was a very smart man, so the kid would think about it some more on the long box car ride. He nodded a final goodbye to his new friend and slipped away, across a field of tracks, a man still running for his life but this time armed with a brand-new name.

CHAPTER ONE

Six months later, in the rainforest, twenty miles south of Manila, the Philippines

Exhausted, Corporal Ethan Cooper took a knee, using his rifle for support. As he shed the wet campaign hat to dry it over the rifle barrel, a torrent of perspiration poured from chestnut hair down his dirt-caked face into a pair of tired blue eyes. His sweat-soaked cheeks bathed greedily in the mid-day sunlight, a just reward for a day spent humping dark jungle trails and hacking through a solid wall of vines in a steady rain. A small sip of water and he was a new man.

He had stumbled onto the perfect observation post, towering over the peaceful coastal village below. He could even see the women gutting fish on the beach beside the drying racks. Turning to his companion, Private Alamo Jones, he said, "Okay, Jonesy, as the youngest man on the ridge, you rate the privilege of humping back down the hill with a report for the lieutenant. Tell him we found a village. I'll wait for the patrol here where I can keep an eye on the place, get an idea of what's going on. We did all the hard work on the way up here, so you'll have a decent trail to follow."

"Sure, Ethan, I'll head out now."

"There's no hurry, so take your time. You got water left?"

"Plenty."

Their mission was to track down the insurgents who ambushed an army supply convoy on the trail to Manila, killing two troopers in the process. Lieutenant Hobbs had sent Ethan and Jonesy ahead to follow their trail and, hopefully, find their camp or staging point. This village was as close as they would come, Ethan figured, but Hobbs would be disappointed. It was just a scattering of families eking out a living quietly on the sea. No suspicious characters, no commotion, and no sign of the stolen mules.

Resting his rifle against a tree, Ethan flopped his bone-weary carcass onto a patch of thick jungle grass along the high ridge. He could easily have dozed off in the sunlight, but Hobbs was not the forgiving type when it came to sleeping on duty.

Ethan had been in the Philippines for over five months now, and, by and large, Jimmy Jeffries' son had delivered as promised. The man with no name would never have chosen the army, with all the discipline and the rules and the vulgarity, but the anonymity it provided was a precious commodity. Ethan would tough it out for as long as necessary, even reenlist if he had to.

ETHAN WAS BARELY AWAKE AND RESTING AGAINST A TREE WHEN he heard the lieutenant's voice. "All right, Cooper," said Hobbs, "let's hear your report."

"Well, Sir," he began, collecting his thoughts, "we tracked the raiding party as far as the river where the tracks veered off. Looks like four or five bad guys. I'd say they're back in the interior hills safe and sound by now. You wanted to know if there was a village nearby. This is the only one," he added, pointing down the ridge toward the shore, "but there's no indication at all that the insurgents came from this village. I'm sure Jonesy showed you where their tracks led off into the hills in another direction."

His report did not appear to please the baby-faced Lieutenant Hobbs. "Damn it to hell, Cooper," he chided. "We have two empty supply wagons and two dead men. There were two boxes of new Krags in one of those wagons. I'm not going back to the captain with a report like that. You haven't even been into that village. You can't possibly know those people are innocent."

"I'm only reporting what I saw, Sir."

Hobbs was clearly annoyed and maybe a bit over-anxious. "Sergeant Tours," he said, "come with me. You too, Cooper."

While the other men rested, the three moved up the ridgeline a bit with the telescope to have a better look. It was hardly necessary, Ethan thought. The whole village, what little there was of it, was laid out right below them. Eight or ten nipa huts, houses built on stilts with grass, bamboo, and coconut palms, spread out around a partially cleared common area. It still looked like what it was, a sleepy fishing village.

Hobbs strutted back to the small clearing like the fate of the Union was in the balance. He looked nervous too. The lieutenant, Ethan reminded himself, had joined the outfit only a couple of weeks ago in Manila.

As Hobbs laid out his plan to enter the village, Martin Tours whispered to Ethan, "This won't be pretty, my friend."

"What's he going to do?" Ethan asked softly.

Marty hadn't heard him and addressed Hobbs directly. "Sir, does anyone know how to say, *Come out of the hut* in Tagalog? It would be helpful. I just can't remember. It's been a while since I burned a village."

Nobody spoke up. It was a miracle, Ethan thought, that Marty managed to keep that third stripe, but everyone in the outfit knew how he'd gotten it, with suicidal bravery. One of these days, Marty would poke fun at some officer as smart as he was. Then again, Ethan hoped, maybe not.

Hobbs seemed to think for a second, then said, "Say it in English, loud, and wave the rifle barrel. They'll get the message." Hobbs clearly was not the man.

While Hobbs didn't recognize the sarcasm, Ethan didn't like the sound of it, but he fell into line directly behind his friend, Sergeant Martin Tours. It had become kind of his natural, unspoken place over the past several months. They had hooked up last winter when Ethan was assigned to the unit straight from San Francisco.

Roughly a half dozen "friendly" troopers, mostly savvy veterans, gravitated toward Marty's group without a word spoken, and the two groups moved carefully down the ridge. Marty's group split off just inside the jungle's edge, hacking slowly through a solid wall of jungle to take position from the south. When they were in position, Marty whispered to Ethan, "I hope Hobbs behaves himself." In a slightly louder whisper, he said to the men, "Just keep a good angle on the other group. I don't want anyone taking a .30 cal from a Krag rifle."

They waited in dead silence. Then Marty whispered, "I know damn well those insurgents didn't come from the village. The supply wagons use that trail every week. Nobody ever bothered them before."

"I told Hobbs that, Marty," Ethan replied, "so what's he going to do?"

Marty gave him a scolding look and said, "Come on, Ethan. You know Hobbs doesn't care where they came from or where they went. The village is *conveniently located* to pay for the attack on our supply wagons and the killing of our men. You haven't been around long enough to see what we do to *conveniently located* villages."

Ethan was light on experience, but not stupid. He was apparently going to see something new today, something more involved than the brief jungle skirmishes or endless dead-end patrols that generally resulted with one or two American casualties. He knew Marty well enough to know the man had just given him an ominous warning. The army had given Ethan another life as a new man but, truth be told, he didn't know much about that man. Apparently, all that was about to change.

Ethan heard the single shot in short order, and the group moved out from the thick jungle eight abreast, Marty in the middle, walking in the open, midway between the lines of huts. They took the villagers completely by surprise. Five or six women around the town well scattered in chaos toward the various huts. A few old men rambled down bamboo stairs from the huts carrying bolos, obviously to defend their homes. Two of them immediately collapsed in a hail of gunfire from the north, as children scurried for the safety of thick jungle. Ethan had still not seen a firearm.

Smoke rose from the north side of the village. To his right, Ethan spotted Private Alamo Jones on the front steps of the nearest nipa hut, screaming at the top of his voice and waving his Krag. Two women and a boy hurried down the steps, hands up in terror and crying hysterically. Another trooper was already splashing coal oil on the hut.

A burst of flame down the trail, then another and another. Two troopers were torching one of the last huts as Ethan and Jonesy approached the front doorway. They both shouted in response to agonizing pleas from inside. Ethan kicked in the flimsy bamboo door just as the flame roared, engulfing the dried kindling structure immediately in an explosion of flame and thick smoke. "Come out, you fools," he screamed. He tried Spanish. "Sal de ahi."

Without warning, Jonesy walked straight into the flaming hut and emerged seconds later, coughing, hair on fire and uniform shirt smoldering, behind a group of four terrified but unharmed villagers.

Ethan thought if he'd stopped to piss, he'd have missed the whole operation. It was over that quickly. With the entire village in flames and already awash in the nauseating aroma of cooked human flesh, seven or eight troopers stood near the hut guarding a circle of about twenty "prisoners." As Jonesy approached with the four natives, one of them yelled, "There goes a nigger lover in action." Most of the others laughed in a show of contempt for Jonesy's actions.

Ethan didn't respond. He was in this army to get along and mark time. There was no upside to defending Jonesy's stupidity.

"Who gave the order to burn the village?' Marty asked no one in particular.

Hobbs was approaching the group from the north and hadn't missed the question. "I did," he announced. "We were attacked by insurgents armed with bolos. Besides, we found a storage hut at the north end of the village. It had three bushels of rice. Rice was on the supply manifest for the wagons. The rice is proof this village was at least supporting the insurgents and hiding some of them."

"What are your orders now, Sir?" Marty asked.

"Burn everything to the ground and kill the animals. I saw two carabao back near the north end. Leave nothing of use to the enemy. Set up a perimeter on the beach for the prisoners. I'll send two men back to the post to request water transport. We'll load them on our transport steamer when it arrives tomorrow. Nice work, men. I will make sure the captain gets a full report of your gallant actions here today." Then Hobbs looked at Marty and said, "You're a veteran. Who taught you to walk straight up into a fight out in the open like you were going to church?"

One of the hard cases laughed and another one said, "It's what he does. Tours thinks he has magical powers that shield him from bullets."

"There were no soldiers in this village," Marty replied softly.

"What about the bodies?" Someone asked.

"Count them and burn them with everything else," Hobbs answered.

As Ethan and Marty walked away from the group, Marty said, "Three bushels of rice would barely feed this village for a week. By the time Hobbs makes his report, it will be a hundred and three bushels and hand-to-hand fighting." He looked at Ethan and added, "Did you learn anything today?"

"I'm in the infantry," he replied coldly. "I do what I'm told."

"Well, your buddy Jones may be a few cards short of a deck, but he's got spine."

After five months in the jungle, Ethan's body had finally adjusted to the oppressive heat and humidity, the dirt, the incessant rain, the abject poverty, but this smell of cooked people was new and clung to his wet clothing like the spray of a dozen skunks. He would never forget that smell, he knew, and grabbed the bandana from his pocket, tying it tightly around his nose to block the stench.

"It won't help," Marty said quietly. "Some of these men love that smell. Most just get used to it. Those are the ones I truly pity."

EARLY THE NEXT MORNING, THE DETAIL AND THEIR CACHE OF ragged prisoners boarded the gunboat USS Laguna de Bay for the journey back to camp. A steady breeze on the water tempered the humidity, offering the men a chance for a refreshing nap on deck. Ethan took a spot along the bulkhead, near the rail, next to Private Alamo Jones.

The "prisoners," basically a pitiful herd of about twenty women, children and old men, were locked below deck for the day-long voyage back to the company HQ. By later afternoon, the old gunboat was approaching the river mouth from Manila Bay and the group of soldiers was seated on the deck around the bulkhead.

"What we fixin' 't do with all these women and kids?" Jonesy asked.

"What's it to you?" Ethan asked.

"Just curious, I reckon."

"They have places for them around the outskirts of Manila. They call them *settlement camps*. That's what I heard." He'd heard a lot more about the camps but saw no point discussing it.

The old Spanish fort with its stone walls and gun ports covered the mouth of the river like a blanket and even a lowly corporal couldn't fail to recognize the tactical advantage of its location in a real war, an old-fashioned war. In a war like that, an entire invasion force could be killed without ever reaching the shore or firing their rifles or even setting eyes on the jungle. This was not one of those wars.

Dozens of great merchant ships lay moored in the bay, just beside the fort, outside the river mouth. The river meandered east from its mouth through the city and past the old, walled, Seventeenth Century city of *Intramuros* on the south side. A line of carabao-drawn carts was visible, waiting in traffic to enter the diminutive, arched gateway into the old city from the river side.

While they were talking, Jonesy removed the entire bolt mechanism from his Krag-Jorgensen rifle. Ethan wasn't sure why. Then he could see Jonesy had chosen this moment to clean the Krag's bolt assembly.

Disassembling the bolt was tricky, even for old veterans. It was a tight, finely crafted mechanism, and disassembly required focus and a stable platform. If you mishandled the firing pin on reassembly, even a little after compressing the spring, both parts could launch twenty or thirty yards, like a pebble from a slingshot.

"Jonesy," Ethan scolded, "get that rifle back together before you shoot your firing pin into the river."

"Okay, Ethan. So what are them camps like?" Jonesy asked.

"Sometimes I think you just set out in the morning to annoy me, Jonesy." Ethan replied.

"Look, Ethan," Jonesy said, pointing. "Them *cabrios* is bad tempered like a Texas Longhorn. Ain't they heard o' horses?"

"Carabaos, Jonesy. They call 'em carabaos. They're not even close to Longhorns. They're domesticated."

"Like horses?"

"Sort of, I guess. They use 'em for everything. Plowing the fields, riding, everything. They'll even cook one up in a big pit sometimes for a festival."

Jonesy's baby-smooth face looked to curl up in a passel of wrinkles. His mop of curly black hair always hung limp in the humidity and drooped over his eyes. He smiled, inevitably revealing a half dozen spaces once occupied by young teeth. "Be like eatin' your horse, I 'spect."

"What?" Ethan said.

"Eatin' one them carabao things."

Good Lord. Would he ever just shut up? "Give it a rest, Jonesy. And when we get back, go straight to the medical tent and have those burns tended. Then get someone to cut that hair. You look like a sheep dog after work."

Everywhere on the river, children bathed, women washed their traditional clothing and carabao did what nature commanded. Drinking that river water, Ethan knew, would be a soldier's quickest ticket to Hades.

18

"Ethan, git a look at that gal holding the net on the left over there." Jonesy said, pointing. "If'n that dress was any higher or wetter you could see her religion. Sure got her some fine gams too."

Her religion, Ethan thought. Only the Lord knew what Jonesy was doing in the army and only his mama knew why. Ethan pegged his age at no more than seventeen. The boy's slight stature and slender frame were likely permanent. He was from somewhere in Texas, tough and fit, but maybe the most annoying youngster this side of the equator.

Jonesy's father was old and had apparently served in Lee's Texas Brigade in The War. According to Jonesy, the family had not fared well during the Reconstruction. It was all unsolicited jabber accumulated from Jonesy's non-stop trap yapping. Ethan never wanted to hear it and Jonesy never stopped spouting it.

Jonesy obeyed orders generally but harbored an unhealthy attraction to local potations. Ethan was also concerned that the youngster's actions yesterday had earned him enemies among the hardened killers of the company. To the men, Jonesy had made a display of risking his own life to save some goo goos. It made him different and, in the infantry, different was dangerous.

With the exception of rare examples like Martin Tours, the pack wouldn't tolerate anyone "different," anyone whose actions or beliefs threatened the pack mentality. The term "nigger lover" was reserved for a specifically loathsome breed of outcasts. Jonesy would need to be careful going forward.

"This is Manila, Jonesy," Ethan cautioned. "You will see that kind of *religion* everywhere, Boy. Just make sure you don't see the nasty itch that can come with it."

Suddenly, the young woman in the wet skirt smiled and waved to the troopers on the passing gunboat, triggering an outburst of hoots and hollers that would wake the dead. The girl's mother promptly dragged her from the river by the arm, earning a round of playful catcalls. But the mother was wise, Ethan thought, wisdom gained through experience, most likely. *Americans bring only death and fire*, she knew.

"The niggers here around Manila is mostly all civilized now. Right, Ethan?" Jonesy asked.

"Jonesy, I swear you coulda' drove Lazarus back into the tomb with all that bothersome chatter. Now, I don't mean to be persnickety, but you don't even make sense sometimes." Ethan already regretted losing his patience with the young trooper. "They just gave up fightin' around here for the most part. I don't know all the details of it, and I don't think of it that way. Now, I don't want to see that bolt out of your Krag unless it's in a tent or in your barracks. And remember! Captain told you directly not to use that word to describe the locals. I don't hold with the word either. It doesn't even make sense, since they're not even black. Now wrap it up."

Just past *Puente España*, the Bridge of Spain, the river snaked to the south and back north again, teeming with commerce. The barges everywhere were loaded with abaca, coconuts, and bananas.

A few more miles upriver, civilization thinned out in favor of jungle and Ethan recognized the layout of Camp Sheridan on the south bank.

Approaching the dock at Camp Sheridan, Jonesy laid his reassembled bolt mechanism on the half-rotted deck wrapped carefully in an oil rag while he wiped inside the bolt chamber. Before he could reach down for the bolt, a filthy Russet shoe skimmed the deck beside him, launching the package overboard and the bolt, firing pin, spring and all, disappeared beneath the dirty water.

Both men looked up to see a smiling Private Josiah Mason nonchalantly launching a chaw spit over the side. He turned to Jonesy with brown dribble creeping inevitably toward his chin and smiled maliciously. "Sorry 'bout that, Reb. Didn't see that rag. Hope it weren't nothin' important."

From nowhere, a hand locked onto the collar of Mason's shirt from behind and another to his service belt. In the time it takes for a sweetheart to unbutton her overalls, Mason was lying prone on the deck beside his Krag with a filthy Russet shoe on his neck.

"You're meaner n' a dog with a sore ear, Mason," growled Marty Tours, smiling down on Mason's contorted face.

With his foot still planted firmly on Mason's neck, Marty calmly picked up the man's Krag, removed the bolt assembly from the stock and handed it to Jonesy. "It's not as clean as the one in the river, Boy, but you can fix that later."

Ethan simply gave Marty a nod of approval as Mason scurried off to find less risky amusement. Killing had a way of making good men mean, Ethan thought, and mean men damn near intolerable. Jonesy was an exception, and the difference could get him killed.

Life in the infantry appealed mainly to the most hardened sort, Ethan had learned quickly as a naïve youngster. Such men confused kindness with weakness and bravery with contempt, all qualities to be devoured or destroyed. Private Jones would either figure it out for himself—or not. As they prepared to disembark, Ethan put a hand on Jonesy's shoulder and said, "Keep your mind where it's supposed to be, Private Jones, and keep your damn mouth shut."

As for the young corporal from Western Pennsylvania, this patrol had shown him that getting to know the man named Ethan Cooper might prove a painful task.

CHAPTER TWO

The five company NCOs, including Ethan, were billeted in two bedrooms of a handsome and strategically placed guest house, part of the original estate, less than thirty yards from the villa on high ground. Ethan was exhausted but pleased to be back at Camp Sheridan from the patrol. After a shower and a hot dinner, he was ready for a good night's rest.

"Beats sleeping in the jungle," said Marty Tours, Ethan's bunkmate, as he flopped onto the Spanish-style, carved-wood bed beside the lamp table. The bed was big, big enough to fit two standard army-issued mattress pads. Each man had been issued one pad before leaving patrol and neither had yet to enjoy the fine new digs. Ethan preferred a pad directly on the bamboo floor.

Marty was a slight character of rigid posture, a bit taller than Ethan, with a generous crop of sand colored-hair but looked suspiciously older than his fellow sergeants, at least thirty-five, Ethan thought. Somewhat of a mystery to men and officers alike, the man was well-spoken and obviously educated. He professed to hail from New York, but Ethan had concluded the claim was more likely a part of some tomfoolery with the Army. It sounded like a Midwestern accent.

Alamo Jones appeared in the open doorway and said, "In case you fellas is interested, they say the company's mail is in Manila. Should catch up with us tomorrow. The boys is purdy excited."

Mail call only interested Ethan because it was the best way to find newspapers. Families would forward them to their loved ones from all over the country. A few times, he'd even gotten ahold of The Pittsburgh Post-Gazette. Last he'd heard, the world's richest man, his personal nemesis, was just getting richer and fatter every day. At sixty-two, the sidewinder could live another twenty years feeding on lobsters and steak and French wine. But you never know, he thought.

Marty never expressed interest in the subject of mail unless he'd ordered some book or other and was expecting delivery. Like Ethan, his name was never heard at mail call. Speculation abounded in saloons and around campfires regarding Marty's former life.

By one account, Marty had been a professor somewhere and joined the army in New York under an assumed name to avoid prosecution for killing his wife. In another, he was an officer who had deserted under fire in the Indian Wars and reentered the fray as a common soldier under an assumed name to seek redemption. It was a subject Ethan scrupulously avoided for fear of drawing unwanted attention to himself. Anonymity required careful nurturing; Ethan knew.

The ranks were filled with these second-chance soldiers, Ethan understood, not to mention wanted fugitives, like himself. In his meager experience, such a man would either desert again, go to prison or conquer his demons and become a real soldier, like it or not. But unlike most men, Ethan understood now that such a man would always be a prisoner, running inside a big wheel while praying the wheel would never stop turning, yet yearning for the day it could.

As Jonesy left, Ethan walked over to the open window holding his canteen, hoping to mitigate the heat while digging for some clean clothes. Marty said, "So what do you make of all this provost business?"

"How would I know? I'm only an enlisted soldier, not even a sergeant. I guess they figured the regiment could spare one company to help out as policemen."

"Let's have a drink," Marty said, sitting up on the bed. "Grab your mess cup." The whiskey bottle was never far from Marty's reach, and, somehow, it was always decent whiskey.

As Ethan settled into the rocking chair and extended his cup, Marty said something strange like, "Belinsky was just like Krylov's Inquisitive Man, who didn't notice the elephant in the museum."

"What?" Ethan snapped. "What the hell does that mean?" This was one of Marty's most obnoxious routines.

"It's from a book called, *Demons*, by a Russian named Dostoyevsky."

Had someone else said that Ethan would have been annoyed, but he knew Marty wasn't trying to mock his lack of formal education. Still, it got tiresome. "Don't start tonight, Marty. Please? It's been a long two days. If you need to say something, say it straightaway in American."

"It means you helped turn around a dozen live human beings into charcoal yesterday, my friend, and you pretend like it never happened. It's not healthy. How do you feel about it?"

Before he could reply, Ethan spotted the beefy, pot-bellied frame of First Sergeant Flood in the doorway. "No leisure time tonight, boys," Flood barked. "Report to the main house in thirty minutes to formally meet our newest VIP prisoner. Look sharp. NCOs and officers only."

Marty said, "Right, Sarge."

Flood turned back like he'd forgotten something and said to Marty, "What's this I hear about Jones recklessly endangering lives on that patrol? The lieutenant didn't actually see it, but I'm getting a troubling account from some of the men."

"There's nothing to it," Marty said. "I was with him the whole time. He reached into a burning hut and pulled some people out. He did what he was told."

Flood looked like he wanted to spit on the floor but realized he was in a nice house. "Well," he said, "keep an eye on him. I don't trust him. You know how those rebs are."

"We'll keep an eye on him," Marty said.

Flood wasn't finished. "Busy day tomorrow. You boys are policemen again. I want these troops from the patrol cleaned up, shaved. I want clean uniforms and shoes. Are we clear?" It was Flood's favorite rhetorical question. He slammed the door behind him without waiting for an answer.

Flood had effectively defused Ethan's annoyance. Before leaving the room, he flashed Marty a stare, fully intending to convey his feelings on the subject and said, "You drink too much, Marty."

"ATTEN...TION," CAME THE CALL FROM THE FIRST SERGEANT, AND the four company buck sergeants snapped into line horizontally with the half dozen or so corporals behind. The company's officers took positions on opposite sides of the door as their VIP prisoner, a particularly short Filipino with a thin face and sloping shoulders strutted into the room. The bizarre scenario felt more like an inspection of troops by a foreign dignitary.

"A nigger in clean clothes," came the muffled whisper from the back row. "What will they think of next?"

The man was finely attired in a white linen suit, wrinkled but spotless. Curiously, his mustache appeared to bend around thin lips at precisely the same angle as his shoulders. The addition of abnormally short legs gave the appearance the man was fighting gravity just to stand. *Chinese Mestiza*, Ethan thought. He looked nothing like a prisoner of war. "Who in hell is he?" Ethan whispered.

"Who knows?" Marty answered. "Probably some general."

The scene was a first for Ethan Cooper, and it completely baffled him. You would think this character *invited* the American soldiers here. There had to be politics involved somehow, but that wasn't Ethan's business. Marty was the expert in politics.

"Gentlemen," Captain O'Brien began, "I'd like to introduce our distinguished 'guest,' *Mr. Smith.*"

Even Martin Tours wouldn't be able to make sense of this, Ethan thought. They were living in a world gone mad. Even so, they could have done better than *Smith*.

The men remained at attention while the captain informally introduced the officers by their real names and the group engaged in some idle chit chat. Their captain, Lawrence O'Brien, was slight in stature, shorter than Ethan, and a couple of years older at twenty-nine. His wide, squared face sported a luxuriant, bushy black mustache with matching eyebrows. The oversized head carried a sparse crop of hair, receding nearly to the crown. The combination formed a strange contrast in which the forehead looked enormous. The result was a tyrannical appearance. One of the privates, a young lad from Colorado, had dubbed the new company commander, "Mount O'Brien."

O'Brien turned to his newly-acquired personal servant, Renaldo, a native Filipino in the employ of the U.S. Government, fluent in both Spanish and English, but before Renaldo could begin, the little VIP prisoner raised his hand. "Not necessary," he declared softly in excellent English. "I speak your language well enough."

Not quite like a Smith, Ethan thought.

Ethan watched with the other company NCOs as the diminutive man in the ill-fitting, white suit offered his hand to Lieutenant Hobbs. The little man clearly discharged a warmth and quiet magnetism in personal communication, but Ethan found the air of superiority annoying. The two officers fawned over the prisoner for a full minute with horseshit, nearly to the point of disgust. *Why?*

Just over a year ago this same *hombre* might have been a top general of the Philippine Army, even an official of the short-lived Philippine Republic. It was irritating how they all deferred to him like he was the fucking Emperor of China.

Well, Ethan Cooper did not pick horses among enemies, nor was he a man to hold grudges. If General MacArthur wanted to lionize some Filipino in captivity, fine with Ethan Cooper. He would do precisely as ordered earlier by Flood, and he didn't give a whore's hair if some of the boys objected.

"Mr. Smith," O'Brien began again, although his gaze was focused fore square on the two lines of smartly dressed sergeants and corporals, "these are the NCOs whom you will encounter day to day as officers of the special guard." And one by one, each man stepped forward as his name was called. Ethan Cooper was no exception. At least they were not forced to salute, he thought.

When the esteemed prisoner made his exit, O'Brien addressed the collected NCOs, now standing at ease. "The first sergeant will post new assignments in the orderly room. We'll send out regular patrols on both sides of the river. Formal hostilities on this island are over, as you know, but there are insurgent forces out there with no intention of surrendering."

As Flood left the room with the entourage, Marty put a hand on Ethan's shoulder and whispered, "Can you really blame me for drinking too much?"

"It's not my problem," Ethan replied with a sense of frustration. "Do what you like, but why the hell do you stay in the army?"

"Simple," Marty answered, as the two stepped into the sweltering hot courtyard from the sweltering hot palace, "I have nowhere else to go." Ethan honestly couldn't tell if Marty was serious, and that fact troubled him.

EVERY THIRD EVENING IN THOSE WEEKS LEADING UP TO THE installation of William Howard Taft as the first Civilian Governor General of the Philippines, like tonight, Ethan logged a shift as officer of the guard.

"Good evening, Corporal," came the accented voice from behind him.

Ethan turned from the desk to see *Mr. Smith* browsing through the well-stocked bookshelves. It was not the first time the prisoner had appeared from the door to his quarters on Ethan's night watch. "Didn't hear you come in, Sir. Sorry."

"How do you like our Philippine mosquitos, Corporal Cooper?" Smith asked. "I am curious about how they compare to those in Cuba."

Ethan always reminded himself to be polite and respectful during encounters with this prisoner. "Not much difference, Sir. Big as Hummingbirds. I hear they killed a lot of men in Cuba. We've learned something about controlling them, but they still kill more people than bullets do."

"Yes," Smith replied, taking a seat on the plush, green sofa opposite the desk. He was holding a book. "I have read about the new evidence connecting the mosquito with Yellow Fever. Your Army doctors, in particular Major Walter Reed, have done laudable work on that subject. I admit Filipinos have benefited immensely."

A knock on the outside door to the exterior patio rescued Ethan.

"Come in," said Ethan.

Private Jones entered the room and came to attention before the desk. To Ethan's relief, he did not salute the prisoner. "All four posts relieved, Ethan. I'm sacking out for a couple hours." He smiled and nodded at the prisoner. "Good evenin', Sir."

Smith smiled back and nodded. "Good evening, Private Jones."

There was something odd about the exchange, Ethan thought. An unexpected, maybe even a curious familiarity. When the eight-foot double doors had closed behind Jonesy, Smith said softly, "Curious how we are capable of turning on each other so quickly and so viciously." Turning back to Ethan, the man recovered his train of thought. "Yes, the work of your doctors has helped everyone."

Good guess. "Well," said Ethan, "if the soldiers are dead there is no army, I suppose. That motivates the generals. They say that in Cuba we lost ten men to disease for every one killed in combat. Most of those were Yellow Fever. It's much better now with the improved mosquito bars, better netting, and the draining projects, but I'm curious why the locals don't seem to suffer as much. In Cuba, some thought it was a secret weapon being used against us." *You're talking too much, Ethan,* he scolded himself.

The man chuckled. "The Spanish were never that creative," he said, "but I'm certain the Americans will find the answer in time." Ethan wasn't sure of his real meaning. "But tell me, how did you learn Spanish, Corporal? I have heard you using it very efficiently with our people."

"No. It's not that good, but my father was a schoolteacher. He thought it was important to learn another language. We learned it together when I was a little kid. I just seemed to pick it up kind of naturally."

Smith said, "May I ask if you are a supporter of President McKinley?"

"No good could come of that discussion, Sir," he said, "I never object to learning something new, but, for a soldier, politics is trouble. I do not engage in it, Sir, and not from some deeply held conviction. There's just no point in an enlisted soldier even bringing such thoughts to mind as they cannot be acted upon."

"Pity," Smith said, rising and extending his hand. "General MacArthur's views on the subject are so intransigent. But I do appreciate honest talk, Corporal Cooper. Tell me, where are you from?"

You didn't need a trip to India to see a snake charmer, Ethan thought. "Honest talk, Sir. My orders are to treat you with respect, but I'm not looking to make new Filipino *amigos.*"

"Fair enough Corporal, but surely we can be pleasant to each other."

"I agree, Sir, and in a spirit of pleasantness may I ask, are you acquainted with Private Jones somehow?"

"Not at all. I only know the man because he frequently accompanies me on walks in the garden as my guard. Why?"

Ethan didn't know why, not really. Their greeting had just seemed a little too informal, even intimate. "No reason, Sir."

As the mystery man reached for the door to his quarters, Ethan could not help himself. "What's that book, Sir, if you don't mind my asking?"

"The Adventures of Huckleberry Finn," the man replied. "One of my favorites."

CHAPTER THREE

"This will be the last patrol before inauguration and July Fourth festivities next week," Ethan announced to the small group gathered on the mud in a light drizzle outside the main enlisted barracks. Most were still nursing bad coffee on stumps and makeshift benches in the soupy, morning swelter. To a man, the soldiers found the standard issue rubber ponchos useless and oppressive and had long ago abandoned them.

"How long and how far?" asked Private James Kayne.

"Patience," Ethan replied, removing a crude, rolled up map from inside his shirt. "Be happy you will be out of the limelight for a couple of days. This place will be crawling with brass while we're gone. I know MacArthur is hardly ever here, but that will change this week."

"What're we lookin' for this time?" someone asked.

"It's a routine patrol. The mission is the same as always. Scout the designated area for signs of insurgent activity and report back," Ethan answered. "Remember, the captain says we're engaged in 'Benevolent Assimilation,' not war, and this will be primarily urban and industrial areas. Don't shoot anyone unless he poses a threat. We'll be out overnight."

Ethan held up the map of Manila and gave them a brief review of the route, and no one seemed to care. The rain stopped as he ended the briefing. Nobody cared about that either. Wet with rain; wet without rain, Ethan thought. No matter but for the occasional monsoon downpour.

FROM THE RIVER, THEY FOLLOWED AN OLD DIRT ROAD ALONG A WIDE canal into the heart of the target region. The patrol moved in single file. "Keep an eye open for anything out of place," Ethan said. "An unusual cart, animals, too many people, anything like that."

"Did y'all ever notice that carabao shit is bigger around than horse shit?"

The remark had come from near the rear, but Private Lucas's animated voice was unmistakable. His crackpot sense of humor had a way of easing tension on a long patrol. It was the reason Ethan chose him.

The line trudged along as a carabao-drawn cart passed them up heading south toward the industrial area along the main canal. The thing was filled to three times capacity with bundle upon bundle of freshly combed Manila hemp fiber. The old man with the reins did not acknowledge them, but the young boy waved.

By early afternoon, the patrol entered the outskirts of the industrial area, and the water in the canal darkened as jungle gave way to city. The air thickened with an odiferous fog, and the general sense of filth multiplied several times over. *Barotas* and barges lined both sides of the canal. A flat barge crept up the canal loaded with barrels of coconut oil. Two little barefoot men on each side with long poles struggled to push the heavy craft up water in unison. They paid no attention to the soldiers.

"You reckon they do that all day without stoppin'?" Jonesy asked no one in particular.

"They's niggers," said Private Clay. "Niggers don't have no concept of tiredness and such. Even the ones over here. It just got bred out of 'em. Them boys will pole that barge til they drop if you tell 'em to."

"I doubt that," Jonesy retorted. "I seent some mighty tired niggers back in Texas. Besides, ain't nobody never owned them niggers. They bred all on they own how they wanted."

"Never thought about that," Clay had to admit, scratching his head.

They reached a cigar factory on a busy main intersection and stopped to rest in a shaded area beside the canal. A group of three young boys and a girl approached, each carrying a basket of fresh fruit. Street vendors were everywhere in Manila. The oldest, a waif of about twelve, spoke to Ethan in crude Spanish. Ethan translated. "He says they have fruit. Cash up front."

As there was no official Philippine currency, the youngsters were happy to accept the odd assortment of Spanish peseta and half peseta coins in exchange for a delectable feast of local fruit.

"So, Ethan, are we just waiting to get shot at or what?" someone asked through a mouthful of mango. "What's the point of this?"

Ethan ignored him. The young Filipinos hadn't moved or spoken since the transaction but remained focused on the group of soldiers like their business was not finished. *"Que' mas quieres amigo?"* Ethan asked their young spokesman.

30

"You have guns, *Señor*," the boy answered with unconvincing bravado, "but we are not afraid. Your friends have cheated us. We brought them camotes, rice, sugar, and fruit three days now and we should be paid."

"What's he saying?" Clay asked.

"Shut your yap for a minute," Ethan scolded. The provost outpost was nowhere near this area. Addressing the ragged Filipino boy, Ethan asked, "What friends? What do they look like? Why do you say they are our friends?"

Ethan was armed with a recently drawn map. The only U.S. Army assets in the target area were located a mile east at the provost outpost. He knew there should not be any other American soldiers in the area.

"They have the great blue wagon of the *Americanos* and horses. Two are soldiers. One white and one with dark skin of Filipino. Darker. They refuse to pay us."

Ethan rose from the dirt, searching his pockets for a coin or two. The information the vendor had given had a foul smell to it. "All of you, find a few coins for these kids. There's something going on here."

With a few more coins in the game, the kids were happy to stay and chat as the soldiers gathered around. Some had rudimentary understanding of Spanish. According to the kids, Ethan explained, at least two Americans, one a Negro, were holed up with an army wagon near a rope factory nearby. The party included up to a half dozen Filipinos with enough small arms to go around. If that wasn't suspicious enough to investigate for insurgent activity, Ethan figured, nothing was.

When Ethan gave a sign to keep voices low, somebody said, "We should go back and report, Ethan. This is a patrol. It's not our mission to attack insurgents or capture deserters, especially if we could be outnumbered."

"And what happens if we do that? These kids could tip them off within the hour. Anybody in this neighborhood could. Look around you. You want to kill everyone who's seen us?"

"American soldiers?" exclaimed Kayne. "What in the name of Hades is goin' on here? Why are we worrying about a couple of American soldiers.?"

"Keep it down, Kayne," said Ethan. "There are things you don't know. Back in '99 there were four Negro regiments fighting in the Philippines. The Philippine Army was more like a real army then, not this guerilla ambush horseshit. The American coloreds were good fighters, but not all of them wanted to fight for our side. Story is a half dozen or so deserted. One is David Fagen. They say Fagen deserted in November of '99. That was also when the legendary Emilio Aguinaldo, General and former President of Philippine Republic, turned his army into guerilla fighters. Some American deserters actively joined the Filipinos and took up arms against their own side. Fagen was the first – and supposedly the worst."

"You mean there are Americans out there trying to kill us?" someone asked.

"I suppose that's the gist of it," Ethan replied. "They're fighting alongside the insurgents."

"Who's David Fagen?"

Clay pitched the remains of his mango into the road, agitated. "Hell's fire," he said. "I know damn well who David Fagen is. He's a goddamned lunatic, a butcher. He's like the fucking Filipino Robin Hood. His favorite pastime is killing and mutilating white American soldiers. He deserted from the 24th Infantry."

"Don't get carried away," Ethan cautioned. "We have no idea what this is about until we investigate, but Clay's not all wrong about Fagen. Supposedly he's a captain in the insurgent forces now. The Filipinos call him *General*. He's one of the few deserters who voluntarily fights and kills Americans, black ones too. He's dangerous and brutal. If he's in Manila, we have to know."

"How do we know he's killed Americans?" Jonesy asked.

"Interrogation of prisoners mostly," Ethan explained, "but we've seen recruiting posters with his image posted in the villages. Some of the images would turn your stomach. Of the half dozen or so colored soldiers who deserted only two or three are known to have taken up arms against us. Fagen is the most dangerous of them. Where else could a Black American get an army and a load of guns to get revenge? If I was a Negro, I could see it that way."

"So how we gonna play it, Sarge?"

"Let's find the place they're holed up. Then we'll decide."

From a tactical standpoint, the hideout had clearly been chosen to defend against a direct assault, offering a virtually clear field of fire for at least thirty yards in every direction. It looked like a small garment factory or weaving operation, a plank structure with a grass roof and living quarters in the back. The natural growth had been cut back some thirty yards in the rear and the yard was littered with rubbish. Schneider had found the army wagon on his scouting trip, hidden along the east side of the structure and covered with a tarp.

The patrol lay crouched in the ditch forty yards down the dirt road peering at the single coal oil lamp scattering traces of light from the rear, clear to the front windows. Someone stood watch at the front of the building and walked the perimeter at fifteen-minute intervals.

Ethan whispered to Jonesy. "If there's good news, it's that this road is the only way out for the wagon. They have it for a reason, so they won't be quick to leave it."

"Ain't got no horses here anyways. If they get scared and scatter out the back or toward the canal, we'll never find them in the dark."

"So let's wait them out," said Ethan. "Gorman."

Ethan could hear Gorman sloshing through the water that lined the trailside ditch. He could feel it seeping over his shoes. The rancid odor gave him a good idea what was in it.

"Here, Ethan."

"You and Clay head back up the road and confiscate a wagon or a couple of horses, something that will get you back faster. Report to O'Brien and tell him we'll sit on the location until he can get here in force."

"Right."

"And Clay," Ethan added.

"Here, Ethan."

"Please try very hard not to kill anyone."

As the two scurried back up the ditch toward the canal, Jonesy asked, "What you think they're up to?"

"It's no good, whatever it is. If they were just deserters looking for a better life, they wouldn't find it in Manila, especially not traveling around in an army wagon."

Nothing moved for an hour. Then a frantic whisper. "Everybody get down." It was Schneider from the far end of the ditch. "Horses."

Near total blackness concealed the source of the rhythmic thuds and only heightened the threat from approaching hooves on dirt. A low whinny. Another, louder. *Two horses? Three?* No creaks or squeaks of a wagon or cart. Now close enough to see the breath of two horses erupting into the thick, tropical air, Ethan sprang from the ditch, knife in hand.

Schneider had been quicker, all twelve inches of his Krag bayonet buried in the man's back just under the left shoulder blade. The man was alone, and such was Schneider's efficiency that the two horses had barely whinnied. Ethan gathered the reins, nodded, and handed them to his silent killer.

"We can't kill the horses," Schneider whispered as Ethan dragged his dead victim into the ditch.

The popular Schneider was a veteran who'd fought in the 1899 Malolos Campaign with a different outfit and distinguished himself. Until that moment in the ditch, the man's natural shyness and humility had defined him throughout the company, but every man on the patrol had watched him dispatch the unfortunate horse tender with the ferocity and stealth of an Apache. They would need to revisit their collective judgment.

"Walk them up the goddamn road and tie them to something," Ethan growled. "Can't kill the horses, eh?"

Schneider returned within a few minutes, and Ethan said, "Well, we're in it now. Those had to be the wagon horses. If I'm right, they'll miss them before long, so our timeline is moved up. My guess is they were getting ready to hitch up the wagon and move out."

Looking at the Filipino corpse, Jonesy said, "This goo goo looks about military age. One of the Luzon *insurrectos*."

"I hope so," said Ethan. "General Tinio's bunch. So if there is a Negro deserter inside, fair chance it's David Fagen himself. We want the Americans alive, if possible, and maybe another prisoner. They will want somebody to question."

"Schneider, get up here," Ethan whispered with authority. Five minutes ago, the call would have gone out to someone else. "Make your way around that clearing to the east side and crawl up to that wagon. Kill the guard quietly when he comes by. Then get a look inside the wagon if you can. Make sure it's not filled with dynamite. When it's clear, signal with your rifle in front of the light and we'll rush the building. Maybe we'll catch the peckers with their britches down."

"Jonesy, you go with him. Stay in the tree line and cover the front door best you can in case it goes wrong. Listen up everyone. Five-yard intervals in the ditch. If it goes wrong, we'll fill that building with lead and do this the hard way."

"Will do, Ethan," Jonesy said.

"Tully, make your way around to the back from the other direction. Get yourself up high in that old Banyan tree so we don't shoot you. Focus on the door opening if it goes hot. There may be light for a second or two when the door opens. Open up and keep them inside." With Tully on the move, Ethan whispered his final orders. "The guard just made his rounds so move out and remember not to put yourself in our line of fire. And, Schneider, make sure you give them time to get into position."

Their sentry walked the perimeter twice more without incident. Soon after the second pass, the crack of a lone Krag rifle declared an end to the brief siege. Four more shots in quick succession told them Tully had emptied his rifle toward something or someone in the rear doorway of the building. The plan had imploded. The guard sprang from his chair, rifle at the ready. A single crack from the east and a muzzle flash revealed a silhouette dropping lifeless through the filtered window light onto the porch.

Before anyone could speak, the lamp died, and blackness descended on the building. The brief, deadly silence was an overture to the chaos that would surely follow.

Instinct kicked in. "Fire," Ethan ordered in full battle voice, and the night came alive with powder, flash, and thunder from three directions. Their combined Krag output poured .30-40 caliber bullets upon the structure at the rate of six per second for a full two minutes before Ethan gave the order, "Cease fire."

Combat was fast, unpredictable, and chaotic. Plans were often scrapped on the spot, this time in favor of simple, overwhelming firepower. Ethan knew instinct and training kept otherwise dead soldiers alive. Some shit box in the building had to take a piss and it was war again.

No return fire from the building. "Move in. Stay low. We go in from the front. Tully has the back." He knew Tully had the sense to stay high out of the crossfire to pick off runners. Ethan would rather they all escaped than lose one of his own men.

No sooner had they stepped off than the anemic moonlight slid behind a passing cloud bank. The momentary darkness offered perfect cover but was so pervasive Ethan nearly fired on the sound of steps at his heels. "It's me," said Kayne. "Sorry."

Shots from the rear. The distinctive pop, five to be sure, told him Tully had been trying to discourage runners or had even dropped a few and was reloading. Still no return fire. They converged around the porch. Five more shots and Tully's Krag went silent again. "Keep your interval."

On Ethan's signal, Schneider breached the door and three men barreled through the opening, bayonets fixed. "Good here," said Schneider.

Lucas posted to the front door while Ethan scurried into the darkened working space with Kayne. An old curtain or sheet separated the main space from the living area in the back. Ethan ripped at the curtain with his bayonet and the patrol dashed in low, hugging the walls of the one-room living area. A few mats, a crude cook stove, and a small table adorned the final resting place of three very dead bodies in various poses spread over the floor, each in close proximity to an old Remington, breech-loading rifle.

Someone fired the lamp and Ethan saw Tully appear in the doorway. "There's one dead out here," Tully said, eying the other three. "Looks like all goo goos, Ethan."

"Nope," Ethan replied, turning one of the corpses onto its back. "This one's American, white, just dressed like one of them."

"What about Fagen?" Asked Jonesy.

"At least two of them got away out the back," Tully said. "Fagen mighta been one of 'em."

"Couldn't be helped," Ethan said. "So let's check that wagon and figure out what the hell was going on here."

Before they could get to the door, a Filipino walked in, hands high with a terrified expression and a bayonet against the small of his back. "I caught this one outside," Schneider said, grinning.

Under a canvas tarp, in the wagon bed, stood twin M1895 Colt-Browning Machine Guns, complete with instruction manuals, each mounted on a tripod and fitted with a seat for the operator. Behind the driver's seat they discovered a cache of uniforms.

"What in the name of God are these?" Tully asked. It was not a rhetorical question.

"The latest in killing power," Ethan replied. "The Army doesn't even have them yet. Too new and untested, I suppose, but the Navy has them deployed over here. I saw one on the Laguna de Bay."

Lucas said, "I'll be damned. A ride-along machine gun. I wonder if it drives itself like one of them horseless carriages."

Tully was already looking at the manual in the window light. "It's air cooled," he said. "Says here it can fire 400 rounds per minute without overheating. Think how much damage two of those could do in one minute. You can't crank out a quarter of that with our Gatling guns."

"Especially lethal from a moving wagon," Ethan added. "They must weigh a hundred pounds each with the tripods and seats. When you put these together with the wagon and the uniforms and two deserters, the whole thing adds up to big trouble."

Ethan jumped down from the back of the wagon, ambling around to the front where Kayne was sorting through a stack of uniforms recovered from the storage box under the driver. "What we got here, Kayne?"

"Looks like three complete U.S. Army private uniforms, all current and pretty new, I'd say. The white ones are from the Makabebe Scouts."

"Everybody, listen up," Ethan announced. "We're heading back right now with everything. Can't wait til morning. Schneider, take somebody with you and go get those horses. Make sure they're watered and hitch them up. The rest of you saddle up. Tie and gag the prisoner and throw him in back with the dead deserter."

In that moment, Ethan was grateful to be a lowly sergeant. No real decisions to make. No strategy to plan. No responsibility for disaster. Just get back to camp fast and make the report. He remembered the NCO training on writing reports. *Report only what you saw and heard. Never report what you think. The Army doesn't care what you think.* Fair enough. The name of David Fagen would neither pass through his lips to superiors nor through his pen to paper.

Ethan had seen the wanted posters himself. General Funston had personally posted a $600 reward around the towns and villages for the capture of "Mad Dog Fagen." And no wonder.

Whatever grand scheme Ethan's patrol had fortuitously thwarted, the schemers themselves, especially Fagen, posed a far greater danger to the successful subjugation of this little, brown race than one operation. Newspapers all over America had trumpeted "victory" in the Philippines and repeated the official line that "isolated pockets of disorganized resistance" would be purged from the islands. Ethan Cooper now knew better.

Any inference, however vague, that Fagen was in Manila and actively involved in an *insurrecto* plot to assassinate William Howard Taft or Arthur MacArthur would ignite a bonfire of terror at command level. Americans were still being ambushed on the roads, murdered in the towns, and cut down on the trails by deadly traps. But Command had been pushing the narrative to the American newspapers that the war on Luzon was virtually won. Ethan couldn't reconcile the disparate realities.

No one had told the Filipinos on Luzon they were beaten. Their leader and former President, Emilio Aguinaldo, had supposedly pledged allegiance to the Americans after his capture some months back, but this was a new kind of war now, one with new rules or no rules at all. Aguinaldo no longer controlled them. An oath of allegiance did not necessarily spell defeat for the Filipinos. A dozen Aguinaldos, worse than the original, if Ethan were to believe reports, operated with impunity on the surrounding islands, and terrible things were happening on both sides.

Even a corporal could see there were bad days ahead in the Philippines. Was it possible, he wondered, that the brass just couldn't see it coming? He hoped that was the case because the only other possibility sickened him. That they would intentionally lie to the world, to their own countrymen, about the state of affairs here in the Philippines? About their intentions? Would Ethan's own government intentionally deceive the nation for the sake of profit or politics? Unfortunately, his personal experiences over the last couple of months made that possibility increasingly likely.

He was fortunate, indeed, to be a lowly corporal, but confident that his secret identity was secure in the hands of fools who believed a thing true only because they wished it so. His work as an angel of death would go on for now. And David Fagen? Fagen was the least of his problems. *Report only what you see and hear.*

CHAPTER FOUR

I n Ethan's hand was the summons bound to seal his fate, dated June 29, 1901:

From: Headquarters, American Forces, Philippines, Major General Adna Chafee, commanding

To: Corporal Ethan Cooper, Office of the Provost Marshal, Special Detachment, Camp Sheridan

Subject: Choose one enlisted provost escort. Report to Office of the Civilian Governor of The Philippines, Ayuntamiento Building, Intramuros, Manila, 11:00 a.m., July 2, 1901

Sitting on a red velvet chair in Manila's cavernous administration building, Ethan felt like a man attending his own funeral. Located prominently on the *Plaza de Roma* in the old walled city of *Intramuros*, The *Ayundamiento* was in every respect a palace. "It looks like pictures I've seen from inside Notre Dame Cathedral in Paris," observed his "escort" on this day trip downriver.

"Never seen anything like it, Marty," Ethan added. They were almost whispering, but every word seemed to echo between the soaring, gilded ceiling and the black and white, marble floor. The pair had been directed to the waiting chairs along the wall beneath a brass plaque reading, *Governor of the Philippines*, as three enormous crystal chandeliers hovered over the space. In two more days, Taft would effectively be ruler of these islands.

Nothing good could come from this summons, Ethan thought. If that Pinkerton had found him, he'd be in the brig already, not running free around Manila in a clean uniform. The summons was almost certainly related to that last patrol. Anyone with a lick of sense knew that those new machine guns had been intended to kill William Howard Taft and Arthur MacArthur on July Fourth. But if they were going to give him a medal, why at the Office of the Civilian Governor?

It would most likely be all right. The thing that could hurt him most was a photograph in the newspapers back home. He had carefully courted anonymity, but a picture in The New York Times or any of the Pittsburgh papers would signal his death knell. A

39

tycoon like Allen Winslow did not require much outside assistance to service his vendettas. Someone would surely recognize his photograph. He thought it ironic that faithful performance of his duty would be what finally did him in. *No photographs under any circumstances.*

"What are you so nervous about, Ethan?" Marty asked. "They'll just pin a medal on you and send us on our way. Might even make you famous."

I should have brought Jonesy, Ethan thought. Marty had a way of making a bad situation worse—and he could just be right. "That's what I'm afraid of, Marty. Let's just say the unwanted attention makes me nervous and leave it there." Ethan wouldn't mind getting out of the army, but he wanted to leave *for* something better, not *to* a jail cell or a hangman's noose.

Maybe it's just as well, he thought. He'd already inflicted a storm of pain and death as a soldier, essentially all to maintain his anonymity. Now they might honor him for it and make him famous, thereby sealing his demise. Marty would find some dark irony in that. But at least exposure would bring Ethan peace. It would end the waiting—and the killing.

An attractive, young Filipina appeared from beyond the doorway and announced in a gentle voice, "Sergeant Cooper, His Honor, Governor Taft, will see you now." Her English was nearly perfect.

Ethan rose from the bench and turned to Marty. "Okay, here goes. I'll either see you in a little while or I won't." Then he addressed the young woman politely, "It's Corporal, Ma'am."

She smiled coyly and said, "You may bring your friend."

The office was as expected; the fat man standing behind the hand-carved mahogany desk was not. He was enormous in both stature and presence in his white linen suit, striding around the desk toward his victims with an effortless gait. Oriental rug, vertical windows, and dark paneling created an expectation of oppressively stagnant heat, but a steady breeze of curious origin powered a pleasant, moderating effect throughout the large space. A relentless humming sound infused the cavernous room.

The big man's warm smile nearly outstretched his elegantly groomed, handlebar mustache. When Ethan saw his chestnut hair and blue eyes, he thought he might be meeting his grandfather for the first time. At least 6'2" and 300 pounds, the man towered over Ethan with a massive, outstretched hand. "It is my great pleasure to make your acquaintance, Sgt. Cooper. I've sent for refreshments while we talk." He dared not correct the man for such a minor mistake.

The appearance and the voice reminded Ethan of mismatched socks and adjusting to the mix required some effort. Had he not been facing the man, watching the lips expel words, Ethan would have pegged the source of the soprano voice as an old female secretary. The governor's grip was firm, sincere and seemed to reinforce his words, dissipating the awkwardness in short order. "Thank you, Sir," Ethan replied. "The pleasure is mine." *It looks like you're not in trouble, not yet anyway.* "But it's 'Corporal,' Sir."

The man looked fat but moved into position behind his desk with the confidence and agility of a wrestler. The high-backed, leather chair might have been crafted for Goliath himself, Ethan thought.

"This is my friend, Sir," Ethan said, "Sergeant Martin Tours."

Taking Marty's hand, he said, "Delighted to meet you, Sergeant. Tell me, were you on the patrol also?"

"No, Sir," Marty said. Ethan noted that it was a rare example of Marty struggling for words.

Taft continued to address Ethan's friend. "Is that T-o-u-r-s?"

"Yes, Sir," Marty replied. It sounded more like an admission than an answer.

Taft held out an open gold box. "Cigar?" he asked.

"No, thank you, Sir," Ethan replied. He had to raise his voice over the steady humming. Marty pocketed two.

"Curious name, Sergeant," Taft observed. "May I ask is the name somehow related to Martin of Tours, the Patron Saint of Soldiers? I think he was French, 17th or Eighteenth Century, if memory serves me."

"Yes," Marty replied. "I've heard about him, Sir. There are stories, but I won't bore you with them."

The door opened behind Ethan, and a male servant approached the desk with a tray of drinks. He'd brought a friend, a guy in a dark suit with a winged collar and a cravat, just like the big man's. "Sergeant Cooper," Taft began in his most formal soprano tone, "meet my Chief of Staff, Elton Schaffner."

41

Ethan participated in the obligatory formalities, then offered the necessary correction, again. "It's Corporal Cooper, Sir, not Sergeant."

Taft laughed and Ethan swore the floor shook. "That's one of the things we'll discuss." He pointed to one of the leather desk chairs and added, "Take a seat, gentlemen."

Feeling a bit bolder, Ethan said, "Sir, I'm wondering, what is that humming noise?"

Seated behind the hand-carved desk, Taft expelled the soprano version of a belly laugh, and the man's belly actually appeared to respond in kind. "Look up," Taft instructed.

Ethan looked up, way up, maybe twenty feet. It was a fan, all right, twirling all by itself. "It's called a ceiling fan. Runs on its own," Taft said. "Water-powered, they say. It's the latest thing and really helps with the heat and humidity. You become accustomed to the noise."

Taft pointed to the tray where the servant had poured three glasses of something pink. He said, "Have a glass of lemonade, gentlemen. Afraid I'm not much on alcohol."

Ethan passed on the *drink*, and Taft leaned back in Goliath's chair. "May I call you Ethan?"

"Of course, Sir."

"Ethan, I brought you here for one reason: to look you square in the eye and say thank you for saving my life. That's very likely what you did on that patrol."

Maybe it will be as simple as that, Ethan thought. No crowds, no newspapermen, no photographers. He was about to say something humble when two more men entered the room. The one in the plaid suit and bowler hat was lugging a big picture camera on a tripod. The whole show had gone south in a heartbeat. His partner was a young army lieutenant.

Before Ethan could even respond, Taft addressed the photographer. "You can set up over there in front of the sofa, John," he said. "We'll get a shot under the President's portrait."

Ethan said what would be expected. "It's not necessary, Sir. Actually, we were just lucky."

Taft chuckled. "Nonsense, my boy. Nonsense. Where are you from? Tell us how a hero is raised."

You should have known this would get personal. Why didn't you think of this? If you tell them you're from Pennsylvania, it's all over but the gallows. Ethan's first instinct was to lie, but his first instinct was generally wrong, so he resolved *not* to lie, not much anyway. It was a lose-lose situation. "Sir," he said, "that's a hard question to answer. Kind of embarrassing really because some of the story I don't even know. My parents died when I was young. I kicked around with relatives." The truth worked sometimes.

Taft nodded, seemingly accepting the answer—or taking the hint. He made a show of donning his specs as he held up a sheet of paper from the desk. "I have here a special order from General MacArthur, Son, promoting you summarily to the rank of sergeant." He reached over the desk, handing Ethan the order and adding a disclaimer. "It's not much of an acknowledgement for what you did, but it's the best I can do. It seems they can't give you a medal because…well…"

"I understand, Sir," Ethan said, "and I'm grateful for the promotion." He noticed Taft had not invited the others to sit.

"I won't drag you into politics, gentlemen, but a lot of people back home would love to see us fail over here. There are powerful men who believe we should not be engaged in foreign ventures, especially on this side of the world. We cannot allow them to prevail. Control of the Philippines is vital for our trade and security.

"Still, I don't believe the Filipinos are ignorant savages. I'm no fan of Kipling and the Manifest Destiny crowd. I agree with Samuel Clemens that the Filipinos are an industrious, intelligent people, capable of governing themselves, *eventually,* and we will see to it. In the meantime, we need a strong presence here and a firm hand until they are ready. My assassination, or MacArthur's for that matter, might have upset the apple cart of public opinion back home and turned it completely against expansion of our influence to Asia. That would have been very unfortunate."

In that moment, Ethan was only thinking about how to avoid a photograph. He nodded and lied through his teeth. "Yes, Sir,"

They all rose, and Taft moved from behind the desk. He handed Ethan a business card and said, "If you ever need anything, Son, I want you to find me and give this card to someone from my staff. Do you understand?"

"Yes Governor," Ethan replied.

They shook hands and Taft added, "Come on. Meet my liaison officer, and we'll get a photograph taken. Are you ready, John?" he asked the photographer.

"Yes, Sir," replied the man in the bowler hat, fidgeting with his tripod.

Taft turned to the patient lieutenant. "Lieutenant Alex Crane, may I present Sergeants Ethan Cooper and Martin Tours?"

Not waiting for a salute, Crane offered his hand.

The photographer said, "Would you like the usual shot in front of the sofa, Governor?"

"Fine, fine," said Taft, taking Ethan by the arm.

Ethan just couldn't do it. He couldn't commit suicide by camera. His life hadn't amounted to much at nearly twenty-seven, but he wasn't about to help anyone tie the noose. He stopped dead with the governor's hand around his arm. "I have to tell you, Sir," he said, "I'm pretty shy about picture taking."

Taft patted his shoulder in a kind of fatherly way. "All right, Son," he said. "It's all right."

Then he looked at the other men and said, "Give us the room for a minute, boys."

Taft pointed for Ethan to join him on the sofa. When they were alone, he said, "I won't ask you any more personal questions, Son, but I want to tell you something in plain language. You won't be reading about this in the newspapers, and you most certainly will never see a picture of yourself on display anywhere. That picture is for you alone. No one will ever know what you did. Do you understand what I'm saying?"

"I think so, Sir."

"Well, I know you're not stupid, so think about this. The war on this island is officially over, and the vast majority of the people are eager to partake of the prosperity that will result from American administration. We want to help them help themselves. We can't achieve that goal if Americans back home doubt our motivations and sincerity.

"Think how it would look if this whole assassination plot became public knowledge. People back home are being told, rightly or wrongly, that the resistance here has been crushed. The war is over, but we know better. Can you imagine the public outcry if it became known that these insurgents nearly assassinated General

McArthur and me? Son, I'm saying nobody will ever know about this incident unless you tell them."

It sounded good and bad at the same time. "I never thought about it like that, Sir."

Taft slapped him lightly on the back and smiled a big, warm smile, so big it threatened to become a bear hug. He said, "Whatever you're running from, Son, I will never slow you down. But someday, when you're an old man telling this story to your grandchildren, you may want something to prove it. Now, do you want that picture or not?"

Ethan smiled. "I'd like it very much, Sir."

"Oh, I almost forgot," Taft added. "Our government is hosting an Inaugural Reception on the evening of the Fourth right here. You will both be my guests. Lieutenant Crane will get you billeted and take you to the Quartermaster tomorrow morning to have a dress uniform issued. He'll get you everything you need, show you where to eat, haircuts, shave, everything. You can participate in the ceremony with your unit in the afternoon. Then, you join the evening reception. I may ask General Chaffee to issue an order assigning you to my staff as personal security for a week or two."

Ethan didn't see that pitch coming. The last thing he wanted was unwanted attention, but he was still a young man of limited experience in a big world. An opportunity like this would never come again.

"You will both receive invitations. Crane will see to it. I hope you enjoy yourselves. Oh, Crane will also give you a few days per diem for spending around Manila. There will be plenty of fine food and only the best liquor at the reception. All right, now call those people back into the room."

"Would you gentlemen care to order breakfast?" The waiter asked in a heavy Filipino accent. The man looked impeccable, groomed like a Sunday preacher, and dressed in a fake American sailor uniform, the white summer uniform but with no insignia. All the waiters wore them. The whole room sparkled with a marble floor, tablecloths, and even the window shutters swung open to give the illusion of dining outdoors in the garden.

Marty showed the waiter their hotel pass and politely asked, "We were told breakfast is included. Is there a choice?"

The waiter nodded. "Of course, Sir," he said, "whatever you like." They both ordered ham and eggs with a pot of coffee.

Ethan knew they had a busy morning planned for them. Pick up the new uniforms at the tailor, haircuts, and a buggy tour of *Intramuros*. He said, "We have an hour until Taft's adjutant meets us in the lobby. I'd like to walk around and get a better look at this place."

When Marty laughed, he spilled coffee onto his uniform shirt. "At least it wasn't the new one," Marty said.

The Army-Navy Club was far and away the fanciest establishment young Ethan Cooper had ever visited, a grand hotel and reception center for American military, families, and visiting VIPs. Located smack in the middle of *Intramuros,* the hotel was walking distance from the *Ayunamiento.* An elongated front porch/entranceway dominated the pure white façade, tucked behind a half dozen massive archways. The archways, in turn, supported an elaborate second story featuring Roman columns across the façade framing floor to ceiling windows.

The waiter appeared with a fresh pot of coffee. Ethan offered his cup and said, "I heard about those toilets that flush but never saw one until last night. They would sure come in handy in the wintertime. Say, what was that talk about the patron saint of soldiers yesterday?"

"Nothing of consequence," Marty answered. "Idle chatter." For whatever reason, Marty didn't want to talk about his name, and that was all right with Ethan.

He moved to change the subject. "Sounds to me like we won't be here much longer. I didn't understand everything the governor said, but it's clear he wants to give these people their independence. It can't happen too soon for me."

Marty looked annoyed. "Don't believe a word of it," he cautioned. "The key word in his little speech was 'eventually,' Ethan. It's not in the cards or in their long-term plan either."

"How do you mean?"

"I mean I don't buy what they're selling. Old McKinley wants us to kill the hard-headed Filipinos. Then he wants the rest to work for us. It may take a while, but before long, we'll be stealing their stuff while they sing, *The Star-Spangled Banner.* Everything will be back to normal here. We might even put some of them in uniform and send them off to kill yellow people for us somewhere. They have no intention of recognizing an independent Philippines."

It sounded to Ethan like Marty hadn't heard a word of Taft's explanation. "Marty, I don't take to what we're doing here now any more than you do. But we stole the West from the Indians with guns. Hell, we took California and Texas from the Mexicans with guns. People had to die, but everybody's better off now. People get killed all the time in a righteous cause. Innocent folks too, often enough. No decent person likes that. Maybe It'll be different here now that their leader has surrendered. McKinley knows what he's doing. Remember, you killed more than a few yourself."

Marty put down a tip for the waiter, and the pair started to walk along the long porch beside the garden. "Don't remind me but tell that to an Indian when you get home. Let's take a rocking chair here and wait for this Lieutenant Crane. We'll see him coming." When they'd settled into the chairs, Marty said, "Look, I can't change any of it, but you need to call this what it is, Ethan. The other day we helped kill innocent people, women, and Hobbs will likely get a medal for it. I'm just trying not to normalize all this butchery, not to pretend it was justified. I know you don't like it either, but you need to stop making excuses for it."

"I'm in the army, Marty. I do what I'm told. I don't moralize about it." Ethan did not mention that similar thoughts had plagued him lately.

Ethan had witnessed Marty's self-righteous outbursts several times before. It wasn't anger, exactly, but the attentive ear could detect the conflict that raged within his soul. Maybe it was why he liked Marty's company, a kinship of secret misery—maybe some mystery too, but he said, "You can't have it both ways, Marty."

"I wish you were right, Ethan. Maybe it's worse when you have a clear sense of your own crimes like I do. People make jokes about how the Filipinos were all cannibals and headhunters before the Spaniards came and put them on the road to civilization. Well, there are all kinds of cannibals, my friend. We're running with the worst of them right now. They don't eat flesh. They eat souls and devour humanity."

CHAPTER FIVE

To a kid from a little town in Western Pennsylvania, the main hall of the *Auyunamiento* that evening was lifted from a storybook of kings and queens and noble heads of Europe. The great chandeliers were electric powered with hundreds of little bulbs showering several hundred people with a soft, shimmering luster. An orchestra at the opposite end of the room played some classical selection or other as the gathering gained momentum.

As Ethan and Marty entered the ballroom, they each handed an invitation to one of the two sergeants assigned to guard the main entrance. The guard gave Ethan a double take before even looking at the invitation. To the man's credit, he offered no wisecrack or comment of any kind but thoroughly examined the document for authenticity. Marty's experience appeared to be similar.

"I wonder if this is what the White House looks like," Marty quipped as a formally dressed waiter appeared balancing a tray of champagne glasses. They each lifted a glass.

They started a slow reconnaissance around the room's perimeter to access the environment. The men were all dressed in black formal wear of the day, complete with stiff, winged collars, or in military uniform. Ethan counted generals from at least seven countries, of which only the Americans and the British were identifiable. Curiously, the recently relieved Military Governor of the Philippines was apparently not in attendance, Ethan noted. "I don't see MacArthur anywhere," he pointed out.

"Disappointed?" Marty asked playfully. "Were you expecting to have a brandy with him?"

"You're a real jackass," Ethan said. "I should have brought Jonesy."

"Taft just took McArthur's job. He's unemployed at the moment and likely not happy about it. These big shots throw their little fits just like everyone else."

Ethan couldn't help but notice the large number of prosperous-looking Filipinos in attendance, both men and women. He thought it must be the cream of the Philippines' high society, most likely business owners, local officials, lawyers, and plantation owners.

High fashion was the women's uniform of the day, and the hall swirled with color as ladies of all ages mixed and mingled. Petticoats, huge hats with feathers and fruit and flowers. All but a few Filipinas seemed to have shed their traditional fashion in favor of Western opulence. Ethan Cooper had entered a door into a new world.

The sergeants scooped two more champagne glasses from a passing tray and took defensive positions, backs to the wall, plotting their next maneuver, when a portly old fellow with a bushy gray mustache and mutton chops tapped Marty on the shoulder. "Excuse me, old boy," he began, "but would you be so kind as to hurry over to the bar and bring my wife a small sherry?"

Ethan had no clue how Marty would react to being taken for a servant, but Marty promptly snapped his heels together and bowed from the waist, smiling. "Of course, Your Excellency," he said. "And yourself, Sir?"

"Whiskey, Irish, please. No ice. We shall be just over there," he said, pointing to Lord knows where.

Marty leaned over and whispered, "The English think everyone is a servant. Let's move on and make our way over to the food tables."

As they feasted on smoked fish, caviar, and a dozen varieties of cheese, Lieutenant Crane appeared, looking as if he had just successfully completed a mission. "There you are," he said. "Governor Taft would like to see you gentlemen. I'm happy to show you the way."

"Give us just a second, Lieutenant Crane, if you would." Marty replied, like he was addressing a private. "I'm dying to try just one more of these delicious chicken legs."

Crane was a good sort, wet behind the ears and completely clueless with no apparent need to fool anyone about it, and they both liked him. He looked around like he was deciding if it was safe to talk. Then he whispered. "I'm taking a chance telling you boys this, but the governor likes you, and I don't think he would mind. You just have to swear to secrecy."

Crane had their attention. Marty even forgot about his chicken leg. They both swore to keep his confidence. Then Crane whispered, "Your company will be reassigned in a few weeks to a combat post down south on another island, one of the big ones. They have an active insurgency down there. The governor knows, and I'm trying to get his help."

"Help with what?" Marty asked.

Another champagne man passed and walked away down three glasses.

"I want a transfer into your outfit. It's perfect, a combat assignment. What's left of this war will be over by next spring, and I've never seen combat, nothing but a glorified valet."

"You're not missing much," Marty said. "It's pretty dirty."

Ethan felt really old in that moment. "When are we leaving?" he asked.

"Sounds like the end of the month," Crane replied. "There's a guerilla general named Martinez down there giving our forces fits."

"I've heard of him," Marty said. "He was one of Aguinaldo's top generals on Luzon."

"Uh oh," Crane said. "There's the governor waving at us. Let's go."

Taft was drinking lemonade again and standing with a trim, middle-aged man and a beautiful young Filipina. The Chief of Staff was with them, Elton something or other, Ethan remembered. The governor greeted both sergeants warmly, then stepped back and turned to his two companions, obviously for the introduction. Ethan squirmed in his shiny new leather shoes and momentarily wished he and Marty had gone back upriver with the company. Then he saw the woman up close and held his breath.

"Charles Grayson, Dr. Tala Espinosa," May I present two personal friends?" Then he pointed. "Sergeants Ethan Cooper and Martin Tours."

Ethan let Marty lead the way as they exchanged handshakes and awkward greetings. It seemed like Marty had done this kind of thing before, but Ethan could feel the perspiration creeping down the back of his neck. He'd had no training for this, not in the army and certainly not before.

Looking at the woman, he had the sense this entire evening was something out of a museum or a living picture book, a fantasy world. Look but don't touch. To his amazement, the "doctor" extended her hand. She looked about his age. "I'm very pleased to meet you, Sergeant Cooper," she said in a quiet, confident voice. It was a Filipina accent no doubt, but with a perfect command of English.

Her tiny fingers were elegant but not the hands of a debutante. They had known work but not in the fields or in the jungle, nothing involving dirt or pain. He'd never shaken a woman's hand and wasn't sure if there was a protocol for it. *Don't say anything stupid*, he reminded himself.

He took the hand gently like it was fine china. She stared at him through warm hazel eyes. The eyes conveyed a serious look but also a sense of sadness. He thought it might be the high, gently curved eyebrows. Unlike every other woman in the room, the doctor wore neither paint nor powder, her straight, black hair drawn to the left and tied in back with a simple gold ribbon. A small, oval mouth completed the face, with full lips rounded under a delicate nose, definitely upturned in a smile at the moment. Makeup could do nothing for this woman, he thought.

The older man was talking again. *Her husband?* Charles Grayson? American? He looked old enough to have seen Christ crucified. The man might have said he was Canadian. *Charles Grayson?* What was he doing in this woman's company?

Her dress was different from the other women's as well, Ethan thought. He was ignorant on the subject, of course, but she wore no petticoats, no hoops or fancy hat. The dress was a wispy-light honey color, not quite gold, a long, slender gown with white gloves and three-quarter sleeves to just above the shoulder. The gown featured just enough lace to make the other women stare. A gold satin sash around a tightly drawn waist allowed the skirt to fall swiftly from slender hips to marble floor, like a frame on a great painting.

Charles Grayson? A charlatan, no doubt, or a wealthy deceiver of young women. He felt a poke in the side from Marty. Her escort had apparently asked Ethan a question. Marty said deftly, "Sometimes Sergeant Cooper has to think about where he's from, Mr. Grayson." Apparently, Grayson had been speaking to Ethan.

Taft chuckled and said, "Well, he's from the army now, and I'm happier for it."

"So, what do you do, Mr. Grayson?" Marty asked. *Why didn't you ask him that?*

The Canadian was wrong for this woman, Ethan thought, with his weather-bitten, wrinkled skin and a receding crop of graying hair. He was in fairly good shape at least, but ancient, maybe even late fifties. Slightly reddish cheeks under a pair of finely crafted eyeglasses announced a frequent drinker of good whiskey. *Wait, Taft said her name was Espinosa, Tala Espinosa. What would she see in a man like this?*

The Chief of Staff was apparently allotting the governor's time for the evening and picked a polite moment to intervene. The enlisted men had exceeded their allotment. "Excuse me, Sir, but I see General Chaffee has arrived. I know you wanted to speak with him, and he will be delighted to meet Dr. Espinosa."

When they were out of earshot, Ethan said, "I don't think she's his wife. They have different names."

"Get the artillery plugs out of your ears next time" Marty teased. "She's his *guest.*"

"Hmm…Well, it's none of my business. Let's head back to the food tables. Maybe we can find some more champagne on the way."

Four glasses of champagne and two whiskies later, Ethan thought he was getting the hang of this "embassy duty," and if he had to spend the next twenty-five years in the army, he might apply for it as permanent duty. Dancing had pushed the drinkers and talkers around the perimeter, and by eleven o'clock, the party was in full swing. The alcohol had fueled Ethan into an interesting conversation with a general's wife about the scarcity of upscale department stores on the *Escolta* and another with a tipsy British banker about his wife's infidelity.

He was about to go searching for Marty on the way to the exit when an angel in a golden dress tapped his right shoulder ever so lightly and said, "Would you like to dance, Sergeant Cooper?"

He was ambushed and orderly retreat was not an option. "I…I…"

She kind of shrugged her lace shoulders and smiled. Until that moment, it never occurred to him that God manufactured skin in such smooth and blemish free form, even on a woman. "I understand," she said, and turned to leave.

"No! Wait!" He pleaded. "You *don't* understand."

"Yes?"

"It's not that I don't want to. I don't know how. I've never danced."

His embarrassing admission cried out for some form of humorous response, at least a laugh, but her face expressed none of that. "I don't dance often myself anymore," she admitted. "We could just talk a bit, if you like."

He was thoroughly tongue-tied and moderately inebriated, but there was no retreat in him tonight, even for the hope of a five-minute conversation with another man's *guest*. He said, "I'm willing to try dancing. I mean I want to try, but you could get a general to dance with you or a senator or something."

"Don't be so sure, Sergeant Cooper. You looked uncomfortable when we met. We Filipinos are a very hospitable people. I thought maybe it was something I said."

"Oh, no," he said. "That's not it. It's just that I've never been to an event like this. I'm just a soldier."

Curiously, she chose that moment to laugh, then said, "I was about to say the same thing to you."

She was laughing at herself, not at him, and the gesture disarmed him. "I'm a doctor, not a princess. Besides, I've only been a doctor for a week."

The entire ballroom, with its glitter, color, and opulence, existed in that moment only to serve her extraordinary beauty. He remembered one of the tactics principles from his non-commissioned officers' training. *No one ever captured ground from a defensive position.* He held out his arms and said, "Well, I'm in your capable hands, Doctor."

The orchestra was playing classical music of some kind, as though he would know the difference. She smiled, guiding one of his arms around her tiny waist and holding his opposite hand high in her own. "The key is to relax," she said. "Don't worry about the steps. We'll just kind of sway with the music, small steps, moving in circles. Come, let's try."

She was a good teacher, he thought, easy to be with and patient, especially when he stomped her toes. He wanted to bottle her intoxicating smell and take it with him for long nights in the jungle, but in the time it takes to pull a trigger, reality crashed his new world, shattering the magic around him into a million pieces and ensnaring him again.

Directly over Tala's shoulder, not thirty feet away, stood the governor's chief of staff, whatever his name was, talking to a broad-shouldered man with a grayish beard. Even without the fiddler's cap and greatcoat, there was no mistaking the Pinkerton of his worst nightmares. *In the Philippines and in the same building at the same time. They found you.*

53

Cold fear locked his knees and feet. Sheer panic nearly sent him running for the door.

"What's wrong?" Tala asked.

"I'm sorry, Tala, but I have to leave—now."

She turned to look behind her. "Is there something over there that upset you?" she asked.

He held her shoulders with both hands, pleading with his eyes. "There's a man with a beard just over your shoulder talking with the governor's man," he said "I can't explain now, but this was a mistake. I'm sorry. I have no right, but I need your help."

"What do you need?"

"Walk with me slowly toward the doors, like we're going to get a drink."

She asked no more questions, but took his arm and smiled, as they sauntered toward the bar—and the doors just beyond.

"Have either of them moved?" he asked quietly.

"No, they're not even looking this way."

Ethan looked into her eyes and said, "Goodbye, Dr. Tala Espinosa. This was the most wonderful night of my life." He could still feel her gaze as he slipped quietly into the street.

A blizzard of possibilities flooded his head on the walk back to the hotel. Would they come for him in the night? If he'd been identified, they could pick him up any time they wanted. Why had they shown no interest when he left the reception? Why would the Pinkerton even bother going to the reception? None of it made sense. Still, the Pinkerton was in Manila for a reason, and the reason almost certainly related to the man now called Ethan Cooper.

And the woman? It was all a cruel dream; a ridiculous fantasy intended only to distract and taunt him with ambitions of normality. He preferred the reliable comfort of nightmares, but sleep was not in the cards for tonight.

CHAPTER SIX

Lt. Crane had it right. The company's reward for thwarting the assassination plot was a three-day, mid-summer cruise south aboard the USS Benson to another of the seven thousand Philippine islands, one of the largest. A converted cavalry horse transport, the ship's cargo space amidships was crammed with a web-like network of hastily welded iron piping that formed a three-tiered colony of enlisted bunks. It looked like a beehive and smelled like a manure factory. Ethan didn't mind the torturous journey because, a month later, the anticipated dustup from the Pinkerton had never materialized, although the danger still hovered.

On the second night, a monsoon condemned the company to the converted horse stalls below. An hour or so before dawn, the rain stopped, the seas calmed, and Ethan momentarily opened a small porthole, a minor crime, to inhale the hint of a cool, clean breeze. Sleepless, hot and sick from the smell, he fumbled his way up to the main deck, blanket in hand, making his way to the bow. The air was cool and clean. It revived him instantly.

Leaning over the bow rail of the ship in the pre-dawn light, he marveled at a dolphin pod, at least a dozen animals, playfully escorting the converted luxury liner into the heart of the bay. Dolphins might be playful, even friendly, he thought, but they had no more sense than the average common soldier. The more adventurous adults appeared to engage in a competition, each trying to swim closer to the slicing bow stem than the next, keeping always just ahead of disaster. Well-informed dolphins, he thought, sensible ones, would swim great distances to avoid encounters with an American ship, any American ship, in the Philippine Islands.

But at least he'd gotten off Luzon before the Pinkerton with the limp showed up at Camp Sheridan to grab him. The man's presence at the ball could not possibly have been coincidence. From all indications, the steel tycoon had put that bloodhound on Ethan's trail until the job was done.

What could they know? If they knew what name he had taken, surely it would all be over. If they knew what unit he was in, he would be in the brig at this moment.

The Pinkerton was following up on partial information. It was the only logical conclusion. Most likely they had roughed up old Mr. Jeffries or his wife at the Hanover Grill and found out he'd gone to Chicago to enlist. But Jeffries was a smart old coot as well as a good man. That was why he didn't want to know names, not his old name and not his new one. If fifty people enlisted that month in Chicago and ten of them fit Ethan's description, maybe they had narrowed it down to three or four candidates. That was too close for comfort.

"Sergeant Cooper," came the quiet voice from behind.

Ethan turned to find the company physician, Major Lawrence, the oldest of the officers at around forty-five, with him at the bow. The major had joined the company the prior day up the coast at Santa Rita where The Benson dropped off another company at its new posting. Ethan knew the man on Luzon. A gentle fellow with closely cropped, prematurely gray hair and squinty eyes, the doctor had a nervous habit of constantly cleaning his spectacles.

"Ah, Sergeant Cooper," he said. "It was good to see you yesterday."

"Same here, Sir."

The major produced a flask from his pocket. "Drink to a safe voyage? We should be moored off Apostol soon. Join me, please," he said, offering the bottle.

"A little early for me," Ethan replied.

"Or late," the doctor added. "Depends how you look at it. I hope you don't mind my saying you should have been decorated for what you did on that patrol back in Manila. I heard about it at headquarters the next day, and there were those who advocated for citations. It caused quite a ruckus. Are you aware of that?"

"No, Sir." He lied. Ethan just wanted the whole episode buried, just like the army brass did.

"Do you know why nothing was said?"

He would lie again if necessary. Ethan knew better than to lower his guard with an officer, with anyone in the army other than a trusted friend. Burying the entire company in an obscure outpost, he figured, was the army's way of killing the story. He'd been expecting something like this since his conversation with the governor. The last thing the politicians back home wanted was to see an award citation detailing exposure of a plot to kill Taft and MacArthur, not to mention the implication that David Fagen, the infamous Negro deserter, was likely involved. They could have accomplished that goal with a simple order and avoided condemning the company to three days in a floating horse trailer.

Whatever the real story with the insurgents, the very mention of Fagen's name struck fear into the brass at MacArthur's HQ. That much was clear from his visit with Governor Taft. But in this army, curiosity killed more NCO careers than bullets, kind of like Yellow Fever without the fever. William Howard Taft's induction ceremony had been executed like clockwork, without so much as a hint of trouble. Taft thanked Ethan personally, and that was that, hopefully. This major seemed like a decent enough fellow, but sometimes it was better not to stand out.

"I never thought about a citation. Major. It's nothin' to worry about anyway."

"Politics, my boy, politics, but I think, in your own way, you understand all that." Then the major patted Ethan on the shoulder and said, "Enjoy your solitude, Son. I'm going to try for an hour of sleep."

"See you later, Sir," Ethan said, returning his attention to the dolphins, still playing their death-defying game.

He remembered his first voyage into Manila Bay five months ago, when he watched two bored infantrymen shooting the fun-loving dolphins in a drunken gambling competition. By this time, it should be as clear to every living thing in these islands, as it was to that mother in the river, that Americans bring only death and fire, Ethan thought. He wished the dolphins well.

JUST AFTER DAWN, THE SKIES CLEARED AND SEVENTY-ODD MEN OF the company-sized detail emerged for breakfast on the aft deck. Even the humidity cooperated to foster a cool, moist breeze in the storm's wake. The ship had moored off the coast, facing a decent sized coastal town directly off the port side. Ethan reeled at the magnificence of the view. How unlike Manila this place was. Crystalline water from shore to horizon, calm and protected within a large bay, and sparkling in the reflected morning sun. Beyond the beach, a line of banana trees spanned the river mouth, and the tops of coconut palms framed the town in every direction. A Spanish-style church along the river, recognizable by its bell tower and steeple, centered the peaceful-looking *pueblo*.

"I'll be damned," Ethan said, looking down from the rail.

Straight down, the sandy bottom glittered with a kaleidoscopic display of fish; their brilliant colors mapped the courses of intersecting schools. He felt a hand on his shoulder and turned to see Corporal Isaiah Feldman pointing to a spot in the bay, off the bow, to the east of the emerald-green hills. "What in the name of God is that Ethan? Ever seen anything like it?"

He hadn't. Not fifty yards out, a lumbering gray creature, perhaps ten feet in length, floated upside down, its colossal, pale belly soaking in morning sun. A massive, bubble-shaped head supported a tree trunk nose. "Never in my life," was all he could muster. "But it looks friendly enough."

"So does that crowd on the beach, Ethan," Feldman replied. "But you know better than to believe it." The crowd was growing. Men, women, even children gathered near the shore around the dugout fishing boats and bamboo racks loaded with drying fish.

"It's called a Dugong," said Marty, joining them at the rail with what passed for his morning coffee.

"Looks like a floating elephant," Ethan replied.

"They're common enough here but docile," Marty added. "They hang around river mouths and the shallows of the bay. That one looks kinda like Flood in his bunk. As for the crowd, we shall know soon enough."

The crowd on the beach had quadrupled to several hundred in the course of their conversation. "Hard to make out," Ethan said, "but I don't see any guns. Lots of women and kids, I'd say."

"This is the middle of nowhere," Feldman observed. "Where the hell are we?"

"Your guess is good as mine," Marty said, "but I'd say Leyte or Samar. All I know is the army calls the place X-104 and the natives call it Apostol. It's pretty isolated."

"What do we know about them?" Someone asked.

"They're different," Marty replied. "Have their own language and culture distinct from anything we've seen on Luzon. Farmers, traders, and fishermen. They're said to be fierce and independent but not unfriendly to strangers."

The crowd was growing, even as they spoke.

Ethan could see a crowd of VIPs gathering on the foredeck. O'Brien and the ship's officers had cleaned up for the occasion, sporting dress uniforms, swords, and medals.

"I wonder how they like uninvited strangers," Ethan said.

"Oh, I wouldn't be overly concerned," Marty replied. "They have no guns to speak of. Not much they could do to a fully armed company of infantry. I'm more worried about our own allotment of knuckleheads and serial killers. There are no whores here. If they start acting up, there will be trouble. That's bad for everybody."

As more men joined them at the rail, a group of four or five Filipinos on shore split from the crowd and boarded a double-outrigger canoe someone had dragged from off the beach. One was wearing a priest's outfit. "Looks like we'll be having visitors this morning," Ethan said.

"That's what the captain's been waiting for," Marty said. "They'll send a delegation of dignitaries out here to take our measure. They'll have a pow wow, and O'Brien will spell out the rules and the logistics."

"Why are we even here, Marty?" Ethan asked.

"Aid to the insurgency. These coastal towns along the rivers are important trading ports for the bigger islands. Growers in the hills ship their abaca crops downriver for transport to ocean-going ports.

"The coconut palms grow like weeds here. The coconut trade more or less sustains the towns, and they export them upriver and up the west coast. This is the perfect place from which to resupply insurgent forces."

The canoe had set a snail's course straight for the Benson. In the bow of the small vessel sat a strange-looking, little man wearing, of all things, a Nineteenth Century naval hat. It was a classic triangular officer's hat, likely of Spanish Naval origin.

The canoe held four people, not five, and their faces began to take shape behind the almost comical figure in the bow. He held a long cane or staff with a string of gold tassels, obviously some cultural symbol of his authority. The priest wore the traditional black cassock, and one of the paddlers resembled the *Indios* on Luzon. The fourth man seemed almost out of place. Tall, even by American standards, his ears, so expansive they might have wind-powered the little canoe, set low around a long, hollow face. A strong physique and careful grooming emitted an air of authority or importance.

59

Parted hair suggested a military man while his white, Western-style undershirt told Ethan he may have shed a uniform shirt for this occasion.

"Little guy with the sailor hat and staff holds the rank, I'd say," Ethan observed. "Looks like Napoleon."

"He's just the ranking civilian," Marty suggested. "The priests have called the shots all over these islands, not just on Luzon, but it doesn't make sense. That priest is a Filipino and I've never seen one who isn't Spanish."

Hobbs took leave to join the reception committee: the ship's captain, his Executive Officer, O'Brien, Dr. Lawrence, Renaldo, and a few ship's officers. Some sailors hurried to place a small table and benches on the forward deck, and another released the portable stairway for the reception. With the forward deck roped off to all but a small guard armed with Krags, the soldiers gathered round out of earshot, clueless witnesses to the diplomatic engagement. The sight of Captain O'Brien accepting a basket of fresh coconuts and mangoes apparently announced the surrender of Apostol to a superior force.

There would be no storming of the beach, no firing on the town, no slaughter of civilians. As with everything else in the army, details would trickle down in time, but Ethan could already read the disappointment in the faces of the company's most willing and accomplished killers, already smelling a turkey shoot.

An hour later, when O'Brien and Flood headed for shore in a launch with a rifle squad, everyone on board the transport knew the trip was to negotiate for, or to appropriate, if necessary, suitable headquarters and billeting in the town.

ANOTHER NIGHT ABOARD THE USS HORSESHIT DIDN'T KILL ANYONE. In the evening, Ethan and Marty attended an NCO briefing on the aft deck, where O'Brien addressed their mission.

The bad guy, he explained, was a general named Martinez. He was originally sent here by Aguinaldo's so-called Philippine government. Not a local. His headquarters was up in the hills. There had been guerilla attacks, some even by locals, against other companies garrisoned in this part of the Philippines. Martinez ran the *insurrecto* operation and had a base of operations deep in the jungle somewhere. He was completely autonomous and got supplies and men from the coastal villages, especially minor ports. Nobody had been able to find him, so the company's mission was to starve him out.

AT DAWN, THE ASSEMBLED COMPANY WATCHED AS A SMALL FLEET of native dugouts, *barotas,* set course for the Benson to ferry troops and supplies. Flood had briefed the company noncoms on the logistics with the aid of a crudely drawn map of the town center. It was a simple layout, not much different from those in small town USA: a town square about the size of a baseball field, framed by two stone structures, the Spanish-style church to the west along the river and the municipal building, facing it on the east. Prominent homes lined the north end of the square with concentric dirt roads or trails sprouting in three directions from the square. Everything faced the square.

Essentially, the *principalia,* a loosely defined group of influential citizens, according to Flood, had "agreed" to temporarily vacate three private homes on the north end of the town square for NCO billeting. The first floor of the stone municipal building would serve as enlisted quarters with the Company HQ in the foyer. The armory and quartermaster would occupy the second floor.

The church annex, a two-story living quarters for the priest, was designated the officers' quarters. The idea, Ethan knew, was to control the space around the beach and the wharf on the river, near the church. Outside the square itself, the entire town seemed to exist purposefully under a canopy of thick vegetation, even between the individual huts.

As the group moved cautiously into the town from the beach, Ethan noticed that the homes, including the houses, were virtually all built on stilts and constructed almost entirely of bamboo and abaca with large window openings, replicas of the huts on Luzon. The window covers adjusted manually with a bamboo pole to account for the sun or the weather generally. A plentiful supply of coconut palms provided leaves for the thatched roofs throughout the town.

The family or their proxies were still clearing out personal items when Ethan and his dozen or so newly billeted barracks mates arrived with kit at their assigned quarters. Ethan's assigned home structure had been designated Grant Barracks. This place was a fine house, in relative terms, two stories with a large bedroom across the top floor. The room was accessible from a bamboo ladder on the inside and on the outside from a ladder at the north end of the house. The private homes had been assigned to noncoms. As the municipal building could not accommodate all the privates, Flood had been careful to house the company's most notorious troublemakers with the sergeants and corporals as an extra security measure.

As they were all unpacking and sorting out their new quarters, Marty walked in with a full kit. Ethan had reserved him a good spot under the window. "Okay, boys," Marty announced. "Listen up. They're setting up the mess tent now. I have the guard rotations for the rest of the night and tomorrow. I'll post the order on the wall here. Settle in, but don't let your guard down. This place may look peaceful enough, but it can kill you just as quick as Manila. Welcome to the end of the world."

CHAPTER SEVEN

"I have a few points to make clear to every man in this company," O'Brien began, addressing the full, assembled company, as confirmed moments ago by the morning roll call. "Our mission here is to close the port and to prevent resupply by land or water of insurgent forces in the hills."

The company stood, fully armed, twenty abreast and four rows deep, minus the four posted guards, facing the church and flagpole. Hundreds of locals, men, women, and children had gathered around the perimeter, just inside the encroaching vegetation for their first glimpse of these foreign invaders with modern rifles. Some appeared curious, others afraid, but neither hostile nor particularly friendly. If there was a general sentiment in this crowd regarding the invaders, Ethan could not detect it.

These people looked distinguishable from the Tagalogs of Luzon, barely, though not by fashion of dress. The men appeared larger, more muscular. A slightly lighter skin tone seemed to define the village population. Some of the women were uncommonly beautiful.

"We will be living and working amongst the local population for an undetermined period of time. Remember, this is not Manila. The hills to the north and the east are controlled by the insurgents. Some of them may be in the crowd today," O'Brien added, pointing around the perimeter. Ethan found the captain's last sentence unsettling, but Marty had already warned the men against complacency.

Before O'Brien could finish his tiresome monologue, a young boy burst from the crowd, running full speed directly past the front row of the formation. The kid was making funny faces and holding out his belly mockingly, causing the entire company to burst out in laughter.

"You are at attention," O'Brien screamed. "Now, we are not here to kill or confront people. So long as the population cooperates, we will extend them courtesy and friendship. You will have unavoidable free time here. Rules will be posted in writing for every man to see. Be clear. There will be no fraternization with the local women. There are no prostitutes here, men. We will conduct ourselves as Christians. We will be friendly, when possible, but remember you are on hostile ground. Your Krag will remain within reach. No man travels outside the compound alone. If you patronize a local drinking establishment in your free time, keep in mind I won't tolerate drunken behavior.

"As you know, the natives have their own language here. You will find no English speakers and very few speak Spanish well. Sergeants will meet with First Sergeant Flood for assignments following drill. We'll make this filthy place sanitary and in secure military order with dispatch."

One of the head cases in the back row couldn't resist a whispered comment. "Last thing I'm going to do to these buxom cows is have a conversation." Ethan could hear the low chuckles in the back row. It sounded like an omen of bad things to come.

"Finally," O'Brien said, "Sergeant Tours, you will immediately organize a search for weapons and an inventory of food supplies and livestock for the entire town. See Sergeant Flood to arrange logistics. You will begin first thing tomorrow."

O'BRIEN HAD ALLOTTED MARTY JUST THREE DAYS TO SEARCH A decentralized town of at least two thousand people. He and Ethan had appropriated five men for the detail, including Corporal Brock, unofficial orderly to the officers. The inventory team, including Brock, was to meet the local police chief at the adjoining church. The chief would assign a translator and a few native laborers to aid in the work. Renaldo, whose translation services were much in demand, accompanied the detail just in case of communication issues.

The chief with the ears and the padre were waiting in the vestibule of the church when the inventory detail arrived after breakfast. The police chief wore a khaki uniform shirt with no insignia, and the priest a cotton shirt with his religious collar. There was a young woman with them. To Ethan's surprise, she stepped forward alone without prompting. Looking Marty directly in the eye, she said, "Greetings, *Sargento.*"

"Good morning, Miss," he replied.

Perhaps twenty-eight, the woman was tall and full-figured for an island girl, with sharply defined features and deep, Hazel eyes, unlike any Ethan had seen. While darker than Tala's, her skin was just as smooth, like it had never seen the sun, with no trace of the dust and dirt that plagued all the hard-working, outdoor women of the Philippines. Odd in such a place as this, Ethan thought.

She wore plain, flat shoes, a sign of status, and a dark cotton skirt falling well below the knees above trim ankles. It hung loosely around strong thighs and rolled like a gentle wave when she shifted or moved her ample hips. Her blouse was pure white with puffy sleeves under bare shoulders and cut precisely low enough to stimulate a healthy imagination. A crop of silky, black hair dropped straight along both cheeks to frame a strikingly sensual face. She was undeniably Filipina in appearance and in dress—and much more.

"I am Asuncion," she announced matter-of-factly in Spanish. "Welcome." The girl turned and pointed a beautifully sculpted hand at the police chief. "This is Señor Mariano Obrador, Chief of the Constabulary." Then the other hand. The woman was no field worker. "Father Vega is our Pastor and spiritual advisor. Señor Obrador speaks some English and excellent Spanish. I am the only one here fluent in both. *She's answered the question of why she took the lead, partly,* Ethan thought.

As the preliminaries continued, Asuncion addressed Marty and Ethan simultaneously. Smiling, she asked, "You gentlemen are both sergeants with three stripes. May I ask which is the leader?"

Marty tipped his hat. "I guess I am, Ma'am," he said eagerly, like a teenager noticing a nice pair of jugs for the first time. This was a new Marty. He was one of the few men who rarely, if ever, sought the comfort of the bar girls always within arms-reach of an American outpost.

With introductions complete, the group gathered around a table in the vestibule to discuss logistics while the privates and laborers waited outside. The chief provided a crudely drawn map of the town that looked extremely useful to Ethan.

Obrador addressed the group in Spanish with Asuncion providing a running translation. Ethan didn't need it. "If it is acceptable to you, Sergeant Tours, Asuncion will take you on a tour of the town to assist in your task. We have notified all residents that you will have unlimited access for the purpose of your inventory. I would take you myself but for the fact that I am meeting later with Captain O'Brien regarding cleanup of the town. May we assume your soldiers will conduct themselves respectfully?"

"Of course," Marty replied.

On their walk out of the church, Brock said to Marty, "Sarge, you know if these people are hiding anything, they might be inclined to give you a doctored map to throw you off the track."

"I thought about that," Marty said, "but the map will save us a lot of work. We'll keep a special lookout for any structures that don't match up. Those would be the most likely places to find weapons or undeclared food stocks, so a doctored map helps us."

There were no addresses on the map, so Marty simply assigned a number to each building, adding or moving a structure on the map where required. Brock would later record the inventoried items for each number in his notebook. The woman was cooperative but nothing approaching friendly.

The bamboo huts lay largely clustered around cleared vegetation off the trail. O'Brien's primary interest, other than weapons, lay in stores of rice and Asuncion led them straight away to three storage huts full. It didn't seem much of a reserve for an entire town, Ethan thought, certainly not enough to share with an army.

The dirt trail widened into a kind of main street, where a few modest shops and small vendor stalls lined both sides, offering fruits, vegetables, fish and even rice. Ethan counted four tuba stands, all with drinking customers. Everywhere, natural vegetation between and around the bamboo huts threatened to literally swallow them. The huts all had personal gardens.

A mutual sense of wariness seemed to prevail with every contact. Even on the main street, the locals stared while taking pains to avoid interaction. Everyone knew the woman and deferred to her. A bartender, a lone exception to the shyness, smiled and motioned the group toward his tuba stand for afternoon refreshment. Over the entrance, Ethan spotted a freshly painted sign reading, *Ryan's Bar.* Either the man's name was Ryan, Ethan figured, or he was soliciting American patrons. The proprietor's language, of course, was incomprehensible but friendly in tone. There was apparently a profitable side to occupation, Ethan thought.

As the dirt street receded back into the jungle trail, Marty and the woman kept just far enough ahead to be out of earshot. Non-stop chatter told Ethan the pair were having no trouble communicating. They reached a group of huts on the slope of a hill at the eastern end of town to wait for the rest of the group. A pack of young boys went nearly wild with excitement at their appearance and began to congregate around them. The rifles seemed to consume the boys' attention. Asuncion scolded them in Waray, the local language, but failed to discourage their performance. They kept walking, and the children followed.

"Why is the rice supply so low in this town and why is it not growing here?" Marty asked.

"We trade for most of our rice," she explained, with Ethan's help. "It comes from upriver, in the hills. They can grow it year-round up there. Here, on the coast, we have only one harvest per year. That is in May. If you close the port, *Sargento* Tours, will you allow us to trade for what we need?"

"I'm only a sergeant," Marty explained. Ethan knew nothing of rice, but he knew something about farming generally and he knew about seasons and rainfall. Her explanation made sense, as did her request, but he thought it best to keep his mouth shut. Then Marty surprised his friend when he added, "Let me think about it. I might be able to raise the issue."

After Brock recorded the four chickens, one pig and endless bananas, the group resumed its walk with the boys in tow. Ethan was close enough to hear Marty say to the woman, "It would be helpful if you could come with us tomorrow as well."

"If you like," she replied without emotion.

Marty smiled like a horny schoolboy. "In the meantime, I'll ask our lieutenant about your problem with the rice." There was no harm in asking, Ethan figured. If O'Brien was sincere about not wanting any trouble with the locals, maybe they could all broker some kind of deal these people could live with.

"We are all grateful for your help, *Sargento* Tours" she said with no hint of sarcasm and no smile. *Oh, no. He's going to say, call me Marty.*

Sure enough. He blushed and gushed, "You can call me Marty."

At that point, Ethan decided to interrupt. He said to Asuncion, "I'm curious as to how you learned English and what your function is in the town. I mean no disrespect, *Señorita.*"

She showed no hint of annoyance. "I am an assistant to our priest and the people of our church. My work includes cooking and cleaning for Father Vega, even maintaining his account books. I was fortunate to attend the Spanish school for several years."

"Then who is really in charge here?" Ethan asked.

She seemed not to have heard the question-maybe.

As they emerged from the jungle near the town square, a young boy appeared, apparently to deliver her a message. They spoke in Waray. Then she said, "I'm sorry, *Sargento* Tours. I must return to my duties. Please inform me what your lieutenant says about our rice. Thank you."

After she walked away, Ethan said to Brock, "That's all very strange. That woman has her nose right up a coconut tree like she's the Duchess of Asia."

Marty smiled like a child and said, "Yeah, isn't she something?"

A FEW HOURS BEFORE DAWN, NATURE SUMMONED ETHAN COOPER from a sweat-soaked mattress in the Grant Barracks. Escaping from the mosquito bar and unencumbered by clothing, he managed to find his Russet shoes in the blackness. The Philippines was home to a hundred crawling things that could kill a man silently in the dark. Outside, he could see the glow of dim lamplight from behind the house in the area of the makeshift privy. He would have company on the privy log.

"Good evening, Marty," he said, resting his ass on the scratchy log beside his friend, careful to avoid the parallel ditch underneath and just behind.

Looking up and framed by the dim light, Marty said, "Good evening, Ethan. Beautiful night. In a week or so, the bark will be worn down. It won't be so damned scratchy. People will flock here at night just for the view."

"You never stop, Marty."

So they sat there, side by side, beneath a canopy of stars. "What are you doing here, Ethan? Marty asked pensively. "I mean why the army? I know you don't want to be here."

Marty was his best friend, his only friend if you didn't count Jonesy, but a confession now couldn't help either of them and might even put Marty in jeopardy. As long as Marty was in the dark, nobody could credibly accuse him of concealing a fugitive. So, he told his friend a small part of the truth. "My old man was with the 62d Pennsylvania in The War. It kind of defined him. You know?"

"Yeah, I get it. *I wanna be like my father.* That's one of the outfits in the fancy French uniforms. Lifelong glory and respect. Well,

Ethan, you missed your war. No glory here, but you already know that."

The nocturnal jungle behind them offered only silence, save the clatter of crickets. There they sat for a fair spell, two bare behinds under a crescent moon on the edge of the jungle at the end of the world. For a long while, neither man felt the need to break the silence. Then, just as Ethan had decided to tell his friend about Tala Espinosa, Marty announced quietly, "I'm a priest, Ethan."

"What?"

"A Roman fucking Catholic priest."

Marty's startling revelation had neither solicited a response nor invited further inquiry. If and when his friend chose to elaborate or entertain questions on the disclosure, he would surely say so. Ethan waited patiently for more information as spear-wielding mosquitos began to venture from the jungle's edge to assault his bottom. His wait was rewarded.

"My real name is Martin Pisiewski. My parents were immigrants from Poland, or what used to be Poland. They settled in Chicago where I was born, and my father worked in a meat packing plant at the Chicago Stockyards. Their lives were something out of *Dante's Inferno,* living hand to mouth, barely enough money to eat and shelter us. Somehow, they managed to keep me in the Catholic school, to pay for it while still giving money to the Church every Sunday. A priest at the school recognized that I had the potential to learn and be of use to God...and well..."

Marty's revelation had nearly knocked Ethan off the shit log. It made him feel even worse about not coming clean with his friend.

Ethan heard leaves rustling around his feet and saw a brown and white-spotted snake traversing the top of his left shoe. He hated snakes. He sprang to his feet, trying to kick the damn thing off his foot, but forgot that his trousers were around his ankles. The first kick sent him reeling face first into the mud.

Marty nearly toppled backward into the ditch, laughing. "It's only a damn wolf snake, Ethan. It won't hurt you."

Someone yelled down from the second floor of the barracks. "What the hell is going on out there? Can we get some damn sleep?"

"Sorry," Ethan said, angrily reclaiming his warm spot on the log. "Wouldn't surprise me if you put the damn thing there, Marty. So,

69

finish the story already. The priest saw you were smart. What happened?"

"…He conscripted me into God's service, you might say, a first class, university education for free, specializing in Jesus. My father died of consumption just after I left, and my mother died three months before I became a priest. She dropped dead doing other people's laundry. But for them, I would have quit years earlier. Anyway, with no other marketable skills, I decided to proceed with the plan and become a carnival barker for Jesus. I always resented that the Church should flourish by vacuuming money from the very people who looked to it for advocacy against injustice and poverty. Ethan, would you pass me a handful of those leaves?"

The big, soft ones were favored for certain hygienic tasks and Ethan had gathered an ample supply to be safe, plenty to share. Ethan couldn't restrain himself. "So why New York?"

"Well, as a young priest, I preached of love and virtue and the evils of sin. When I visited the homes of my parishioners and treated their misery with the sign of the cross, the self-loathing began to consume me. I had become a link in the very chain that bound these miserable human beings. *There is no God*, I finally admitted to myself. I quit and looked for the most anonymous place I could find outside of Chicago, far away. New York was a natural choice. I took a new name and taught school for a year. Turned out it wasn't anonymous enough. One morning I thought, why not join the army and see what the rest of the world is like? Maybe you can find a place even more miserable than this. So here I am."

"Why pick the name of a Catholic saint?" Ethan asked. "Isn't that kind of rubbing it in?"

Marty laughed. "Sure. Self-flagellation. That's the point maybe."

For Ethan Cooper, the revelations had been a lot to absorb, so he sat silently for a minute as Marty finished his business. Finally, his thoughts collected atop the shit log, Ethan looked at his forearms and said, "I have my own story, Marty, but I just can't talk about it. I hope you can understand. See, it's not that I don't want to. It's just that it would put you in a tough spot right now."

The damned Pinkerton in the fiddler's cap could show here tomorrow and have him clamped in irons. He just didn't want Marty in a spot where he had to lie. They'd put him in the brig without batting an eye.

"That's what I thought," Marty replied. "Well, don't worry one bit. Tell me or don't tell me, in your own time. Makes no matter to me. We're partners."

Then Ethan looked at his two forearms and said, "I will tell you about the girls."

Marty's malicious smile penetrated the darkness. "Well, that ought to be entertaining."

"It was on a trip to the Black Hills for my twenty-first birthday. I was between farm hand jobs and figured it was time I saw something outside Pennsylvania. Deadwood was still a pretty wild place back then. So, I got to drinkin' and gambling there and kind of met up with these twin sisters, Nona and Mona. They were half-breeds, Cheyenne, I think. I had some winnings in my pocket, and we all spent a few days together. Met them on Thursday and married them both, I think, sometime Saturday night. When the fog cleared, I learned their father was the town marshal, so I headed back East real quick, with the tattoos, not the girls, as I recall." He pointed to the left arm and said, "This is Mona, I think, and the other one is Nona."

"But how did you get a judge to marry you off to two women at the same time?" Marty asked.

"Simple. He was drinkin' with us."

CHAPTER EIGHT

"Give it up, Sarge," one of the privates hollered from his position at first base. "That kid'll never be Honus Wagner."

"Shut up and give him a chance," Ethan quipped. Then, turning back toward home plate, he took the bat from the boy's hand and started again. "No, no, no. Use two hands. It's not a bolo. Like this...Wait for the ball. You're swinging too early." The instructions fell upon a smile and deaf ears, but maybe the demonstration would help, Ethan thought.

"Strike two," said the umpire, Marty Tours, as the boy swung wildly at a pitch well outside the zone. Ethan laughed. It felt good and fun, and for a moment, he was a boy again. But for the bare feet and the unconventional outfit, the image of this skinny, eager youngster at bat mirrored those of his boyhood.

Exasperated, he waved Renaldo, O'Brien's interpreter, over from the sidelines. "Explain to the kid we're not trying to harvest crops or clear the jungle. It's about rhythm and timing. Two hands on the bat, eye on the ball. Wait for the pitch."

The infielders all laughed. The third baseman, the company cook, said, "Show him how it's done, Sarge. See if you can put one in the bell tower."

"No, thank you," Ethan replied. Looking out to the pitcher, he said, "Come on. Lob a few in there for the kid, Jimmy."

"Okay. Put him in the batter's box."

Marty stepped out from behind the plate, taking the bat from Ethan's hands. "Step aside while I show you how to coach," he said.

He handed the bat to the youngster, adjusting his hands to the right position. "Not too tight," he cautioned, signaling for a translation. "¿Cómo te llamas?" he asked the boy.

"Pollito," the kid answered, smiling. Almost everyone in the town understood a few simple Spanish phrases.

Ethan watched along the sideline as the young batter awkwardly fanned on pitch after pitch. He yelled, "Renaldo, tell him stop holding it like a rifle. Keep the hands together."

Before the next pitch, Ethan heard the doctor's voice from behind. "Well, Cooper, enjoying your new job as Community Liaison, I see." He nodded at Marty. "Morning, Tours."

They did not salute, in accordance with leisure activity protocols. "Good morning, Major Lawrence," Ethan said.

"So how is the baseball coach thing going?"

"It's going well, Sir," Ethan replied.

Marty looked over from behind home plate smiling and said, "If they don't pick it up soon, Sir, we can always burn them alive in their homes."

The major just shook his head. He was getting to know Marty. Maybe they were even kindred spirits, Ethan thought.

Marty just couldn't keep his mouth shut, but he knew the old doctor had no interest in military discipline. Protocol aside, Marty's comment made sense. Community baseball had sounded like lunacy when Flood gave them the assignment a couple of weeks ago, so the idea must have come straight from Captain O'Brien. Burn people alive in their homes one day; teach them baseball the next. Still, Ethan and Marty were both warming to it. Ethan had forgotten that a man could have fun without liquor or bar girls.

The major said, "Well, that young man batting looks about military age, sixteen anyway. The more of those we win over, the better." Then he pulled out his specs and began wiping. "By the way, gentlemen," he added. "Yesterday's patrol just returned and reported no insurgent activity again. That means no trouble since we arrived."

The crack of a bat interrupted their conversation. By the time Ethan could focus on the action, the ball was rolling past the right fielder, and Pollito was streaking full-steam and barefoot around the bases—the wrong way, with a smile that required no translation. Marty was going wild, and the crowd of two dozen or so locals cheered and clapped like it was a National League game in Pittsburgh. Ethan spotted Asuncion in the crowd, standing near the town well with an old woman. She was clapping wildly, radiating a smile with the power to span oceans and defeat armies. She was a very beautiful woman, and Ethan had already entertained romantic thoughts. He could tell Marty had not escaped her charms either.

"I see the game is catching on," the major said. "Are we trying to impress a lady?"

As Pollito crossed the plate to a cheering crowd, Marty stepped over to join the conversation. Major Lawrence added. "You're doing a fine job here, Sergeant Tours."

When the chaos had settled a bit, Marty said, "Thank you, Sir. Oh, have you heard anything about the town's request for some exceptions to the trading ban and port closure? I spoke to Lieutenant Hobbs about it."

"Nothing at all and, frankly, I wouldn't hold my breath, but Hobbs did raise the subject. Captain O'Brien follows what you might call a narrow interpretation of orders, as you know. Probably not wise to be advocating for the townspeople, Tours. I'd be more concerned about the temperature of the town if I were you." The major was telling Marty to mind his own business, that O'Brien did not appreciate sergeants engaging in diplomacy.

Looking disappointed, Marty said, "I understand, Sir, but accessing the mood here's not so easy. We can't get a read on it."

"Hostility?"

"Not right off, Sir. Not really. Just a feeling like maybe these people haven't decided that yet."

As the defense started running off the makeshift field, Ethan realized the game had ended, and he started collecting equipment.

"I'll let you know if I get any helpful information," the major said to Marty. "The Police Chief, Obrador, is coming by the officers' quarters after dinner. We've been playing chess. I must say I like the man. He's educated and thoughtful, but who knows? Maybe he just likes my Scotch whiskey. Anyway, I will raise the subject with him."

"Thank you, Sir," Marty replied. "If you don't mind my asking, Sir, what does Captain O'Brien think about this? Our situation with the locals, I mean."

The doctor appeared to consider the question, then said, "Walk with me, gentlemen. I'm off to dress for cocktails and dinner. That means clean the mud off my shoes and brush my hair." As they passed the Meade Barracks, he said, "I'm glad you asked that question. Between you and me, I think our captain should be less worried about women's clothing and more worried about whose side these people are on. That's the big question."

"Women's clothing, Sir?" Ethan said.

"He's talking about regulating the female clothing in the town. Thinks it's too provocative, might trigger some unchristian or violent behavior by the troops. Oh, right, you haven't heard. Well, he's also thinking about banning cockfighting."

"No, Sir," Marty replied. "We hadn't heard."

Ethan said, "I see." *Careful, Cooper*, he told himself. Ethan wasn't about to discuss one officer's shortcomings with another, even after an opening like that. No future in it.

The major chuckled. "Relax. I'm not trying to involve you in mutiny, Cooper, but keep your eyes open and an ear to the ground for me. I'll provide our God-fearing captain solid advice. That's all we can do."

"Yes, Sir. We understand," said Ethan.

The crowd had largely dispersed, but Ethan spotted young Pollito at the well talking with Asuncion and the old woman and saw an opportunity. The kid had been hanging around her for a couple of weeks. This time Asuncion was barefoot, and the skirt was dark and tight, a wraparound.

Ethan had to admit his fascination with the woman. Her beauty was obvious; everything else about her was subtle, even mysterious. She was educated though not refined, assertive though not confident, and clearly a woman set apart from the ho hum experience of life in a poor coastal village. *Exotic* was the word that came to Ethan's mind with a kind of serpentine-like attraction.

True to form, Marty had seen her first and said, "Come on, walk over there with me."

At the well, Marty said, *"Buenas tardes, Señorita. Hace mucho calor hoy. ¿Puedo tener una taza de agua?"* That was about all the Spanish Marty knew. Ethan knew he was showing off for the girl.

Before Asuncion could even reply, Sergeant Major Flood came barreling toward him from the nearby orderly room.

"Cooper," he said, "tomorrow is Sunday. The captain wants you to pick a detail of eight men and conduct an observation at the cockfights. You know where the pit is?"

"Of course, Sarge."

It appeared the doctor had his finger on the pulse of X-104. "All right, observe and make a full report. The captain is interested in anything unusual, suspicious characters, large amounts of money, any vice or other violence. You understand?"

Ethan sensed immediately that such a conversation in the woman's presence was ill-advised. She spoke English better than

Flood himself, yet the sergeant major gave her no more consideration than he would a rock or a tree. "Yes, Sergeant," Ethan replied in a low voice. "They do it right after Sunday mass. I've got it."

"The captain may even stop by himself to get the lay of the land." Flood plodded off to hunt his next victim as the group around the well had dispersed except for Asuncion and a few youngsters. She offered Marty a bamboo ladle, and he pretended to drink. She might just as easily have offered it to Ethan. The woman almost smiled, Ethan thought, but when she lowered her head, the wide, round brim of her conical straw hat covered the clues. The well water was almost certainly good, but Ethan and Marty had seen too much dysentery and other disease to risk it. She showed no interest in leaving.

Marty said something to Pollito in Spanish. Nobody could understand it, not even Ethan.

"My brother only speaks Waray," Asuncion said. "We are working on it."

Ethan was surprised. He said, "Your brother? Oh, I see." Marty seemed to have taken it in stride.

"He is not *really* my brother," she explained, "but he and another boy live with me in the convent. I take care of them with the assistance of Father Vega."

Then Ethan addressed Pollito in Spanish. He knew the kid wouldn't understand. "You hit the ball well today. I hope to see you out there again."

He could have been talking to the well, but when Asuncion translated, Pollito's smile was warm and sincere in any language.

Ethan knew she had overheard the conversation with Flood, so he decided to give her a bit of lead and see what happened. "Señorita," he began in English. "I know you heard the conversation about cockfighting. I'm curious as to how you would feel if our captain shuts it down."

"*¿Por qué?*" She seemed surprised, then switched back to English. "Why?"

"Obviously, it's an important event in town."

She laughed. Then Pollito laughed. Finally, Marty joined in. Only this woman knew the joke. "Yes," she said. "Cockfighting is *muy importante*. The practice allows every man in town to spend the afternoon away from his children. It allows poor men to squander what little they have on gambling and tuba. Those same men blaspheme and scream like animals to taste the blood of chickens slaughtered in mindless violence.

"But it's not that simple," she continued. "Jose Rizal used the cockfight in his novels to help show us the origin and depth of our enslavement by the Spanish, but Rizal personally deplored all blood sports especially the cockfight. He thought the sport degrading and corrupt. Rizal preached non-violence and education. That did not work with the Spanish, so they hanged him. I cannot speak for our men, *Sargento*, but you will offend no women here by banning the cockfights."

"Rizal was a doctor and novelist," Marty explained. "He's a national hero and martyr, an advocate of peaceful revolution."

Apparently, the two were better acquainted than Ethan knew.

"I must go now," she said, reaching down to lift the big, clay, water container.

Marty said, "Let me help you with the jar."

This time she definitely smiled. "It's called a '*balanga*,' *Martin*, and we are quite adept at carrying them." *Martin? So much for Ethan Cooper's budding exotic romance.* Marty had been keeping a big secret, and Ethan felt like a dunce.

The woman was desirable, no doubt. Maybe it was only jealousy, but she seemed to play Marty like a fiddle, arousing Ethan's suspicions. There was nothing he could put his finger on, maybe just a soldier's instinct for caution, but it had served him well in the past.

They were in a strange place among strange people on a largely hostile island. He liked these people as much as Marty did, but things are not always what they seem, he knew. Ethan should not have been surprised when she addressed his friend as *Martin*, since Marty's bed had been rarely slept in over the last couple of weeks. Ethan wasn't the only one who'd heard him tiptoeing into the barracks before Reveille, but he had not connected the clues.

Nobody paid attention to the captain's "no fraternization" order. Nocturnal wandering was the norm. It was Martin Tours himself that worried Ethan. He worried for Marty because with all his education and knowledge of history combined with all his natural skepticism and cynicism, Marty was pitifully inexperienced with women.

Marty didn't normally charge too aggressively or trust too easily. Apparently, this woman carried a natural ability to breach his defenses. The real question was whether she had an agenda. Was she employing too much effort in impressing Marty? If so, why? There was an uneasiness in the air, and Martin's vulnerability to this woman was beginning to look like a character flaw that could get him killed. Ethan hoped he was overreacting. It didn't take an education to see that Asuncion could be a formidable and dangerous adversary. Over the past few years, the Filipinos had crafted creative and deadly methods of resisting occupation. Taken together, this raised the bigger question of whether there was some organized plan of resistance afoot.

BY SUNDAY, STILL SHORT OF A MONTH INTO OCCUPATION, THE Pinkerton had still not shown his face, and the men had learned firsthand that Sunday mass was really a warmup to the week's main event. The Sunday Cockfights routinely drew hundreds of male spectators, gamblers, drinkers, both rich and poor, from the nearby barrios and even some neighboring islands. Locals had also hosted two lesser, "unsanctioned" cockfights in the evenings earlier that week.

Cockfighting, Ethan knew, was the equivalent of the Philippines' national sport and attracted virtually every male over the age of sixteen. Several of the other troopers had also figured out that Sunday after mass was the safest time to court the town's shy but eager young ladies. The back doors and hidden beaches were awash in cavorting troopers.

All year round, they would gather at the cockpit behind the main street for the great sadistic spectacle. Merchants, traders, fishermen, farmers, and an assortment of bust outs routinely assembled to watch the cockers and the murderous chickens themselves in a bloody round robin of death. The event brought wild cheering, money, and plenty of the local tuba. Sometimes it brought trouble, Ethan knew. They were about to learn what the addition of eight armed American soldiers would bring.

As the cockers readied their birds for the first match that Sunday, Ethan had found himself standing beside none other than Mariano Obrador. "On duty, Chief?" He asked.

"It depends," answered the chief. "A few of my men are always here just in case. When you mix tuba and violence with gambling, sometimes you get trouble."

Before he could respond, Ethan spotted the company commander, O'Brien, standing on a nearby slope, hands clasped together in back, around his hips. The cockfights on this Sunday, Ethan knew, would be judged from a Biblical perspective.

"It's a bit strange," Ethan observed. "The men come out of church and head straight for the death matches, kind of like the Christians and the lions. How does the Church feel about it?"

The chief let go a laugh until his ears wiggled. "It's all taxed by the church," he said. "Father Vega will get his cut of the wagering tomorrow morning. In the time of the Spanish friars, the padres encouraged the sport and pocketed a hefty tax from the wagering for their personal coffers. Try to cheat them and you'd be off in chains on the next ship."

"And you have no problem with that?" Ethan asked.

"Not anymore. Our current padre is Filipino. He is one of us, a good man who uses the tax for everyone's benefit."

"I've been to the cockfights in Manila," said Ethan, "and always wondered how they make the fight matches."

The crowd went silent as the referee dropped his hand for the duel to begin. Each of the two crouching men in the pit slid the protective sheath from the razor-sharp blade fastened to his bird's leg. They held the birds closer together for a moment, allowing them to peck at each other in anticipation of the fight. As the men moved away, the birds circled one another warily.

"They try to match them by size and weight," the chief explained. "There will be eight or ten matches. The shortest kill time is the winner."

A minute passed and nothing happened. The crowd began to boo as the circling continued. "What happens if they don't fight?" Ethan asked.

Before the chief could answer, a roar erupted as the two birds collided full force in mid-air with a thud, wings disappearing into a whirling weave of colors and dust. Flashing steel and splashing blood sparked a ghoulish euphoria in the crowd. When the dust cleared, the smaller chicken lay stone dead in the dirt as the winner crowed over the body.

"A clean kill," said Obrador. "If it has to be done, that's the best way, quick and merciful."

As the bets were settled and the new cockers entered the ring, Ethan sensed an opportunity to find out something about the woman, maybe something about this police chief as well. He said, "I'm curious about the woman, Señor Obrador. She seems to be widely respected here, a person of influence even. I've been here long enough to know that's uncommon."

One of Obrador's policemen stepped between them, offering the chief a jar of tuba. He took a long drink and handed the jar to Ethan. "Enjoy yourself," he said. "Everyone is behaving well."

"Thanks. I will."

"I will tell you about Asuncion because we are proud to have her with us. She was near thirteen when her parents disappeared on the bay somewhere in a *banca*. We had a Spanish friar back then as did every Catholic *pueblo*. The friar was the real power in every town and village. Some were kinder than others. This one was particularly cruel and sadistic. He offered to "mentor" little Asuncion after the accident and moved her into the convent. He ensured that she was educated, but his charitable motives ended there. Before long, everyone in this *pueblo* understood what "mentorship" meant, but no one lifted a hand to help her. The abuse went on for years until just before Spain's war with the Americans when the friars abandoned this part of the island."

"But doesn't she still live there?" Ethan asked.

"Yes, but by choice and by the grace of a good man, Father Vega." She helps him with his work and takes care of the church while she raises two orphans in the convent. It is we citizens who are shamed by what happened here, yet Asuncion has forgiven us and given herself over to a life of service."

Ethan found it a moving and powerful account but noted the briefing did not include her possible connection to a certain Filipino general running around the hills making war on Americans. He decided not to push for now.

BY THE NEXT MORNING, THE CAT, OR RATHER THE COCK, WAS OUT of the bag. As expected, the *Principalia* erupted over the very suggestion of a cockfighting ban. The mayor, complete with hat, led an irate preemptive committee to Captain O'Brien's office in the orderly room where Ethan's watch as sergeant of the guard was about to end. O'Brien had left instructions not to be disturbed, a *de facto* assignment of his dirty work to Lt. Hobbs.

Hobbs, Renaldo, Ethan, and two armed sentries confronted the group outside the main entrance of the municipal building. They communicated through the translator Renaldo. It didn't take a linguist to catch the gist of the confrontation. The group wished to register a protest and requested a face-to-face clarification of the rumor in a meeting with Captain O'Brien. Hobbs informed them it was no longer a rumor. Cockfighting was done, and O'Brien was too busy to meet with them.

A burly police sergeant stepped forward from the group. He seemed always to be silently present when the *Principalia* interacted officially with O'Brien or his Headquarters. No one was certain of his role or function. The man was plainly dressed, with broad shoulders and light features. The eyes hinted at Chinese and set him apart from the locals in physical appearance. He was out of place, a decidedly suspicious character, and Ethan decided to discuss the subject with Marty.

The man addressed Hobbs through the translator in excellent Spanish, making no effort to conceal his anger with no hint of timidity. "This is not an affluent place, Sir. The people here depend heavily on the revenue generated by the cockfights. This sport is embedded in our culture and this decision will not sit well with the people."

First Hobbs tried to bully him with logic. "Sir, our commander has determined that cockfighting is neither sport, nor is it art. The cockfights present a potentially lucrative source of funding for Martinez and his fighters in the hills. That's precisely what we're here to stop."

Then the lieutenant tried friendly persuasion. "I would remind you all that no less than General Aguinaldo himself banned cockfighting across the Philippines during the period of his insurrection. He considers the practice inhumane and debasing. As you know, he has now pledged allegiance to the United States' authority here."

Even the lowly sergeant from Pennsylvania noticed that no one in the room dared argue on the subject of Emilio Aguinaldo, but their faces to a man expressed a palpable sense of anger. It sounded more like the voice of Captain O'Brien himself, the intractable moralist and Biblical scholar. Ethan had a clear and ominous affirmation that the citizens of Outpost X-104 had chosen a side— and O'Brien was poking a crocodile in the eye.

CHAPTER NINE

"According to General Hughes," said Captain O'Brien, standing beside a perfectly useless map on his wall, "intelligence indicates a serviceable trail straight up the middle of this island. It may even lead to Martinez's base of operations."

According to General Hughes, intelligence indicates..., Ethan repeated to himself. *Somebody is taking a wild guess.* He regretted being handed this detail already.

O'Brien was fond of his pointer. He ran the tip up and down the center of the useless map. "The island is shaped roughly like Wisconsin, as you see." It didn't look at all like Wisconsin, Ethan thought. "We believe Martinez's safe area is to the north, somewhere west of these mountains in a dense jungle between these two rivers."

O'Brien's pointer circled a completely blank space on the map. To Ethan Cooper, it meant unknown, unexplored jungle. Likely as not, no white man, European or otherwise, had ever seen it. The captain's almost casual treatment of the mission seemed something more sinister than ignorance.

"We know it's dense jungle in the interior. Still, Martinez has no trouble mounting small operations to the south in coastal towns down both coasts. American installations on both the east and west coast have been hit. He can't be relying on the major rivers. We have gunboats patrolling all of them. He must have a trail north up the middle to move men and supplies. We need to find it and close it even if we don't find his base camp. Simple SOP. Cooper will take a six-man patrol in tomorrow."

The group was sitting around a crude table in the orderly room. Lt. Hobbs, surprisingly, seemed to grasp the issue immediately. "That's unexplored territory based on the map, Sir. What's the hard information supporting this theory? Has anyone actually been in there?"

"You know what I know," O'Brien answered. "I get the order from Headquarters, and I make sure the order is executed."

Ethan said, "Sir, can you give me a few locals to cut through this jungle and carry water? This will be slow going as it is, Sir."

"Of course. Conscript as many as you need."

"Three will do, Sir." There would be only six men on the patrol, so Ethan would rather not worry about eight or ten locals running around with bolos, especially at night.

O'Brien rose from the table, pointer in hand. Moving back to the map, he pointed to a spot about twelve miles north of X-104 and said, "You will be able to find where the river starts at this point within a day. We know there is a trail from here up into the high hills to the source of the river. You'll follow the river north about twenty miles to this point where it turns east. This is where your search starts. If you don't find anything in a day, head back. If you find the trail or their camp, report back immediately."

He talked about the "trail" up to where the river forms, Ethan thought, like it was a section of the *Escolta* in Manila, a quaint urban walkway. In a jungle like that, a trail was the only way to make progress, and every step could bring death by ambush or by some fiendish trap. If O'Brien expected them to reach the river in a day, that trail would be their only route.

"Sir," Ethan said, "most likely we won't be able to traverse the riverbank up there. Probably need a raft for the river portion of the trip."

O'Brien nodded. "Draw whatever you need. Rope, axes, whatever."

No one at the table challenged O'Brien's game plan or timeline. For all his good intentions, Hobbs had never been forced to hack his way through thick jungle while under assault from mosquitoes, pythons, scorpions and venomous centipedes, not to mention stifling heat and humidity. Then there was the prospect of insurgents, maybe even headhunters.

Ethan looked over at Flood in vain, hoping for support. Flood had to know better but remained mute as O'Brien presented his ridiculously inept tactical plan. Their top sergeant was a good soldier and a reliable comrade in battle, but his boldness was confined to the battlefield. Flood knew full well that a day's journey through terrain like that could inhale the life from a man all on its own. Progress could be measured in yards, not miles.

Flood also knew that criticizing the plans of tactical command was not a viable path to becoming Regimental Sergeant Major. The top sergeant would send Ethan into the jungle on O'Brien's terms and that was that.

"Sir," Ethan said, "it's clear on the map the mouth of the river is on the east coast. That's well north of where we find the river. You know that rivers don't usually flow north. Do we know if this one does?"

"I don't have that information, Cooper. You'll have to adapt. Draw your supplies."

O'Brien stood, an indication the briefing was over and a signal to Ethan he wanted no more impertinent questions.

Well, fuck him. It's just another stroll in the jungle. Privately, Ethan was still more wary of the situation in the village than of the prospect of trouble on this ridiculous patrol. He knew how to minimize danger in the jungle. Things were far too lax at X-104. O'Brien might have mistaken disengagement for surrender, a potentially fatal miscalculation in a village of two thousand people. He'd made a point of warning Marty of his misgivings. "Sir, can I choose my own men?"

"Sergeant Major Flood will handle the assignments, Cooper. Talk to him. That's all, Gentlemen."

ETHAN'S CREW ASSEMBLED OUTSIDE THE MESS TENT AFTER BREAKFAST under the eye of the sergeant major. Flood, Ethan knew, courted the image of an old-school Indian fighter, gruff and fearless. As a young private in the 7th Cavalry, Flood had fought under Captain Frederick Benteen at The Little Bighorn in 1876. He was with the battalion that rescued Major Reno's command and formed the defensive line. The Benteen-Reno action was credited with saving three-hundred-fifty men of the 7th.

The contemporary version of Sergeant Major Flood, Ethan learned from experience, was more politician than paladin and slipperier than an eel in bacon grease. The sergeant major had allowed Ethan to bring Schneider, Jones, and O'Leary on the patrol. O'Leary was a burly, red-headed Irishman, solid and reliable under pressure.

In exchange for the concession, he had saddled Ethan with two new men, both unknown commodities. Privates Baker and Pots had joined the company on the way down from Manila. It could have been worse. Flood liked to leave everyone with a little sense of give and take.

Ethan pulled three Filipinos from the cleanup crew to hack the jungle. He would have preferred to take a couple of the baseball players but dismissed the idea quickly. There might be serious trouble on this patrol, and he saw no point putting them in danger. His three conscripts were strong and had been around town with their families since the company arrived. He put all three of them at the point for the trip up to the river. If there were traps, the bearers would either show how to avoid them or fall into them before his men did. Locals on Luzon had always seemed to know where the traps were located. It was still a war. He didn't want to hurt innocents, if that's what they were, but better them than his soldiers.

They passed the last huts a couple of miles north of the church. The trail narrowed in a steady rain, and in the next mile, the sky disappeared beneath a green ceiling. The air thickened into a kind of hot, stagnant soup as water dropped from leaves of all shapes and sizes. Only sporadic streaks of light penetrated the canopy.

"Schneider," Ethan said, "move up behind the natives."

"Right, Sarge."

By mid-afternoon, the landscape began to change every few meters. The trail became nearly vertical, and the green jungle floor surrendered to rock. The air thinned, and Ethan felt the hot sun on his back and a life-giving mountain breeze on his face. For an hour or so, the incline was minimal.

"This ain't so bad, Sarge." It was Jonesy, directly behind him in the single-file line.

"We're just starting, Jonesy. Let's get to the top of this hill and see where we are."

The barefoot Filipinos showed no sign of slowing down on the rocks. Finally, they came upon a rock ledge, a highpoint commanding a magnificent view of the Emerald green jungle and shimmering coastline back to the south.

"I hear water, Sarge," one of the new guys said.

"We'll rest here," Ethan instructed. "Take your buddy on up a ways and see what's waiting for us. We're near the top. No more trail once we find the river." The sun was low, and they had about an hour until sunset.

Ethan was unlacing his shoes on a big rock when Corporal O'Leary, the Irishman, sat down beside him. "Tell me, Ethan, do ye really plan on hacking through virgin jungle blind twenty miles downriver? We could just stay here a couple of days and go back with a bloody story."

"Haven't decided yet, Paddy. It's a stupid patrol. I'll give you that, but we have two new boys with us, so we have to be careful. Flood is no fool. Just looks like one. My guess is he knows these new boys better than we do."

Just as the group was getting comfortable, two rifle shots shattered the air and echoed down the rocks. The shots were so close together they could not have been fired by the same Krag. The remaining soldiers grabbed their Krags, hopped into their shoes, and scurried up the rocks a hundred yards or so until they reached a peak of sorts. There were several other higher peaks to the north and west. Not mountains but more like high hills. The group found itself over the entrance to a small rock canyon framed by two stunningly beautiful waterfalls both emptying into a pool of crystal-clear spring water. Two naked bodies lay face down in the water near the edge.

"There's one more behind the big rock there." It was one of the new guys yelling from the opposite side of the pool.

"Hold your fire," Ethan ordered. He could see the Filipinos' clothes along the rocks near the water. Two bolos were clearly visible beside a huge, dead warty pig. The thing was tied around a long pole and had been gutted.

An arm appeared from behind a rock waving a white shirt. It was the same signal Ethan had seen from the Pinkertons on the barge at the docks on the second worst day of his life.

"Schneider, Jonesy, go down there and get him. When he's secured, we'll come down. And don't take chances."

As they started down, the man rose from behind the rock, hands in the air, crying, and waited. Ethan signaled him to move into the open, and he complied immediately.

With the survivor in custody, the new guys, Pots and Baker, joined the others on the rock landing beside the pool. Ethan and O'Leary had already dragged the two bodies from the pool. Ethan looked at the two replacements, and it occurred to him it was for the first time. Baker was a skinny kid like a hundred Ethan had known before, clueless and scared. "Where you from, Private?" he asked.

"Chicago."

"So what happened here, Baker?"

The kid just looked over at Pots. The older man had the black eyes of a killer and sun-wrinkled, leathery skin. Thirty-year-old-privates usually excelled at only one thing, and this one was not shy about it. He took a step forward and said to Ethan, "They came at us with bolos. We got 'em first." Ethan ignored him. "I asked *you*, Baker."

"It's like Pots said, Sarge. They came at us."

Pots was not deterred. "Niggers in the jungle with bolos," he said to Ethan. "That's why we're here, Cooper."

Ethan picked up a ragged pair of pants from the rock. He looked at Pots and said, "Naked? Carrying a pig?"

Pots laughed. "So they ain't cannibals. Maybe they're headhunters or something. They don't like to wear clothes anyway. Look, why don't we just bury the niggers and cook the pig? Then we can go swimming. We killed two insurgents and you got yourself a prisoner for the captain to interrogate."

"Get this straight. I don't like you, Pots, but the company commander will decide what happened here. I'll just make my report, and I guarantee you won't like it."

"What about the pig, Ethan?" O'Leary asked. "We going to just let it rot?"

"They're probably just hunters from the east coast where the river goes from here," Ethan said to no one in particular. "This has to be where the river starts. We're near the top. The north slope starts down just up ahead. I'm betting these guys have a boat down there."

"Sure, Ethan, but what about the pig?"

Ethan shrugged. "Cook a piece of the pig. No. Make Pots clean and cook the pig—after he buries the Filipinos. Small fire, nothing green to cause smoke. We'll camp here tonight. Get our Filipinos to help him. The prisoner too. We'll put him to work."

"Who the hell do you think you are, Cooper?" Pots snapped. "I ain't takin' no…"

Before Pots could finish the sentence, Ethan's right hand was around his throat, launching him against the rock wall. As Pots gasped desperately for breath, Ethan leaned in close to his ear and whispered, "I gave an order. Just nod your head to let me know if you'll obey it. We'll go from there."

Pots nodded up and down vigorously, leaving no doubt as to his decision, and slid to the ground as Ethan released the stranglehold.

Jonesy was guarding the prisoner who was sitting cross-legged on a flat section of rock floor. Ethan relieved Jonesy to grab some food and sat down next to the prisoner. The kid wasn't a day over fifteen, bawling like a baby and ready to shit himself. This child was no insurgent. "What's your name, Kid?" he said in Spanish.

The boy lifted his head from his hands revealing a gap from a missing eye tooth. "Chuko," the terrified kid managed to say. The boy had a name. His name was Chuko.

THE TWO DEAD MEN HAD EACH TAKEN A .30 CAL TO THE TORSO, one in the chest, the other in the back. Something told Ethan it had been a family, a father and two brothers out on a hunt for the coveted warty pig. Pots and Baker had murdered them for no reason. They shouldn't be dead, he told himself, but there was a war on, and bad things happened all the time.

"Sarge, you'd better come up here." It was Schneider from back on the ridge.

He found Schneider standing next to a pile of rope and no sign of their three Filipinos. "All three of them?" Ethan asked.

"Looks like," Schneider answered. "At least they left us the extra canteens. Have to be at least a mile back down the trail by now."

"Well, you can't really blame them, I guess. Let them go. Probably figured we'd kill them too, so I doubt we'll see them again in Apostol. We're not doing all that well making them love us. Are we, Paddy?"

Ethan found a spot near the edge of their small, rock plateau, high above the jungle canopy and away from the others. The night was cloudless, the humidity banished to the jungle floor. They'd all bathed and rested while waiting for dinner. A million stars ignited the sky above and stretched clear across the horizon, transforming the waterfalls and pool into a nocturnal display of color and hypnotic, shifting light patterns. He thought he would have paid to visit a place like this in another time.

Perhaps the Filipino hunters lying buried on the slope below came here for that very reason. A father and his sons. Maybe it was an annual trip, a rite of passage, like his own fishing trips on the Allegheny Railroad with Pop to the Mountains of the same name. They only got to do it twice, but from all the good memories of his early childhood, he cherished those the most, probably even embellished them more every year. When you have so little of something so good, you cling to the memory of it. Every rotten thing life dumps on you over the subsequent years works to strengthen that memory until it's all you have, all you are.

He saw Jonesy approaching with a tin plate and cup. "I got your dinner, Sarge. Fresh pork."

He looked at the pig and remembered the boy's name was Chuko. His father and brother had names too. "No appetite for pork tonight," he said, "but I thank you kindly for the coffee, Jonesy. I'll be along shortly for some beans and hard bread."

Pop had endured the worst of the War for freedom and the Union. He had found glory with the 62nd Pennsylvania and come out of it admired and respected for his service and his valor. Ethan knew that, not from Pop— he refused to speak of it. He knew it from his mother, his neighbors, and the parents of his school friends. Mostly, he knew it from the annual Fourth of July festivities and such in little Bethel, Pennsylvania, his small village tucked into a hill in Southwestern Allegheny County. His father had always seemed to be a reluctant center-of-attention at such festivities. Young Ethan had heard the stories of his valor from the old men in The Grand Army of the Republic.

Pop was, in the end, a gentle man, slight of stature but fiercely loved, whom other men always greeted warmly or made way for. A part of Ethan was happy that Pop had not seen him in action today. Another part wished he was still a nine-year-old who could go fishing with his Pop and seek his advice and guidance in troubling times.

IN THE MORNING, WITH THE LAST OF THE COOKED PIG DEVOURED, Ethan called the men together to issue orders. They assembled on the rocks around the pool, Jonesy guarding their new prisoner.

"Pots, Baker," Ethan began. "You two head back down the trail toward Apostol. See if you can pick up the trail of our Filipinos and get some idea of where they're headed. Don't follow them."

Pots was already grinning like a shot fox. "You want us to take the prisoner back with us, Sergeant Cooper? Won't be no trouble."

You'd like that. Ethan wanted to say. *You'd cut his throat the minute you were out of sight.* "No." he replied. "He may be useful to us in the jungle. Make sure you each take an extra canteen and get moving. Report to Captain O'Brien when you get back. Tell him where we are and what happened. Tell him we're proceeding upriver with the mission best we can."

When the two new guys had disappeared back down the trail, Ethan said, "Schneider, you and Jonesy head down the north side to the river and see if you can find their boat. Me and O'Leary will take turns trying to catch some fish for lunch."

Thankfully, O'Leary kept his mouth shut until Jonesy and Schneider had set off down the hill, but not a second longer. Ethan was sitting on a rock going through his knapsack when O'Leary said, "Now, Ethan, would ye care to explain what just happened? I find it all a bit confusing. That Pots fella will turn this whole thing around when he talks to the captain. Last night I heard Pots runnin' his mouth about you and Jonesy being nigger lovers. He's no feckin' good, Ethan."

Ethan forced a weak smile. "What do I care? It won't change my report, and O'Brien won't do a damn thing to them either way. Pots is right. We're here to kill these poor, miserable fucks. No, I just needed those two to go away."

"Go away?"

"Ah, here it is," Ethan said, pulling out the small first aid kit from his pack. "The safety pins in here are just as good as a proper fishhook if you bend them right. I'm sick of beans."

"Ethan, would you let the fishes swim free for another minute and tell me what the feck is going on?"

He put down the kit and looked at O'Leary. "What's going on is the four of us are going to fish and swim and enjoy ourselves for two more days right in this little slice of heaven. Then we'll go back, and I'll tell our Bible-loving captain a version of the truth. We executed the mission the best we could but couldn't find a trace of any trail leading north or anywhere else."

O'Leary slapped him on the back and grinned. "Ah, but you're a sly one, Ethan, me boy."

Ethan was not feeling sly—or clever. He had no choice. He wouldn't expose his men to any foolish risk and that was that. Besides, he was more worried about X-104. Could he have been the one to recognize the rising tension in the town? "No, I'm not. Don't call me that. I just know what our chances are with only a few Krags and no bodies to cut through the jungle. If we follow our orders any further, we'll all die or some of us will die—needlessly. We'll die of exhaustion or malaria or yellow fever. And that's only if we don't stumble into Martinez's camp on our own. This is a stupid assignment. O'Brien has no idea what it's like out there. We do. I don't mind risking our lives, but I won't do it anymore without a purpose. If we find the bad guys, we die, and if we don't find them, we die. None of it will save the Union or end slavery."

"What?"

"Never mind."

As Ethan applied a clinch knot to the repurposed safety pin, he nodded toward a clump of brush and trees beside the small waterfall and said, "Go over there and get me a good stick to hang this line on."

O'Leary brought back two stripped branches. As Ethan tested their strength, he said, "All you three need to do is keep your yaps shut and let me do the talking. We'll get the story straight in case someone presses you."

"What about the prisoner?" O'Leary asked. "If they interrogate him, they will know it's all horseshit."

"Paddy, do you think I'm an idiot? Now, go get me a few worms."

O'Leary took a few steps, then stopped and turned back to Ethan like he'd just remembered something. "Ethan, did you consider that sending the prisoner back with Pots would have solved your problem? Sure, that kid would never have made it back alive."

Ethan did not look up. "Never entered my mind. Worms, please."

CHAPTER TEN

"What do you mean, 'he escaped?'" O'Brien raged, eyebrows nearly resting on the end of his mustache. "How does one little, brown prisoner elude three armed troopers?"

Ethan was still at attention as O'Brien visibly restrained himself from leaping over the desk. "Only thing I can say, Sir, is that it happened during the night. He shed the restraints and slipped past the guard somehow."

"Who was the guard? I want to know who was on guard duty."

Ethan had anticipated that question perfectly. "No way to know, Sir. We were on three-hour rotations, me included."

O'Brien rose from the desk chair and leaned forward on his hands. "You may well be a private by morning, Cooper. I should give Pots and the other guy each one of your stripes. At least they killed two insurgents. We've been here five weeks, and I don't have a single prisoner. We have located no insurgent camps, not so much as a trail, no weapons. And I have every reason to believe the town is still getting supplies to Martinez."

It just wasn't true, Ethan knew, even if the locals had tried. He'd done the inventory himself. But O'Brien wasn't finished ranting. "The natives have been cleaning up the town for a month, and it looks worse now than when we got here. On top of that, the Inspector General will be here in a few days. These people need a lesson in obedience, and my people need to start doing their jobs around here instead of playing baseball with the natives. Go clean up and report to Flood. Dismissed."

Heading for the Grant Barracks, Ethan surveyed the square. In the three days since he left on patrol, O'Brien had transformed the town into a bona fide war zone. No baseball players. No chatty women gathered at the well. The place looked abandoned but for small details of two or three troopers herding groups of local men at gunpoint toward the east side of the municipal building.

From the barracks, he could see their destination, two large, conical tents just beyond the mess tent, a makeshift guardhouse. He spotted Marty near the tents in conversation, and curiosity drew him to the gathering.

"So, what's this, Marty?" he asked. "I hardly recognize the place."

"O'Brien's orders. It's been a busy little *pueblo* since you left, Ethan. Bad business."

As he spoke, a couple of privates walked up, rifles at the ready, behind a group of four Filipinos. "We got these four in one hut up the trail," one of them said. The second prisoner from the left was young Pollito, and he looked terrified.

Another private, holding a notebook and pen, said, "Okay, line them up and give me their names."

As the young men disappeared into the tent, Ethan said, "What did they do?"

"Who knows?" Marty replied. "I told you. O'Brien's orders."

"What orders?" Ethan asked.

The private with the notebook interrupted. "All four of them refuse to give their names, Sarge. That's pretty much the way it is with all of them. Should I keep trying?"

"Call them One, Two and Three," Marty replied.

Ethan could see clearly inside the first tent. At least fifty Filipinos stood elbow-to-elbow on a dirt floor in a tent designed to accommodate fifteen at most.

"Marty, what the hell is going on here?"

"We had an incident while you were gone, Ethan. Well, I should say incidents. It's been going downhill around here since you left."

In that moment, Ethan spotted Asuncion running toward Marty from around the south end of the municipal building. She wasn't coming to give him a kiss. To avoid a scene, Marty bolted to intercept her between the two prison tents. He risked grabbing her by the arm and said, "Come with me now. A scene here won't help your cause."

Ethan watched as he escorted the woman to a quiet area out of sight. Everything was spiraling out of control now, Ethan thought, for everyone.

The more he could piece together, the worse the situation looked. When the conscripted workers failed to show up for their cleanup assignments for two days running, O'Brien issued an order to arrest every able-bodied man in the town over fifteen and confine them to the conical tents. The uneasy friendship between the locals and the Americans had ended. There would be no more baseball games, chess matches or Spanish lessons at the church. No more days cavorting at the beach or sneaking off to the convent every night for Marty Tours.

During a miserable, sleepless night, Ethan considered his options. Going directly to O'Brien was out of the question. He decided to visit the police chief, the man who had been instructing him in the martial art of *Arnis*, Philippine stick fighting. Like the doctor, Ethan had developed a warm relationship with Obrador since their initial meeting during the inventory process. The man spoke much better English than he had let on at first.

From the mess tent at breakfast, he could see a group of women gathered around the guardhouse tents and decided to investigate. The prisoners were being grouped into work parties, and the women had brought trays of fruit, rice and camotes to feed them. The men were eating in line and the women all crying, all except one.

Asuncion was near the front of the crowd, close to the place where her brother Pollito was trying to finish some mango and a handful of rice. So much had changed in a few days.

Ethan approached one of the guards. "Private," he said. "There are no mats in there. Did they spend the night in those tents like that?"

The private laughed. "Sure did," he answered. "Can't you smell it?"

On the way to Obrador's, Ethan spotted Marty coming out of the municipal building. He looked shaken. "What's up, Marty?" he asked.

"They found Private Woods down by the dock this morning with his head blown off. Ate his Krag last night some time."

Fortunately, Ethan hardly knew the man. It was worse when you knew him. There was always something you'd think about, something you might have done or said differently. He tried to put it out of his mind and said, "I'm going to see Obrador. You never know what I might learn."

Police Headquarters had moved temporarily from the municipal building to a small storage hut a quarter mile north of the square. Ethan was relieved to find Mariano Obrador at his "desk," a couple of planks atop two wooden boxes and more surprised to find O'Brien's interpreter, Renaldo, sitting across the desk. The big man seemed pleased to see him as he entered through the open doorway.

"Come in, Ethan," said Obrador, standing.

Renaldo also rose, offering his hand. "Good morning, Ethan. Your timing is perfect. I was just leaving. Had to deliver a message from the captain."

"Let's go out on my beautiful veranda," said the chief. "We might catch a breeze on the bench."

When Renaldo had cleared earshot, the two settled on the crude bench and Ethan said, "What's the status of our *Arnis* lessons? Seems like the wind is changing, and I'm not sure why."

"No more lessons, I'm afraid, and I suspect you know why. Your captain has imprisoned most of our young men."

"Yes. They were wrapping up the operation when I got back from patrol yesterday. The captain thinks your work crews have been sabotaging the cleanup operation. I can't do a damn thing about it, just want to hear your side of the situation if you care to tell me."

"My side?" said the chief. "My side? In my office? In my *pueblo*?" He stood and descended the bamboo stairs. "Take a walk with me."

They walked around to the rear of the hut and over a crude trail for a few minutes until coming to a clearing. "Take a look for yourself," said Obrador. "Our people cleared these little fields hundreds of years ago. Everyone who lives here grows root crops or corn or staples of some kind in his own yard too. We eat what little we are able to grow on this infertile ground, and we trade our plentiful coconuts and bananas for the other things we need to survive, things like rice and abaca. Out there you see sugar, vegetables, tobacco, all lovingly cultivated in small amounts. Now there are no farmers to tend these fields. There are no fishermen to fill the nets, no climbers to harvest the coconuts. They are all in prison. Why? What will happen to these people? They are *my* people, Sergeant Cooper."

"I get it," Ethan said. "The captain thinks the people here are working for Martinez and his insurgent forces in the hills. He thinks the town is supplying them."

"I can speak only for myself, Cooper. I work only for my people."

Obrador was sidestepping the question, but why shouldn't he, Ethan thought. He was probably getting squeezed and threatened by General Martinez, the insurgent commander, from the other end. It was pointless to ask the next logical question straight out. No one in these circumstances could expect Obrador to come clean. Ethan didn't even want him to, not really. He was looking for something else, something elusive, like the answer to a forgotten question. Obrador seemed to sense his dilemma. He said, "I know your friend has a personal interest, Cooper. The priest knows about Tours and the girl also, but don't worry. Your secret shall remain with us. Not for you, but for her. Things would not go well for her if it became known. This is not Manila, and she is a loved and respected figure here."

It wasn't the girl that concerned him. She was a survivor, cunning and purposeful in Ethan's opinion. Marty was another story. He was hopelessly in love with the woman, and Ethan's greatest fear was that she had been milking Marty for information useful to the insurgents. For all his education and understanding of the world, poor Marty was effectively still a clueless priest.

"I understand," said Ethan. "Thank you. So there is nothing else you can tell me?"

They started walking back to the hut. Ethan could tell the chief had something else to say. Finally, he did. "We Waray are a peaceful people, Cooper, but we have experience with invaders. For hundreds of years, the Moros would launch raids against us. They would steal, rape, kidnap women. The people would retreat into the Mountains in the north. Sometimes we would wait out the invaders, then come back and rebuild from nothing. Other times, we would fight and drive them out."

Was the chief giving him a warning? A threat? Maybe he was only saying the people would never submit. Still, he'd said that for a reason. "What are you saying, Señor Obrador?"

"Only that we wish you would all leave peacefully. Your captain is placing us in a dire situation. If he doesn't let our men free by tomorrow, I will go to him and plead our case. We did not bring this on ourselves. We offered the Americans our cooperation and a warm welcome."

It was a clear warning. O'Brien had ignored their pleas and dismissed every warning sign since the day the company had landed here. Now they are going down the chain of command, hoping someone, anyone would hear them.

WITH TENSIONS RISING, IT WASN'T THE BEST EVENING TO BE heading to Ryan's Bar, but O'Leary could be persuasive. Marty's whiskey supply had run out a week ago, and the local tuba had become a popular distraction among the troopers. The proprietor, a fidgety bald fellow, answered to the name of *Meesta Ryan*, and had begun serving his coconut wine concoction in clay mugs, American style, rather than in the locally preferred tubes. A most adaptable businessman, he'd added a few tables with chairs about a month ago for poker and had obviously become the most prosperous merchant in town. How *Meesta Ryan* would fare when the Americans left was an open question as the local population had been determinedly boycotting his business.

Jonesy was already drunk at the bar when Ethan and O'Leary arrived. A gaggle of the usual ruffians drooled over a big poker pot on the patio as the pair joined Jonesy at the bar. Pots and Mason were among them. As usual, Jonesy was alone, even with seven or eight troopers mingling at the bar. *Meesta Ryan* greeted them warmly, as was his custom, pouring two mugs from a big tuba jar. Tuba and fruit were his only menu items.

He didn't really have a set price because of the lack of a monetary system. Like a horse trader, his prices varied with the number of customers, the form of payment, even the time of day. He liked American money best but would accept Spanish pesetas and just about anything except the Philippine revolutionary peso, which became worthless after Aguinaldo's capture. They settled with Ryan but did not offer Jonesy another drink.

"What's the game here?" Jonesy mumbled. "Ol' Jonesy ain't good enough t' drink with y'all no more?"

"You had enough Jonesy," Ethan said quietly. "O'Leary n' me will have one or two and walk back with you. You're not supposed to be walking in the town alone."

Jonesy beat his chest with a fist. "I'm a Texican," he boasted, loud enough to get the attention of the other troopers. "I walk where and when I please. Hit me agin' here, *Meesta Ryan*."

Ethan and O'Leary had hoped to kill some time in a poker game, but they didn't like the crowd that evening, and Jonesy was just too obnoxious. Ethan managed to settle the youngster down a bit and got Ryan to bring him a bowl of fruit. It had all the earmarks of an early evening, so they finished the first drink and Ethan said to

Jonesy, "Come on back with O'Leary and me. We could all use a good night's sleep."

Jonesy held up his palm and said, "No. I'm all right, Sarge. "I'll just stay here and finish this fruit, then tag along with one of these guys at the bar."

Ethan thought about forcing the issue, but he was just too tired of dealing with Jonesy's troubles. Besides, Mason and Pots seemed to have no interest in tormenting the boy tonight. They were winning.

He patted Jonesy on the back. "That's it then. Don't wait too long. See you in the morning."

Outside the doorway, Marty said, "You could have pulled rank."

"I'm not his father," Ethan snapped. "He could transfer tomorrow to another unit. It's time he grew up."

AT THE COMPANY ASSEMBLY THE NEXT MORNING, FLOOD ANNOUNCED an impromptu NCO briefing in O'Brien's office directly. Alamo Jones was a no-show, and his name was not even called in the rain-soaked roll call. It could only mean they knew he would be absent—and why. Even with all this going on, Marty had barely made it back to the barracks before dawn.

Ethan and Marty walked over to the municipal building together where they found the sergeants and corporals already gathering around O'Brien's corner of the first floor. O'Brien was not in the mood to procrastinate. He appeared from the orderly room and raised a hand calling for silence, then addressed the gathering directly through the bush on his upper lip. "There were two incidents last night, and one of our men was injured. Sergeant Major Flood will explain."

Flood created a space for himself in the middle of the group amid a dead silence. "We have a report from locals that some drunk soldiers attacked a local woman on the trail last night. We have not yet learned if she was, er...violated." *What horseshit*, Ethan thought. There had been at least a dozen assault complaints by local women since the company arrived and this was the first requiring a full briefing. Whatever happened, Ethan concluded, was violent. "Two natives came to the woman's aid and beat the men severely. They are in the medical unit now. The police chief came to see Captain

O'Brien right afterward and returned two Krag rifles taken in the melee."

Ethan looked at Marty in horror. Marty shook his head, indicating the victim was not Asuncion. Whoever was attacked, Ethan was confident Jonesy was not one of the assailants. "What about Alamo Jones?" he asked Flood.

Flood was ready for the question. "It appears that sometime after the first incident, Jones was board-stiff on tuba behind the main street where two or three men approached him from behind and threw a bag over his head. It's likely he was beaten with rifle butts."

"Is he all right?" Ethan asked.

"He's with Major Lawrence. He was awake an hour ago."

"So, who jumped on Jonesy?" Marty queried. "The Filipinos?"

"No," Flood answered. "Jones was attacked after the police chief turned in the missing rifles. That means our own men did this to a fellow soldier, and the captain won't tolerate it. There will be courts martial after we sort this out."

My ass, Ethan thought.

O'Brien then raised his hand signaling Flood to shut up. He was apparently ready to disclose the purpose of the briefing. "Like the sergeant major said, if some of my soldiers assaulted another one there will be hell to pay, and I will get to the bottom of it. Armies do not function like that. Lieutenant Hobbs has already begun an investigation. I expect all of you to report any leads or information to him promptly.

"However, it's more troubling to me at the moment that locals would assume the authority to disarm and beat American soldiers, soldiers who are here for the sole purpose of rescuing them from oppression and teaching them a better way of life..." O'Brien seemed to have already forgotten the same two men had just raped someone.

Abruptly, the captain's gaze turned toward the main door. There stood the imposing figure of Obrador in full police uniform and ears in the ready mode. This would be a busy day for the commanding officer.

O'Brien addressed the sentry standing beside the chief, saying, "Please, ask *Señor* Obrador to wait. I will see him in a few minutes."

Ethan would rather have left with the chief. He wanted to know what Jonesy's injuries were. Who did this to him? Why? There would be time for guilt later.

When Obrador had gone, the captain got down to business. "Sergeant Flood is working out the details of new orders, effective today. Our objective is to nullify the usefulness of this town to Martinez as a source of supplies and men. We will begin setting fire to all food stores, especially common rice storage huts. We will confiscate all livestock in the town. That means pigs, chickens, anything that can be considered a food stock. Finally, we will kill all carabao as they are used to ferry supplies to insurgent forces."

Everything was happening too quickly now, Ethan thought. Events were spinning out of control. *If only I had grabbed Jonesy by the collar and dragged him back,* he admonished himself. *Now O'Brien wants to destroy the town?* Ethan knew these people could become a lethal insurgent army at the drop of a hat.

It wasn't the first time Ethan had heard orders like that, but for the first time, he questioned them. There was no evidence these townspeople were supplying Martinez. Even if they were, killing their animals and destroying their food would kill the town and the people in it, more slowly, sure, but with the finality of a bullet in the head. He also knew from experience they would inevitably shoot a few resisting citizens during the sweep. It wasn't war. He could see that now. It was something else-and it was wrong.

A voice whispered in his head. It was his friend, Jimmy Jeffries, the café worker from Pittsburgh. *You have good in you, Boy. I can see that. It's wild and buried deep like rich virgin soil under a sea of grass. But if you manage to live long enough, listen to it and let it guide you over time. It will show you who you are.* He asked, "Sir, may I inquire why we are doing this?"

O'Brien looked more shocked than angry. "I'm not in the habit of explaining myself to enlisted soldiers, Cooper. Suffice to say, I have concluded that the townspeople are actively engaged in sabotage and in supplying General Martinez's forces. Our primary objective here is to prevent just that. We have offered to show them a new and better way to live, and they reject our help. The evidence is clear. Just look at the rice situation. When we arrived, we found three storage huts full. As of today, there is one."

In for a penny, he thought, *in for a pound*. "Sir, I did the original inventory with Sergeant Tours. Each hut holds only a one-week supply of rice for the town. Seems they have been carefully rationing it. They don't even have enough for themselves. As for the carabao, they use them to plow fields."

O'Brien's face contracted to the point that it resembled an asshole with bushy eyebrows. It was as angry as Ethan had ever seen the man. "That's enough, Cooper. You're on the verge of insubordination. All of you, listen. I have no wish to be cruel. I am a God-fearing Christian. We would gladly have continued to help these people if they had been honest and receptive to American generosity. That is not the case. Accordingly, we will follow orders as best we can. This is still war. Dismissed."

OVER AT THE INFIRMARY, POOR JONESY WAS BEAT HARDER THAN A drum on the Fourth of July, lying flat on his back in the makeshift hospital at the back of the Grant Barracks. Five or six other cots held soldiers with various tropical diseases by the looks of them. Ethan spotted Corporal McCoy, the corpsman, heading for Jonesy's bed. "Make sure there's no mud on your shoes, Ethan, and that boy needs rest. You got five minutes to hold his hand."

"Right, I got it." Jonesy's exposed torso formed a ghastly canvas of purple and blue. Bandages encased his entire head, and his left eye was so swollen Ethan wondered if he still had the eyeball.

"Damn, Jonesy, you look like ten miles of bad road," was all he could think to say, looking down on this broken man-child. Alamo Jones was never going to make it as a soldier. His gentle nature would never adapt in this world gone mad. The boy was just a walking disaster so long as he remained in the army. "Least you're not shot, boy," he said.

"Yeah, them ol' boys got me pretty good, Sarge. It pains me some, I admit. If they'da come at me straight on, Ida whupped 'em sure."

The doctor chose that moment to interrupt the reunion with a visit to his most recent patient. "You're a lucky soldier, Jones. Couple of broken ribs, a concussion. Could have been much worse. You'll be out of here on light duty in a couple of days. What did they hit you with?"

As the major spoke, Ethan noticed a book on the small table beside Jonesy, *The Adventures of Huckleberry Finn*. *Odd*, he thought. *Jonesy can't read.*

"Rifle butts, Sir. Slipped a bag over my head from behind first. Called themselves *'the nigger lover honor guard.'* I ain't feelin' so honored, Major, Sir."

The doctor turned to Ethan and said, "It's a pretty bad concussion. He was unconscious for a long time, might have died, but I think he'll be okay now."

"Major, are you sending him to Manila?" Ethan asked.

"No. I made the mistake of telling Captain O'Brien he was recovering," the major replied. "I should have shipped him out right away on the mail boat."

When the major had left them, Ethan said, "Who did it?"

"No, Sarge, I can't git me involved in that. I told Lieutenant Hobbs the truth. They just jumped me from behind on the trail. I didn't see their faces...but..."

Before Jonesy could finish, two privates walked into the hospital area in shackles and under guard. Both were bloodied and bruised, uniforms in tatters. Ethan couldn't put a name to the short one but the tall, grizzly one was his *friend*, Private Pots. "Morning Major, Sir," said the guard. "Lieutenant Hobbs told us to bring these two over here to get patched up before they see the captain. Morning, Ethan."

"Are they in custody?" the major asked.

The man nodded. "Straight from here to the guardhouse until the captain is ready to see them."

The medic pointed to a cot on the other side of the room and said, "Sit them down over there."

All the while, Pots maintained a hateful stare on the bed-ridden Alamo Jones. It wasn't difficult for Ethan to make the connection.

As the doctor started to clean them up, Ethan said to the guard, "Were these two involved in assaulting the woman?"

"That's what Sergeant Flood said. I guess a couple of locals beat them pretty good."

The major interrupted, "I treated the girl. These clowns raped her and beat her up pretty badly."

"The Filipinos did a good job," Ethan said. *Clearly, there was more to this than Jonesy was sharing*, Ethan thought.

As Major Lawrence busied himself with the prisoners, Ethan moved back to Jonesy's bedside and said softly, "Go ahead and finish, Jonesy. You 'didn't see their faces but...?'"

"You won't say nothin' to nobody?"

Ethan crossed his heart. "My word."

"The one who talked were Mason. No doubt about the voice. It were Mason all right. I suspect he were the one planted that rifle butt on my skull."

"Mason," Ethan repeated. "I figured as much. And you tried to help that woman last night, didn't you?"

Jonesy grimaced and grabbed his side in pain. "Yup. They was botherin' her all right 'n I stepped in. They caught me off guard on my way back. They must have caught up to her in the dark after."

Ethan patted his friend on the shoulder. "Get some rest now, boy. I'll check in later."

He started to leave, then remembered the book. "Oh, Jonesy, where did you get the book?"

Jonesy tried to force a smile. "The high-class prisoner, Mr. Smith, give it to me back in Manila, Sarge. He give me two. First one was about a rascal name o' Tom Sawyer. They was Southern boys like me. Real rascals all right."

"Mr. Smith, eh? I thought you two were getting tighter than a cinch on a horse's belly. Strange character that Mr. Smith."

Jonesy revealed his best version of a smile through the pain and said, "Oh, that weren't his real name, Sarge. It were Ogalando or some such name. He were the President of this place a couple of years back. Told me not to say nothin' 'bout it 'cuz he didn't want no special treatment."

"Well, I'll be damned," Ethan muttered. He should have figured that out long ago, or rather Marty should have figured it out. Jonesy's best friend in the Philippines was a general and the former President of the damned country to boot. "Emelio Aguinaldo." He wondered if Captain O'Brien had known all along.

"Yup. He used to read me the Tom Sawyer book walking in the garden, Sarge. I liked it. The Doc here reads me the Huck Finn book sometimes. They was buddies down on the river, Tom and Huck."

"Yeah. So I hear. But what does he mean callin' you his *brother?* I mean, you bein' a private and all and him a general of sorts. He was a pretty uppity cuss, as I recall."

Jonesy smiled again. He did have both eyeballs. "That's easy, Sarge. That feller Smith, or whatever you called him, was a Freemason, just like me. My pa was too."

"Well, I'll be damned, Jonesy. I'll just be damned. I heard some about Freemasons. But did you ever stop to think that those books weren't his to give? They were in the library at the palace."

"Well, Sarge, I guess that depends on how you look at it. Don't it?"

Jonesy had a point. "Hmm...You keep the books to yourself now. You hear?"

"Sure, Sarge."

Between Jonesy's predicament and his own personal failings the night before, Ethan couldn't get a wink of sleep that night. Instead of lying awake, beating himself up until sunrise, he decided to do something therapeutic. A couple of hours before dawn he slipped stealthily from his bunk and out the door, his shoes in one hand and bayonet in the other.

"GOOD MORNING, MARTY," ETHAN SAID, PLOPPING HIS TIN PLATE on the table beside his friend. "I see from the assignment board we're on the same wagon today. I don't like it."

"Oh, it won't be so bad. Burn and plunder. I'm just bubbling with anticipation. Let's get through it best we can and try to kill as few people as possible, my friend."

"We'll be killing all of them in a way, Marty. The animals, the food, everything."

"Jesus, Ethan," Marty scolded, "you sure are changing your tune. Ready to turn our own country back over to the Indians? Listen. The dumbest thing you can do is to start seeing these people as actual, living, breathing human beings. You are *The Sword of Damocles*, my friend. You kill and burn only in the name of freedom and democracy for the common good."

"Stop it," Ethan snapped. "You should be the last one to talk shit like that, Romeo." The woman had completely scrambled Marty's brain — or unscrambled it. Ethan didn't know anymore which was worse. The man was talking the same old horseshit through his mouth but thinking with his johnson, to the point where his usual sarcasm was sounding more every day like a pitiful cry for help. Marty had *always* seen the Filipinos as human beings, and that was his great weakness.

Marty didn't respond at first but made a little ceremony of dipping his hardtack into the black coffee one too many times until a soft piece dropped off into the cup. Then he said, "Seriously, Ethan. Just do what you're told. If you're disenchanted, don't reenlist. End of story."

Time for a change of subject, Ethan thought. "What do you know about Huckleberry Finn, Marty?"

"Where did that come from? Well, you must mean what do I know about Mark Twain. Why?"

Ethan continued peeling his second banana. "Strange thing. That fancy prisoner and Jonesy became pretty good friends back in Manila. He used to read to Jonesy on afternoons walking in the gardens. He gave Jonesy two books when we left. More than that, his real name is Emilio Aguinaldo."

"Wow! I should have guessed. That explains a lot. Okay, let me guess the names of the two books. Tom Sawyer and Huckleberry Finn, I'll venture."

Lieutenant Hobbs chose that moment to literally burst into the mess tent. "Where's Flood?" he shouted.

Brock, the officers' valet, was near the entrance. He said in a loud voice, "I saw him take a plate over to the Grant Barracks. He's probably at that little table outside, Lieutenant." Hobbs was gone before Brock even finished the last sentence.

"I wonder what that's about?" Marty said.

"We'll find out soon enough. Anyway, you got the right book names, and there's more to this thing. Apparently, the prisoner and Jonesy are both Freemasons."

"Well now," Marty declared, as he stood from the table, "that does add another fly to the pie. Let's kick it around while we're plundering the town."

Before Ethan could drink the last of his coffee, he heard Flood's voice from the front of the tent. "Cooper, Tours, Polk, O'Leary, outside now."

They found the sergeant major waiting outside at the north end of the municipal building. As the four arrived, he said, "A local fisherman just brought in Private Mason's body. He found it floating face down on the sand bar near the mouth of the river. His throat was cut ear to ear. If it hadn't been low tide, he would have drifted out into the bay without a trace. He had the pre-dawn perimeter watch last night. Any of you know anything, anything at all? Did you see anything unusual?"

Nobody said a word at first. They all just shook their heads and shrugged, then Ethan mumbled, "No." He had to wonder why a local fisherman would go to all that trouble bringing the body back.

Then Marty said, "That's a damn shame. He was such a pleasant dinner companion. Was it suicide?"

Flood sneered. "I ain't figured you out yet, Tours, but you're either dumb as a post or...Get out of here, all of you. Lots of work today."

As they headed off to the assembly point, Marty said softly, "We haven't heard the last of that, but do me a favor, Ethan."

"Anything, Marty."

"If there's a next time, try not to look like the cat who ate the canary. I'm worried about you."

CHAPTER ELEVEN

Along every little dirt trail, the word was out, Ethan could see. Families, mainly women and children, crowded around their little clusters of nipa huts, visibly terrified, as his soldiers marauded through the town in a coordinated and well-planned dance of destruction and fire.

Hut by hut, Ethan and Marty watched from the lead wagon as soldiers escorted lingering residents, mostly old people, out at gunpoint before searching for food stocks and bolos. Other soldiers loaded livestock and crops onto carabao-drawn wagons. They burned any food deemed unsuitable for mess consumption.

The caravan halted on a side trail north of the square when someone pointed to some vegetation behind the hut. "Carabao, Sarge," said a private from behind the wagon.

"You know what to do," Ethan replied. "Be warned, anyone who starts hooting and hollering or burns somebody's house down, I'll shoot him myself between the eyes."

While two privates trampled a garden in the neighboring hut, the old carabao came lumbering into the road with his military escort. Not thirty feet in front of Ethan's wagon, the man chambered a round, leveled the Krag behind the animal's ear and fired. The huge beast thudded stone-dead into the dirt, and other troopers promptly began dumping all manner of food and trash onto the pile as women wept and pleaded and babies cried. A good splash of coal oil, not too much as to cause waste, a match, and on to the next hut, accompanied by that nauseating odor familiar to all combat infantry men.

Ever since burning that village on Luzon, Ethan had been consciously preparing to steel himself against the horror and the inhumanity of those moments. He tried to stuff it all in a locked drawer or to think of it as acting in a play. Then the memories might only visit in his sleep.

"So why Mark Twain?" Ethan asked, easing the carabao forward with a switch. "Why those books?"

"I've been thinking about that," Marty replied. "Existential dilemma, primarily."

"What?"

Marty laughed just before both men watched the last rice-storage hut burst into flame. "Existential dilemma. They seem like kids' books but only to kids. Huck is a young kid with no preconceived ideas about race and slavery. He befriends a runaway slave Jim, and they become close. Jim saves him; he saves Jim. You know. Well, Huck loves Jim, but he also feels badly because he's doing something wrong by helping a slave escape. As I recall, he even betrays Jim at one point out of a sense of duty. To most white people, Jim is just a runaway nigger, and Huck is a criminal for helping him."

"So why would this VIP prisoner want Jonesy to read those books?"

"Think about it."

A trooper crossed the road in front of them thirty yards or so ahead into a crowd of women and kids. One of them was a little boy holding his pet monkey like a baby. Without warning, the young trooper snatched the monkey from the child's arms, hurling it to the dirt. Before the monkey could react, the man emptied his five-shot load into its little chest and head, then burst out in laughter.

A state of uncontrollable rage descended upon Ethan Cooper, and he snapped, leaping from the wagon, bayonet already in hand. Before the trooper had even seen him, Ethan locked onto his collar with an iron grip, dragging the man through the dirt and back behind the wagon. With the bayonet in position and poised to sever the man's head, Marty launched himself violently into his friend's torso, and both men rolled to a stop on the dirt trail. The trooper had already scurried away with his life when Ethan came to his senses.

He saw Marty extending a hand to help him from the dirt and quickly recovered his composure. As Marty pulled him up, Ethan said softly, "I don't know which one of us is worse off, Marty."

They resumed their places on the wagon and returned to work with no harm done and almost no time lost, but neither man spoke for several minutes.

Just let it go. It never happened, Ethan told himself. *Just finish the detail and move on to the next one.* Nothing good could come of dwelling on it. Finally, he said, "So what's the answer? Why would he want Jonesy to read those books?"

"Ahh...what?"

"Why would he give Jonesy the books?"

"Well, to make him think, I guess. I mean he wants Jonesy to think about where he stands in a world where people own other people, or one group of people thrives and prospers only through the exploitation of other groups. That's what Twain was trying to do."

"But why bother?"

"I'm not sure," Marty admitted, "but it almost seems like he saw something in Jonesy, something he admired maybe. Innocence, maybe."

"Well, to Jonesy, those are just kids' books. He could never understand all that stuff you said. I don't even think I do."

"Oh, you do, my friend," Marty said, "but Jonesy doesn't have to understand it. That's the point. He just needs to figure out who he is. I do too, my friend. Look at me. I'm a priest out in the jungle killing people and burning their food and houses, in love with a woman I can never have."

If he was going to talk to Marty about the girl, now was the time. But when it came right down to it, what would he say? *She's trouble? Stay away from her?* How about, *She's using you?* In a way, Marty was happier than Ethan had ever known him to be. Asuncion did that, and what they had together was none of Ethan's Cooper's business.

Maybe she really loves him, or maybe it's all true at the same time. If he'd learned anything in the Philippines, it's that good and evil can coexist in the same place, even in the same person. Besides, it was going to end badly for Marty anyway. *Let the man be.*

Ethan knew he hadn't even been honest with Marty about his own troubles. *If only you knew, my friend,* Ethan thought. When the time was right, he would tell Marty everything, but telling him now would only put his friend between a rock and a hard spot. He knew what was on Marty's mind, so he said, "We're never talking about Mason, Marty. Never. You good with that?"

Marty smiled. "Perfectly."

"The thing is," Ethan added, "I still don't understand why some fancy prisoner would care that much about one hillbilly trooper from Texas."

"Freemasonry might explain part of it."

Corporal Isaiah Feldman approached the wagon on foot and addressed them both. "That's it, Ethan. Our section is clear. That trail on the right will get us back to camp quicker. These people won't be happy, but word is they'll be getting most of their menfolk back within a couple days."

"How's that?" Ethan asked.

"O'Brien agreed to a deal, maybe to calm them down. That police chief is out collecting a bunch of tax cheats from the outlying *barrios* to work off their debt. O'Brien's gonna swap some of them out for the town's men."

That was one bright spot on a black day, Ethan figured. Pollito would likely be coming home and that would please Marty. He was the youngest being held. "Okay, Thanks, Feldman. We'll wait here and follow up the rear of the column."

He looked back at Marty and said, "So what about Freemasonry? I heard of it but all I know is it's secret."

"Very. Nobody outside of it knows too much. They have all kinds of secret greetings and symbols. They've been around all over the world since the 14th Century, I think. But I know Freemasons don't recognize class or religious differences, social status or even race, I think…but how are *you* doing, Ethan?"

"I'm fine, Marty. Just lost my temper for a minute. Thanks. I guess that explains the *brother* thing all right."

"Anything else you want to talk about?"

"Not a thing, Marty." *You're my friend, not my mother*, he wanted to say.

THE NEWS OF ALAMO JONES'S DISAPPEARANCE THE NEXT MORNING spread throughout the garrison before the Cook served his first cup of morning coffee, and Ethan had a bad feeling in his gut. The doctor had released Jonesy from the infirmary on light duty last evening, and Jonesy was a no-show at morning assembly. A search of the camp and surrounding area was underway, but the smirks and chuckles were already spilling out. *He's gone over to the niggers,* was tattooed across a dozen faces at the mess tent.

With breakfast squared away, the company clerk lumbered in with two big canvas bags over his shoulders. Mail call was considered his most important duty, a duty he had yet to perform since the company's arrival at "Population Point X-104," known to the natives as Apostol. The news that Lieutenant Hobbs had returned with the mail on the quartermaster's supply ship generated palpable excitement across the outpost, and the mess tent was packed.

Hobbs was right behind the clerk, and the men crowded around to wait for the news of home from family and loved ones. Ethan Cooper was there, as always, because mail call invariably lifted everyone's spirits, even those leaving empty-handed. Hobbs wasted no time in making his announcement.

"You'll get the mail in a minute, men, but first I have some sad news to share from the world. As you know, we have been out of touch here for some time. I got back before dark last night and have reported to Captain O'Brien that President McKinley was shot and killed in Buffalo, New York. The President of The United States and Commander-in-Chief is now Theodore Roosevelt. I will post some newspaper articles in the orderly room for those wanting to know the details."

Ethan could hear some muted rumbling in the crowd for thirty seconds or so, then someone shouted, "What about the mail?" This was not a crowd given to grieving over the violent death of a stranger, even a highly placed one. Even a suicide had failed to generate any sympathetic swell and the only responses Ethan had detected over Mason's unfortunate demise were downright giddy. *Old Mason tried to mount the wrong filly*, was one of the less vulgar ones Ethan had heard since yesterday. From some men's perspective, why should it be different for the man who'd sent them to this *shithole*? Half of them didn't know or care who the President was. They nearly all preferred Roosevelt anyway. He was one of them, and a few of this lot had even fought with him in Cuba.

O'Leary crowded his way in next to Ethan and whispered, "They found Jones's shoes on the riverbank. Brock just told me. Hobbs thinks he's been killed or kidnapped...or..."

"Yeah, I know what *or* means but that didn't happen." In fact, Ethan wasn't so sure. The increasing pressure on Jonesy from the company sadists had been taking its toll on the youngster. Coupled with Jonesy's apparent personal friendship with that Aguinaldo added up to a big question mark in Ethan's mind.

"Well, for now he's just officially *missing*," O'Leary said.

As usual, neither Ethan nor Martin Tours received any mail but stuck around until the end to witness the entertainment that always accompanied the spectacle of mail call. Filing out of the mess tent, Ethan spotted the newly released Pollito in front of the barracks. The young man was heading straight for them.

They met just north of the municipal building. Pollito stopped and held out a note. Marty said, "Good morning, Pollito. What's this?"

When he didn't reply, Marty took the note. By the time he opened it, Pollito was gone.

"Looks pretty mysterious," said Ethan. The note was in Spanish, but Ethan didn't try to read it. "What is it?"

"She wants to meet me tomorrow night at our beach," Marty confided.

Ethan felt a big hand on his shoulder and didn't need to turn to know it was Flood. He said, "Cooper, get over to the orderly room. The captain wants to see you in ten minutes."

"Sure, Sarge," Ethan said.

"Now, Tours, since you boys have no mail to read, perhaps you'd be kind enough to get over to the punishment tents and help get these crews moving. We can do without you boys at drill. The Inspector General is due here this week, and the captain is foaming at the mouth."

Marty said, "I'll take care of it, Sergeant Flood."

When Flood had cleared earshot, Ethan said, "That beach is an hour and a half each way through the jungle. You should think twice before wandering out of camp by yourself to meet her. Things are pretty damn tense around here in case you hadn't noticed."

Marty had rarely been sleeping in his bunk. It was hardly a secret among the NCOs. If he was more at risk this time, that was his business, and it wouldn't compromise post security in any way. Still, Ethan had a bad feeling. "I have a few minutes. I'll walk over to the prison tents with you."

"I hear there's a big *fiesta* tomorrow night," Marty said. "The parish anniversary or something. It should last late. I'll be okay. I'm a big boy."

The new prisoners from the first tent were lined up outside in groups of ten getting work bolos, ready to begin their cleanup assignments. Ethan said, "Do you notice anything different about these guys, Marty?"

"Indeed, I do. They look like some pretty rugged customers."

"Exactly. Obrador claims they're tax cheats from the countryside, but you have to wonder why they're not complaining and grumbling about sleeping on the wet ground in that tent? If you really have to go tomorrow, I could go with you and hang back out of sight. Things will be fine here."

Marty shook his head in an emphatic *no*. "If you show up, she'll think I don't trust her. I'd rather get ambushed by *insurrectos* or fall into a stake pit."

"Well, I'd better get over to the orderly room. I can't imagine why O'Brien wants to see me unless it's to take my stripes."

Marty said, "Maybe it has something to do with that Pinkerton who arrived on the mail boat this morning with Lieutenant Hobbs."

"What?" For a few seconds, Ethan considered stealing a boat that very minute, but there was just nowhere left to go. This guy had tracked him to the other side of the globe over two and a half years and finally cornered him. Ethan's running was over. It was time to face this demon in the fiddler's hat and the man with the deep pocket, but he wasn't about to make it easier for him.

With his heart pounding and his mind racing, Ethan knew he had to collect his thoughts and hold it together. He wasn't sure if the Fiddler could identify him, but he had to buy himself every possible minute to plot his next move.

He stopped at the door to the municipal building and rolled up both sleeves, clearly exposing Nona and Mona to open view and opened the door. O'Brien's "office" was just a space along the wall segregated by vertical bamboo panels for some privacy. Flood had a desk right outside the space. He spotted Ethan coming in the door and said, "Wait here. I'll tell the captain you're here."

Flood reappeared seconds later and motioned Ethan into the office. O'Brien sat at his desk flanked by the man in the fiddler's cap on his left. The Pinkerton hadn't changed. Even the graying beard was identical to one that had stalked Ethan back in Pittsburgh. The Fiddler was standing proudly, like a hunter over his dead prey.

The eyes were a new addition to the man's nightmare profile. Ethan saw no trace of hate or vengeance, just the nondescript, dark blue eyes of a middle-aged stranger. "At ease, soldier," O'Brien said.

Turning to the Fiddler, he said, "So is this the man?"

Ethan tried his best to stare the man down, being certain the girls were fully exposed. Timidity would not serve him well in this encounter. The Fiddler hesitated. Ethan saw doubt in his face until the man's eyes landed on the girls. "That's him. No doubt about it. That's my man. He has two naked women tattooed on his arms."

114

"We all see the tattoos," O'Brien began. "The man made no attempt to hide them, but you could have just made up the tattoos. You said nothing about tattoos in our private conversation." O'Brien pointed out.

"But I recognize his face as well," Fiddler pleaded.

"Well," said O'Brien, "The thing is easily settled. Show me something official that says the man you're looking for has naked ladies

on his arms, and I'll surrender him to your custody. Otherwise, I find your identification lacking."

The eyes turned angry, frustrated. "The file would fill a trunk," the Fiddler protested. "I don't carry it around while tracking suspects. That's him, I tell you."

When the Fiddler produced a pair of handcuffs and moved around the desk toward Ethan, O'Brien said, "Stop. There will be none of that just yet." O'Brien rose from his chair. "Not good enough," he declared. "Cooper is a pain in my behind, but he's one of our best NCOs. I have a mess on my hands here, Mr..."

"Hellman, Captain. Richard Hellman. May I remind you, Sir, that my company's employer is Mr. Allen Winslow, the Pittsburgh steel tycoon? Mr. Winslow is personally pursuing this investigation. With a simple wire to Governor Taft, Mr. Winslow could..."

It was the wrong thing to say to the righteous-minded captain. His face pinched up like an asshole, and with his hands resting on the desk, he leaned toward the Fiddler and said slowly, "Do not threaten me, Sir. If this is your man, you shall have him but not until we are certain." Looking at Ethan, he said, "According to this man, you are charged under a different name with the murder of three Pinkertons in connection with a labor riot at one of Winslow's steel plants. What say you?"

"Captain O'Brien, Sir, I won't lie to you. I never murdered anyone in my life—until I joined the army."

The Fiddler seethed openly. "All right," O'Brien began. "This is what will happen here. You are confined to the post unless detailed elsewhere, Cooper, but you will maintain your duties. We're at a critical moment here, and I need your help. Do you understand?"

Hellman started to protest but O'Brien held up his hand. His mind was made up. "Mr. Hellman, Corporal Brock will arrange quarters for you in the church annex with the officers. You are welcome to conduct your investigation here. You may send for your materials or leave and return with them. You will have access to Cooper's records. If Cooper is your man, you shall have him, but only with proper authority from General Chaffee's Command. The letter you brought instructs me to 'cooperate.' This is my decision. Cooper, you are dismissed."

The Fiddler growled, "I'll be watching you. You're the thirteenth and final name on my list. I know you enlisted with that nigger's son in Chicago, and I know he lied to me. Don't think for a minute this is over for you."

Ethan looked at O'Brien. "May I go, Sir?"

The captain nodded.

CHAPTER TWELVE

The next morning, Ethan was awake before Reveille and saw Marty still asleep. He'd made it back. It took some effort to wake him up. Finally, Marty said, "Good morning, Ethan. How was the *fiesta*?"

"Ahh…I'd say a good few of these boys will be sporting headaches the rest of the day."

"Any news on Jonesy?" Marty asked.

"Nothing at all."

Then Marty was up and looking for his trousers. He said, "What was the general mood at the *fiesta*? I mean considering all the tensions around here lately?"

"Well, there wasn't a lot of socializing," Ethan explained, "but the locals were very generous with the liquor, the ones who are not in custody."

"Did you happen to see Asuncion around the square last evening?"

"I did," Ethan answered, "and I was surprised. She was supposed to be with you."

"She didn't show up," Marty said. "I just made it back here a few hours ago."

Ethan knew a talk with Marty was long overdue. He would tell his friend the whole story, right after breakfast. This Hellman character wasn't about to quit now. They would haul him back to Pittsburgh and start lining up the witnesses. Whatever would happen would happen. He didn't murder anyone, but the truth had never really mattered. Allen Winslow won the battle of public opinion with his money, crushed the organized labor movement, and was determined to have his last measure of revenge. Yes. He and Marty would have a talk after breakfast. Marty needed to hear it from him.

ETHAN WAS STANDING IN THE CHOW LINE WITH HIS MEAT CAN AND tin cup when the chaos erupted. Screams from every direction, a flash of steel from the left, and a powerful *thud* as warm blood spattered his uniform shirt.

He whirled in time to see a head and neck peeling from a uniformed torso. It was a sergeant. He couldn't see who, but the attackers had run past ten men in line to get to him. The man who'd killed him was tall and dressed in a police uniform. *They're going after the stripes first*, Ethan thought.

Swarms of crazed natives barreled through the tent and across the long table-top flailing wildly with bolos. Arms, heads, and pieces of bodies already littered the table. Sergeant Major Flood's torso, identifiable only by its stripes, lay collapsed on the table, still seated as its head lay upside down, eyes staring down the grizzly neck in Ethan's direction.

Instinctively moving toward the Grant Barracks, only yards away, Ethan cursed himself for leaving his rifle in the barracks as infantrymen fought back with fists, plates, and mess knives. Just outside the tent, hordes of wild-eyed bolomen poured into the municipal building as dozens of the new prisoners erupted from the confinement tents into the action, somehow already armed with the curved, war bolo.

Ethan knew immediately this was a coordinated attack, and they were after the armory upstairs, the guns and the ammo, but he had to secure his own barracks first to get some rifles and lay down coordinated fire from a secured location.

Across the square, Filipinos charged from the church toward the Meade Barracks where the occupants were also under attack.

In front of Grant Barracks, Ethan spotted O'Leary and a few others locked in a death struggle with a dozen natives. The troopers had managed to grab their rifles, employing them with great effect from the front doorway. The attackers had already managed to secure some rifles but did not appear to be firing them, Ethan noticed.

Surrendering to a sharp pain in his leg, Ethan collapsed onto the dirt only a few feet short of the house, a clean shot through his left leg. Two bolomen were on him in a second. He rolled, barely dodging a bolo swipe and grabbing the wrist of the second attacker. With the wrist, Ethan leveraged himself to his feet and began beating the second man with his meat can until disarming him. He now had a bolo.

The first attacker showed his back, not liking the new odds, and Ethan joined his comrades attempting to retake the barracks. Someone was lying on the porch in front of the door. It was Private Pots, his head cleaved like a coconut, rifle gone. Slashing and dodging, Ethan glanced left toward the Meade Barracks and saw Schneider, weaponless and staggering toward him, bleeding from the head. Beyond Schneider and to the left, at the church, scores of attackers swarmed out of the side door and through the passageway into the convent—and the officers' quarters. Others poured from inside the church into the square.

The whole square pulsated with screams, blood, gunshots, and the incessant rhythm of beating conch shells and drums in the distance. He watched a crazed pack of armed Filipinos run right past the wounded Schneider, leaving him unmolested.

Ethan was in Grant Barracks now where he saw a few others fending off dozens of attackers. Dead and maimed soldiers littered the first floor. Through the window, he could see more natives climbing the outside ladder to the second floor.

He retrieved a rifle and ammo belt from a dead native and yelled, "O'Leary, upstairs. We can't let them take this house."

O'Leary, now armed with a Krag, nodded and began fighting his way to the stairs. Someone else joined him. From the opening along the stairs, Ethan could see Schneider outside, now wearing a native straw hat to stem the blood flow, and newly armed with a Krag and ammo belt. He'd found a strategic fighting position outside to the west and was blazing away toward the municipal building.

At the top of the stairs, several men were locked in mortal, hand-to-hand combat. As they opened up with the Krags, the surviving attackers scurried out and down the ladder, others jumping to safety or injury from the second floor. Someone writhed in agony against the wall while another man moaned with a third of his head missing. Brains and blood saturated the floor, but the barracks was secured. Ethan knew they now had a strategic point from which to fight. He also knew, in order to live, they had to control the municipal building and the Meade Barracks near the church.

From the front window on the second floor, Ethan commanded a panoramic view of the chaos. He and O'Leary focused on pouring cover fire on the municipal building while others, he hoped, were fighting for control of the all-important armory inside.

Outside the municipal building, the unmistakable figure of a tall, muscular native with elephant ears urged on his Filipino fighters while holding a stolen Krag. Obrador was around the corner before Ethan could get a shot. To Ethan's right, Feldman and his mates were fighting a similar action to cover the men in the Meade Barracks to the west. Marty was nowhere to be seen.

From their position, Ethan and O'Leary did not have a line of sight to the second-floor windows in the armory where natives were firing from the openings and throwing rifles down to the other attackers. Suddenly, Filipinos appeared to be falling out the windows faster than they could throw rifles. From his position behind a tree between Meade and Grant, Schneider was picking them off like flies on the ground and in the window openings, and Americans were picking up the rifles as they fell.

Ethan watched Schneider turn his fire to the concrete pile around the flagpole where three men were holding off a dozen or so attackers by throwing pieces of concrete.

Waiving, Ethan hollered to the sharpshooter. "Schneider, focus on the guns. We got the flagpole." Schneider signaled back and intensified his fire in the area of the municipal building while Feldman and his crew in the west opening concentrated on Meade Barracks. The square was quickly transforming into a death zone for the attackers. Still, they kept coming from seemingly all directions by the hundreds. Ethan could only imagine the struggles being waged inside the municipal building and Meade Barracks.

"O'Leary," Ethan bellowed, "grab an ammo belt and come with me. The rest of you hold this house at all costs until relieved. Johnson, take this window."

They knew how to follow orders in combat. This time, he figured, their survival would depend on it. The three men were down the stairs and at the front door in a heartbeat. Ethan hollered to Schneider outside behind the tree. "Schneider, cover us. On three we'll make a run for the armory."

Schneider signaled and Ethan counted—loudly. On three they were off. The bolomen dared not come near the firepower of three Krag's. Only feet from the municipal building door, a Filipino popped from behind a barrel nearly face-to-face with O'Leary, aiming a Krag squarely in the Irishman's face. The attacker fired on the big man at point blank range and the gun jammed. Ethan shot the Filipino dead. The attackers were having trouble with the blocking mechanism of the Krag. Unless the switch was moved, the chamber could not load a round. Ethan knew it wouldn't take long for them to figure it out.

The three men from the flagpole fight had joined them at the doorway, and Ethan could see Renaldo with Brock and another man in a death-defying dash toward them from the convent. Brock had slowed his pace in order not to leave the wounded man behind. Everyone at the door opened up with covering fire.

They found the main door to the municipal building blocked and bolted. Joined now by three or four other stragglers, the dozen or so soldiers smashed it down using concrete and rifle stocks and rushed inside firing. Ethan saw forty, maybe fifty natives many armed with Krags but largely unable to fire them. Roughly half the natives scurried up the stairs to the second floor as the others escaped the overwhelming firepower through the south door or window openings.

"O'Leary, keep three men and secure the main floor. The rest of you up the stairs." At the top of the stairs, he could see dead Americans, a few horribly mutilated on the floor, blood seeping straight through the bamboo mat. The twenty or so natives, outgunned with no easy escape route, crowded to the north end of the room, and for a moment, the room was quiet. A few dropped their bolos and raised their hands.

Ethan found himself eye-to-eye with the tall policeman, the one who had severed Sergeant Polk's head and neck, and he fired. Then they all fired as natives cried out and dropped or jumped through the high window openings. The municipal building and the weapons, what the natives hadn't already taken, were secured.

As the battle raged, Ethan could hear a shout rising among the various Filipino attacking parties "Udang! Undang! Udang!" It was one of the few Waray words Ethan understood. It meant "stop" or "quit."

From the window opening, he could see Obrador again, calling a general retreat to his troops as the attackers gathered into groups and began an organized retreat into various positions outside the square, beyond the view of the battered infantry company.

"They're retreating, Ethan," said O'Leary.

"There are hundreds of them," Ethan replied. "They could have overrun us in a few more minutes. Can't be more than fifteen of us left alive but he doesn't know that."

Ethan looked over at Brock and said, "Brock, what's the status of the officers?".

"Lieutenant Hobbs and Doctor Lawrence are dead. Hacked to death. Must have been fifty of them who invaded the convent from the church. They were hiding in there. I don't get it. Me and Renaldo were standing in the passageway to the convent when they came through screaming. They ran right by us, Ethan. From outside, I saw the captain jump from the second story. A dozen of them chased him around the church toward the riverfront. He couldn't have survived. There were more of them waiting along the riverfront."

Ethan said, "There was a civilian with the officers. A guy with a beard. He came in early with mail."

"Oh, that's who the civilian was. They lopped his head off, Ethan. It had a beard for sure. Bad time for his trip, whoever he was."

Ethan heard two shots from across the square and saw Marty standing in front of Meade Barracks. Feldman was in the doorway giving cover. They had weathered the storm and were alive. Others must be alive in there too, he figured. Ethan saw the bugler and asked, "Do you have your horn?"

The man, wounded in both arms, nonetheless held up the bugle. It had stayed around his neck during the melee. "Right here, Sarge. Call it."

"Sound Recall. Let's give those guys in Meade cover when they make their break across the square. There could be another attack any moment, so we need to group up and figure a way out of this mess."

"Ethan," O'Leary said, "with the officers and Flood and Polk dead, looks like you or Marty Tours is in command."

"Looks that way, Paddy. All right, boys, here they come. Open up on the convent window holes and anywhere else you see a rifle."

Two men started over from Meade in the open and limping, all but carrying the wounded Isaiah Feldman. All three carried Krags. Everyone who could fire helped fill the square with lead, and not a single Filipino boloman dared brave the fire to get to them.

As they made it through the door, Ethan said to Marty, "How many?"

"Six dead in the house," Marty replied grimly. "Two outside. The dog made it out through a window."

Two less seriously wounded men lay Feldman on the mat in a corner with other wounded and tended to the slice on his leg. Marty plopped onto a hardtack box to catch his breath and Ethan said, "So what do you think, Marty? We have them off balance. Got to check for wounded in the hot zone. We can't leave anybody here alive. Can't leave any serviceable weapons for them. You're in command."

"Agreed," Marty replied. "I'll take five men and check the church and convent. You have enough to do here. Get the company records, some food, water." Then Marty leaned in close and whispered. "Maybe the company records will get lost. The whole company knows why that Pinkerton was hanging around."

"No. They won't get lost," Ethan answered. "In the meantime, we have to figure a way out of here and where to go if we make it."

Everyone in the room was either on guard or tending to a wounded comrade. Someone said to Ethan, "Sarge, you better sit down and let me get a belt or something around that leg. You're bleeding like a pig."

Seated on a desk, Ethan addressed the group. "Everybody, let's count off to get a number. Speak up for anyone too badly wounded." When the men had counted off out loud to twenty-three, including the six at the church, he said, "Okay. Let's hear some ideas on how we get out of here alive and where we go. Seems like boats are our only chance."

Brock spoke first. "The docks are out. When we got out of the convent there were already dozens of goo goos there. They'll expect us. There's a small beach on the bay near the river mouth where the fishermen keep a few canoes. We could make it there if we go now."

Ethan nodded. "Okay. That's it then. Schneider, take five men and ammo right now. Go down there and secure the boats we need. While you're gone, we'll figure out where we're going."

They watched as the detail crossed the square untouched. Everywhere men ejected the firing pin mechanisms from the extra rifles, piling them in a heap. Ethan stuffed company records into a canvas mail sack.

Near the flagpole, Ethan saw someone reach for the Krag in the hand of a presumably dead soldier. It wouldn't budge. Suddenly, the man sprang to his feet and sprinted toward the municipal building, rifle in hand.

"Okay, everyone, take some firing pins and throw them in the bay when we get down there. Brock, take a couple of men and get the colors."

Ethan turned to *Lazurus* and said, "You, since you're not dead, take two men and go across to the Grant. See if anyone is alive. If you play dead again, I promise you will never get up."

They could counterattack any minute. Ethan thought. "Any ideas about where we go?"

The badly wounded Private Chomsky, propped against a wall, chimed in. "On the way down here, we passed another outpost like this up on the west coast, about a day's travel from here."

"Yes," Ethan said, remembering the place. They call it Camp San Juan Hill. That's it then."

"Sergeant Tours is back," someone yelled and held the door open as the patrol rushed in.

After a few deep breaths, Marty said to Ethan, "Nobody alive. We grabbed seven firing pins and found a couple bottles of whiskey. Oh, we found General Sheridan too. He was beheaded."

"I'll bet you knew just where to look for the whiskey, but the dog too?" Ethan asked.

"He fought like ten infantrymen, Ethan," Marty said. "Probably saved a couple of us."

Ethan found a chair near the door and told Marty his proposed plan. He would need his strength for the dash to the beach. The survivors numbered twenty-four, although a few of them would likely be dead by noon. Ethan surveyed the ghastly mess in the orderly room. One poor soul was against the wall, holding his own guts in with both arms, and he wasn't the worst of them. The all-too-familiar smell of fresh blood permeated the room.

"All right, boys, saddle up," came the call from their new commanding officer, Sergeant Tours. "Everybody with two good arms and legs help with stretchers."

Standing again, Marty loaded one in the chamber of his Krag and five in the box, then turned back to Ethan and said, "Pick one strong man, Ethan. The minute we hit the beach, push off in a small boat and make for San Juan full speed. Maybe you can get there in time to help us. The rest of us will pull through with the wounded best we can."

"Marty, I'm wounded pretty bad. Not sure I'd make it."

Marty nodded. "Right. I'll go myself. You're in command." Marty immediately tapped an unwounded soldier and shoved off toward the beach to grab the smallest *banca*.

With the remnants of a full company assembled and ready to move, Ethan addressed the group. "O'Leary will take five men to act as rear guard. Stick together and follow my lead. When we hit the beach, load the most badly wounded into the biggest boats." He named three men to command the other boats and the survivors moved out toward the beach.

They had just turned west, toward the area of fishing boats, when the attack came.

Upwards of a hundred men with bolos and a few working Krags charged before the ragged survivors could disappear onto the trail. O'Leary's rear guard formed a skirmish line as the main body ducked onto the short trail to the beach. In less than half a minute, Ethan heard them open up in unison with a minute-long cascade of lead.

On the small beach, they found Brock with four boats of various sizes and lost no time beginning to load the most seriously wounded onto the largest two.

Ethan spotted Marty and another man already well underway in the bay. "Okay, keep to the plan," Ethan ordered. "Get them loaded."

The rear guard held solid until Ethan signaled that the boats were loaded. The loading had taken less than five minutes. When O'Leary's party reached the beach, the boats were already waist-deep into the bay and engaged in close combat with a platoon sized force of bolomen. A concentration of rifle fire made easy work of the attackers in the water.

With all boats away, the makeshift sailors, bloodied and maimed, paddled for dear life as another swarm of Filipinos rushed the beach in a chorus of hatred and rage and lead.. A few reached the boats and were cut down at point blank in a hail of lead as the retreat had begun.

CHAPTER THIRTEEN

Two arms reached across Ethan's chest to snatch the paddle violently from determined hands. "Sarge, hey Sarge," he heard someone say, "your leg is bleeding again. Here, take my belt and keep the pressure on."

In less than a minute he was paddling again. He could see the Filipinos along the shoreline as the last of his four commandeered *barotas* cleared the sand bar at the mouth of the river. Not a word was spoken in his lead boat until the ragged fleet had paddled beyond the range of the hijacked Krag rifles. His two dozen or so men seemed to sense the momentary reprieve, but the knowledge offered no comfort. They were battle-hardened soldiers and already understood the long odds against surviving the voyage. Ethan raised his paddle into the air in a signal for the boats to regroup.

The bay was calm for the first time in a week, and Ethan was determined to exploit nature's merciful gesture. Shouting was unnecessary in the eerie stillness of early morning. Whispered prayers and cursed moans of the wounded skipped along the blue surface, boat to boat, every syllable, sound, and cough perceptible, inescapable, and incessant to each survivor in the grim convoy. There would be no secrets on this voyage of the damned.

"You all know where we're headed," Ethan announced calmly to his pathetic command. "Looks like clear weather but you never know. Remember to keep an eye on the boat ahead of you, and if you get lost, stay in sight of shore. When we round that point, shore will be on your right, then thirty-five miles to Camp San Juan. We'll take them one at a time."

He knew if any boat lost its points of reference through cloud or fog, it could end up in the gulf, heading west for one of the more primitive islands—or worse. Infantry training did not contemplate encounters with headhunters. There were places in this archipelago so primitive and violent even the Spanish had dared not tread for over three hundred years.

"Ah, Jae'zuz, Ethan, some of these boys won't make San Juan," came the voice of Corporal O'Leary. "It could take us twenty-four hours. Maybe we should be after findin' a defensible position up the coast a wee bit, set up a perimeter, and wait for relief. Sure, they're bound to come for us soon."

"Just keep your eyes and your Krag trained on the shoreline and do your job," Ethan replied, in no mood for insolence. Friend or not, O'Leary could be annoying as hell. Ethan had not asked for command. He had inherited it in the crack of a buggy whip. Sgt. Major Flood, or pieces of him, were still lying back there. They'd butchered him like a Sunday chicken. Who even knew what had become of their commanding officer? With Polk split from neck to opposite waist at the breakfast table, the only sergeants left were Ethan and Marty Tours. Half a dozen people had to die to put him in command, but that was that.

"Ethan, we got company." It was Brock, commanding the second boat. "Three hostile boats coming out past the sand bar." So far as Ethan could tell, Brock was one of the least seriously wounded survivors in what had been a crack infantry company a couple of hours before.

"Okay. Let's get moving, one man in every boat on watch with a Krag. Rotate. Pick one off if they get in range. They can't outshoot us, so they can't get to us on the water. Help the wounded best you can. Stop the bleeding at least. Best thing we can do is get them to San Juan quick time."

Ethan's lead boat belonged to the local padre who had turned it into a fairly decent rowboat for eight people. The most seriously wounded littered its v-shaped hull. Ethan wasn't even certain how many after their chaotic escape. A ghastly brew of blood and sea water pooled shin-deep through the dugout hull, and the men who could bailed furiously with coconut shells to fend off disaster.

They included the disfigured John Love and another bloody wretch dangling a belt from the stump of his left bicep. The bolo was a particularly effective weapon against limbs and faces. With faces obscured, most of his own men were unrecognizable, a hodgepodge of damaged frames covered in blood and makeshift bandaging.

"Ethan," came the voice of John Love near the bow. "Miller has had it. One of those shots from the shoreline hit him square in the temple, looks like."

"Cover him with something and keep bailing," Ethan said. Killing and dying were part of the job, but death sported a strange, new intimacy on board a stinking, native, fishing canoe on the other side of the world. "Pass the word to the other boats. Easy on the water."

Even near the river mouth, the water was too salty to drink, he knew, and most of the fresh water supply had been lost in the attack. The group was down to a few canteens and some hard tack. *You should have chanced a run back for more water and some food. No matter now.* Getting to San Juan before they all bled to death would offer the best shot at survival—or so he hoped.

Without warning, the crack of a stolen Krag rifle drove them all low to the decks.

"They couldn't hit any of us out here except by accident," Ethan said. "Must be half a mile to shore."

"They don't need to hit us, Ethan," someone said from one of the small boats some twenty yards back. "That one got us at the water line, and we've sprung a leak. We'll plug it for now, but we've got to go out farther."

"Okay, everybody, let's take them out another fifty yards." The farther they moved from the shore the greater the chance of getting lost, but he could not allow panic to take hold. It could happen, Ethan knew all too well, even among veteran infantry. These men were no sailors.

Ethan's rowing station aft offered a good position from which to access and manage the situation. Their immediate pursuers from both water and shore had given up the chase. Harris and one of the young kids were his other paddlers. No one else could hold a paddle.

"A steamer! Look!" One of the wounded in Brock's boat was pointing out into the bay. Ethan could see a single line of smoke consistent with a U.S. Army transport ship. It was clearly visible but undeniably a long way out.

As the men of the ragged armada desperately waved shirts and rags to attract the ship's attention, Ethan quickly weighed chancing a volley of shots. The natives likely had them in sight at that very moment anyway and, if not, could easily find them again in minutes without rifle shots.

"Okay, we'll fire a volley and see what happens. Ethan retrieved the fully loaded Krag lying propped against the stern beside him and self-executed the order, firing five deliberate shots into the air with a measured tempo to the bolt action chambering. A breathless silence followed, but the smoke in the distance continued to fade until only the horizon remained. No one felt the need to articulate their common despair.

"Keep rowing and stay alert," Ethan warned. "The whole damned island knows where we are now."

Ethan had only witnessed scattered bits of the chaotic slaughter. He might never know half of what had really happened. It was all over in a flash as quickly as it started. An infantry company of seventy-five or eighty men, almost all at breakfast, instantly reliant on instinct and sheer will to survive, to escape. How did it happen? Why? Who? Had Ethan himself unknowingly aided their attackers? What about Asuncion? He thought he saw her there in the square in the middle of the chaos tending to a wounded Filipino. She knew something was going to happen. She tried to keep Marty out of danger, but had she been involved? Could Jonesy have been involved somehow? Questions dogged him. *There will be time for that later, maybe.*

The shoreline was deserted, but the sounds of conch shell and bamboo drums resonating louder over the bay from beyond the tree line sounded an ominous note. It made him regret the volley and told him the gruesome engagement had simply advanced up the coast with his ragged command. Filipinos were hunting the survivors now like wounded boar.

All the signs were there, and Ethan had seen them, sensed the danger and the tension. It had been carefully planned, brilliantly even, and flawlessly executed by brave men. Many were simple farmers or fishermen defending their families, but the prisoners in the confinement tent had likely been seasoned fighters from General Martinez's forces. Even now, drenched in the blood of his comrades, he could see that. He'd recognized dozens of faces, even names, during the brief battle.

"Look," somebody said, pointing. "There are more in the tree line."

"They don't have any boats," Ethan replied, "so they're only a threat if we make land."

"What else can we do?" someone pleaded. "We drown or get eaten by sharks if we stay in these boats."

"Shut your yaps and row," was Ethan's only response.

Twin, bamboo outriggers made the ancient fishing craft difficult to maneuver and offered a stiff, bumpy ride, but the increased stability just might save their lives, Ethan thought. He scanned the bloodied deck and counted seven mangled bodies aboard, plus his paddlers. Most were in desperate straits with all manner of slash, stab and gunshot wounds but struggling gamely to aid the next man. He figured Marty Tours and the other man were a couple of hours ahead by now in the single-outrigger dugout. With luck, they might reach the camp before midnight. Still, it would be at least an hour more before anyone could launch a relief party. That meant these men would have to paddle into the early morning. Some of the wounded were already living on borrowed time. *Just keep rowing.*

Whatever sorcery had transpired back in Apostol, his company had been nearly wiped out. What if he had left people alive in the village? *Put it out of your mind. None of it will matter if you don't get back alive, if you don't get these men back alive. It's your command now, like it or not.*

Without warning, two cracks from a Krag shattered the silence.

"Dinner," someone cried from the last boat, trailing some distance behind the others.

"What is it?" Someone asked.

"Biggest goddamn turtle you ever seen," a man hollered back.

"Cut it up and spread it around," Ethan said. "Use the shell for bailing if there's anything left of it."

Scattered *pueblos* and small groups of nipa huts dotted the shoreline every few miles or so against the backdrop of hilly, bamboo jungle. Too often the convoy passed tempting groves of banana trees and the occasional coconut palm grove between the shore and the jungle. All the while black eyes trained on the passing armada as the unrelenting sun baked open wounds and labored to extinguish the last breath from these makeshift sailors.

As boredom mercifully descended, Ethan remembered the dead Pinkerton. If nothing else, it might buy him some time. But what is a week or two? Had O'Brien put something into his record yet? Maybe and maybe not, but everyone who knew the Pinkerton was dead. Still, the whole company had heard the story, and each surviving man would be debriefed. Game over.

"Chomsky's dead," someone announced.

"All right," said Ethan. "Cover him and keep paddling."

As they rounded another point to the northwest, the seas roughened. Inescapable, scorching sunlight enfolded them. "We're in open water," Ethan announced. "It will get tougher now all the way."

Within minutes, Ethan could see the last boat increasingly falling behind. Horrific wails from the wounded weakened as the distance grew. He watched as the native craft settled ever lower into the brine, saltwater waves assaulting open wounds and dragging the boat to an agonizing dead stop.

They had lost half an hour by the time Ethan pulled alongside the much smaller *barota*, bobbing aimlessly like a drifting tree trunk. Only the dual outriggers kept it afloat. Ethan counted seven occupants, including Renaldo, the Filipino servant of their presumably deceased commanding officer. The rest looked to be in pitiful condition with the common assortment of gut and head wounds, not to mention the muscle cramps and delirium from guzzled seawater.

Ethan took the two most severely wounded men onto his own boat and handed over two Krag rifles to the rest. He couldn't even remember who was commanding the boat, and the faces had blended into each other hours ago. "Do the best you can, boys. We'll send search parties back soon as we can."

Rough water forced the armada to assume a zig-zag course in the afternoon to minimize flooding and roll. It worked for a while but, by mid-afternoon, Ethan's boat was taking water and losing its struggle to top the waves. Amidst the zig-zagging and the thirst and the unremitting intensity of the sun, progress slowed to a near stop. Bailing with shells became a hopeless waste of energy. They had to lighten the boat or drown, so Ethan made the decision to bury the two dead men at sea. No one objected.

By dusk, the canteens were long ago empty and the paddlers exhausted as the convoy passed a sandy beach. The darkening skyline spilled just enough light to reveal the lush coconut palm grove and several bountiful banana trees beyond the beach. The drums had fallen silent, and the inviting shoreline bore no sign of human life.

Ethan said, "No village around but there's a nasty coral reef that goes out about a hundred yards."

"At least we can see it clearly," someone said.

"We'll risk it. Brock, you have a better chance in the smaller boat. Take a couple extra Krags from us. We'll get as close as we can and cover you from the boat. You got anyone who can climb a coconut tree?"

"Sure. We're good," Brock answered.

Feldman was right as rain about the coral reef, and Ethan's boat held just outside the reef to provide covering fire while Brock eased the small boat slowly over the reef until it grounded. Feldman stayed aboard as Brock and another man, wearing boots, eased carefully over the side. Someone carried a Krag and Brock a bolo as they advanced toward the beach.

As the duo closed to about fifty yards of shore, half a dozen natives sprang from the tree line, yelling all the way as they traversed the sharp coral reef, bolos at the ready. With Feldman's party in retreat, every Krag on the two boats opened up in full magazine mode, and three of the attackers dropped in unison as the others retreated toward the tree line. There would be no coconuts.

Nobody complained openly as the two boats resumed course up the shoreline, not even the two or three notorious malcontents among the survivors.

"SHARKS," CAME THE LABORED CRY FROM OVER THE WATER.

Ethan had already seen the massive fin. The beast glided past the little boat in plain view, not ten feet from his submerged paddle, an enormous creature, seeming to arrogantly mock their desperate state. The sharks had no doubt targeted a carnivorous dinner feast, having lunched earlier on the flesh of their dead.

The wounded were beyond panic and the rowers, like Ethan himself, seemed too terrified to cause a fuss. Ethan had never seen a man eaten by one of these monsters, but it didn't seem a desirable or fitting end for a soldier. He had watched men beheaded like a chicken, gutted like a hog, shot, stabbed, burnt, and trampled. All those seemed merciful to him there in the falling darkness. Maybe at some point, his body would just stop working and, hopefully, it wouldn't matter by then.

Ethan spotted two more sharks in the early moonlight, circling Brock's boat. Before he could fully process the image, he heard what he had been fearing most. "Let me off this thing," came the tortured scream from Brock's boat. "I can't take it no more." No telling who it was.

The boat began to sway. Thuds and racket announced a scuffle until the agonizing scream settled into a harmless whimper.

"It's all good, Ethan," came Brock's bone-weary voice. *No, it's not good.* In the last few minutes, even in the moonlight, Ethan had lost sight of the coast, and he seriously wondered if one could intentionally drown himself quickly by breathing in salt water. *How do you fight a shark?* "Can any of you see the shore?" He whispered softly to his rowers. No answer.

Then he remembered a technique he learned from an old sailor he'd met in San Francisco. In a crescent moon, if you draw an imaginary line between the points and follow it to the horizon, it will point you to south in the northern hemisphere. He guessed the result would be the opposite from the southern hemisphere. If he were wrong, maybe they would at least end up on another island. Better to be dinner for cannibals than by sharks. It was common knowledge that primitive cannibal tribes were still living in remote areas of some islands. Cannibals would most likely kill a man before roasting him on a spit.

Within a half hour, he could make out the line of treetops to his right and happily banished fear of attackers from his fear list, and his thoughts turned elsewhere, to the future—or lack thereof. It was just as well that he was finally caught, Ethan thought, because every day in this army going forward would be a day in captivity. It wasn't necessary to understand all the politics. This was a murderous war without just cause, and this army would never be his father's Union Army.

Maybe it wasn't the army that had changed, he thought, or even the world. Maybe the world was always cruel and heartless, no more and no less now. What had changed for certain was something inside Ethan Cooper. *When enemies acquire names,* he told himself, *war becomes murder.* For the first time, he understood, he felt, what Marty had been saying and, just maybe, took a short walk in his friend's shoes.

Ethan knew his disgust with this pointless butchery now outweighed his fear of arrest and hanging. He had truly become Ethan Cooper now, and that man had outgrown this army. He finally understood old Jimmy Jeffries' final words at the freight yard: *You have good in you, Boy…if you let it guide you, it will show you who you are…or it will get you killed,* he added silently.

Ethan looked down at his hands and watched the meandering lines of blood trail down the shaft of his paddle, disappearing beneath the water line. He was down to bone on the wood paddle but had to keep going. He knew with great confidence that only death could stop him this time. Death was more merciful than surrendering to the consequences of fear. He knew that with certainty.

Silence covered the sea like a blanket. The survivors were beyond talking, parched, exhausted, burned, and bloody. The armada was at least a couple of hours from Camp San Juan, but nearly at the mercy of nature now. The sum of his body and soul taunted him to lie down and rest, end the pain. A search vessel would be looking now, a fleet of vessels, scouring the entire coastline. *No,* cried the voice from inside. *Stay awake. Keep going.*

"Sea gull," someone said, barely audibly, and pointing from up near the bow.

They were no sailors, but any idiot dying of dehydration on the sea knew that gulls needed a place to land. Nobody seemed to know just how far one of the birds could fly from land, but for the first time on the voyage, optimism prevailed if only among those not mad from exposure and thirst.

Something would have to change. Aside from everything else, he had swallowed a belly full of death. Some soldiers enjoyed the killing and relished the sight and smell of death, a few so much that they only tolerated the camaraderie because it was inseparable from the slaughter. Most, like Ethan, saw the killing only as the price of membership in the brotherhood.

The brotherhood could hide your past, conceal shame, and ease loneliness. No doubt he could still kill, would kill if he could face the people who'd inflicted this slaughter, who'd planned it, just not in that workman-like way. Marty's girlfriend had almost certainly been one of them. She even tried to get him out of town before the attack. But what if Jonesy had helped? And where was his friend, Marty?

Ethan had crossed a bridge back in Apostol, and the bridge blew up behind him. There was no going back, ever, and no clear way forward. He was more alone now than the day he enlisted. Still, whatever the answers to his questions, he was no longer running or hiding and loneliness, he knew, was different from being alone.

Someone cried out from the second boat, "A church steeple."

"Camp San Juan Hill," said Feldman, and Ethan could hear hardened soldiers cry.

Ethan checked his pocket watch. It had stopped ticking when he submerged it in water boarding the outrigger. As Acting Commanding Officer, he would need the time for the company log. It read 6:37 a.m. Flood's head rolled onto the mess table at 6:15 a.m., he noted. In twenty-two minutes, an entire company of infantry was sliced and butchered, every one of seventy-four men either carved into pieces or changed forever.

The sun was hinting at its presence just under the hilly, eastern horizon. He would see it rise again after all, but it would never look the same as it had yesterday.

CHAPTER FOURTEEN

"Where am I?" Ethan said, staring straight up at a plank ceiling, his head nearly buried in a cloud-like pillow. His right hand was heavily wrapped, body covered in an army-issued white sheet. Someone was hovering over his face, touching his eyelids. A nurse. She had that white hat with tiny wings. *American*, he thought, *and old*.

She said, "You're in the infirmary at Camp Lincoln, in the Philippines. It was the closest hospital from where you were found. Some of your friends are here as well, but don't get too excited. You were severely dehydrated and exhausted. You might have died from the blood loss. Rest is what you need."

"My leg?" he asked.

"You still have it. You'll be fine. You'll be all right to get up and walk around later. There's a corporal here. He's been waiting for hours to see you."

"Thanks," Ethan said. "Send him in...Oh, Nurse, thank you, but I don't even remember being transported."

"You've been in and out of consciousness with a fever for three days," she answered.

He managed to prop himself up on the bed by the time he saw the red hair and bushy mustache coming in the door of the one-story converted barracks. The infirmary was an open bay with around twenty beds, most occupied. He didn't notice anyone in obviously bad shape. Several men hollered over to him, and he waved back.

"Ahh, you're lookin' fine, me boy," said O'Leary.

"Where are the rest of the men?" Ethan asked. "I only see five or six of our boys here."

"Some are out of the hospital already. Others were never in such as meself. They moved the worst cases to the big hospital in Manila. A few more passed away. God rest their souls.

"Marty?"

"Alive. In fact, he was here when they brought you in here a few days ago. I saw him on the dock. His little boat was blown out to sea or something, but he was rescued. They shipped Marty and some others on to Manila this morning."

The nurse appeared holding a chart and sporting a menacing frown. "That will do, Corporal," she announced. "I said five minutes. Wrap it up."

"Just one minute," O'Leary pleaded.

"Who else is here?" Ethan asked.

"Stop, will ye," said O'Leary, "and listen carefully. Everyone in this room knows the story. The company records were lost with one of the boats..."

"No, I..."

"Ah, hush now. I threw the records overboard. You passed out before we got to shore. All the lads talked among ourselves, and we all took an oath. No one will remember a damn thing about that Pinkerton or why he was at the camp. You saved our lives, me boy. Everyone he spoke to is dead as is himself. So, if O'Brien wrote a report or put something in your file, it's swimming with fishies now. Do you understand me, lad? They will be debriefing you soon, so say nothing about it. You were the commanding officer. If you talk now, they'll have us all up on charges."

It was a lot to take in and raised thorny issues that required consideration, but Ethan said, "Yes...and thank you."

O'Leary waved to the nurse, who was getting ready to grab him by the collar. Producing an envelope from his shirt pocket, he said, "I almost forgot. Marty asked me to give you this. See you later today, me boy."

Ethan picked up the wrinkled envelope and adjusted his position so as not to block the light and began to read:

Dear Ethan,

It was with great relief and immeasurable pride that I learned of your survival and your gallant deeds on the voyage to safety. I tried to see you in the hospital today, but the nurse is a tyrant and shagged me away. By now you must know that Miller and I became lost at sea and were rescued. I will always regret not having pulled my weight in that most decisive and perilous moment in our lives. Know that I tried my best.

The troops at Lincoln are buoyant over rumors that a captain is preparing to sail from one of the ports with a full company of infantry, a burial party really, but hell bent to avenge our dead boys. Rumor has it the natives themselves set fire to the town after the slaughter and escaped into the hills before our men arrived. I am told even the church is now a heap of charred stone walls.

I grieve for the old doctor, a kind man having been condemned senselessly by that insidious purveyor of Jesus, Captain Lawrence O'Brien. If there is a silver lining in this cloud, it must be that, for once, the fool suffered the fate of his victims.

General Jason Bell has arrived here to take command of this district. He is a bad one, indeed, Ethan. The word is he will send a brigade of soldiers into the area to exact revenge and crush the insurgency. They are even shooting unarmed natives around here, sometimes just for walking up to the guard post. It's all very tense and has become a ghastly mess. Supposedly, Bell has issued orders to "kill and burn…kill everyone over the age of ten and capable of bearing arms."

As for Asuncion, I envy her for choosing her people over her personal happiness. I truly loved her, and I know she loved me. They will try to hunt her down in the coming apocalypse. Help her, if you can, my friend. I shall say no more on the subject, only that we have facilitated the transformation of a peaceful race of people, or the eventual survivors among them, into whatever they have become or will become under our yoke.

As I record these words, I await the transport vessel to Manila and will likely have arrived there before you read this. From there, I shall return home, employing that term with no suggestion of emotional bond or sense of belonging. My good friend, I am done with this army and will leave when my enlistment expires, no longer The Sword of Damocles.

My faith in God yet and forever lost upon the wind and my faith in humanity yet mortally wounded, I shall set forth upon a new life's course, antithetic to the one you know, a course absent the burdens of saving souls with fairy tales and lies or plundering foreign lands and slaughtering their peoples. Ah, but what does a life of sin and slaughter prepare me for? I might seriously try acting, for I have surely perfected the art of the thespians in the two failed career chapters of my life to date.

Write to me, friend, as I do so miss your company. In truth, never did I encounter a more supportive or willing audience for my rambling, high-minded self-pity.

138

I will remember you every time I take a dump in the moonlight.
Be well and write me soon.

Your friend always,
Marty

He folded the letter and placed it on the nightstand. He would read it again tonight and likely the next night to be certain he hadn't missed anything. Marty's letter was a bright, shining light upon a very dark time.

BY THE NEXT MORNING, ETHAN WAS UP AND MOVING ABOUT. Deciding to stop into the mess tent for coffee, he spotted the curly-headed Private Pablo Garcia straightaway at one of the long tables near the front. Ethan and Garcia were never particularly friendly owing to the latter's proclivity for running his mouth, but so many things had changed in the last week. Now they shared a lifelong bond, and Ethan found himself delighted to see the half-pint Texan. He plopped his cup and meat can down beside Garcia and patted the man on the back. "Good to see you, Garcia."

Garcia couldn't have faked the smile. "Sgt. Cooper! You look terrible, my friend. You're down to skin and bones, man, and your hair, it ain't black no more."

Ethan slid onto the long bench. "It was never black. It's just clean for a change. Did you go back to X-104 with the rescue party?"

"No. They sent me straight here to hospital but Feldman, Brock, and a few others went. Brock came to the hospital afterward to see some of the boys and told us about it. *Muy malo* what those savages did to the bodies."

"Yeah, I heard from Feldman." Ethan said. "It all happened so fast."

Garcia nodded. "I know. It just kind of swirls in your head. Sometimes, you remember more in the middle of the night, so the picture never sits still for you. Every time you try to put it together, the memories change. You can't step back and see the real show. There were just so many of them. Who figured they had so many fighters in the town?"

Ethan spotted a black-haired major in a snappy uniform with sky-blue epaulets, seated at the officers' table at the very front of the room. The man was facing Ethan, his slick, black mop pleated so perfectly that he might have been glued together down the middle from two pieces. "That's Major Glenn," Garcia whispered, "from Special Detail. You know him?"

"I know about him," Ethan replied. "What's he doing here or, rather, who's he doing it to?"

"Bad business, Sarge. He's been recruiting and training new troopers for his unit. They're working out of a hut down near the beach, mostly at night. You won't believe what they do."

"I've heard about his 'work,' but what do you mean, training?"

"If you're finished, let's walk a bit. I'll show you."

The pair was standing in line to rinse mess kits when a young private addressed the line of enlisted men. The man was carrying a big, black courier bag over his shoulder and wearing the corresponding arm patch. "I'm told I can find a Sergeant Ethan Cooper here," he announced. "Can anyone help me?"

Ethan raised his arm. "I'm Cooper," he said. "Just let me rinse this kit. I'll meet you at that table in a minute."

As Ethan sat directly opposite, the private withdrew a package from his courier bag and handed it to Ethan. He said, "I'm from Governor Taft's Military Attaché Office. This package is from the Governor to be delivered directly into your hands." The man then removed a small notebook from his blouse pocket and handed Ethan a pen. "If you will sign here, I'll be on my way."

"Wait," said Ethan. "You came here from Manila just for this?"

"Not exactly," answered the private. "I already delivered the classified dispatches to the post commander, so I'll have some quick breakfast and back to the boat."

When the man left, Garcia said, "You got a gift from the governor? Are you going to open it?"

Under the plain, brown wrapping was a thin box, 8" X 10". Inside, Ethan found the photograph of himself and Marty with William Howard Taft. The picture was signed under an inscription: *To my friend, Ethan Cooper with eternal gratitude. "There are no secrets except those that keep themselves"—George Bernard Shaw.* It was signed, *William Howard Taft.*

Ethan removed a note and a sealed envelope from the box. The note said simply, *Present this envelope, a letter of introduction, to the Quartermaster Department should you desire a peaceful return to civilian life at the conclusion of your enlistment. Make application for discharge directly from the Philippines. Approval has been arranged. Good fortune, Taft.*

How the hell did Taft find out? Ethan wondered. Was he guessing? Ethan's skittishness about the photograph might have simply painted a general picture for a very clever man, he thought. Maybe it was his Chief of Staff. *What was his name?* Winslow has tentacles everywhere, and Ethan definitely saw the Fiddler talking with that chief of staff at the reception. If Taft knew about his predicament, he had to know the Fiddler was on his trail.

"A picture with Taft himself?" Garcia exclaimed. "What's the note say?"

Returning the picture and note to the box, Ethan said, "More than you could imagine. Come on. Show me where Glenn works."

ON THE LEFT, NOT FIFTY YARDS FROM THE MESS HALL, WAS A SMALL, nondescript, bamboo hut with two uncovered window openings. "That's it," said Garcia. "Every night he takes a Filipino prisoner down here from the guardhouse, and they go to work on him. I looked in one night as I heard the screaming. There were about six of them working on the native. It was bad business. They held his mouth open and pumped dirty water down his gullet 'til he blew up like a balloon. The screaming usually goes on for hours."

"Why are the Filipinos in the guardhouse?" Ethan asked.

"That's the other thing. One of the boys told me when Glenn runs out of prisoners, they go into the town and grab the first three or four goo goos they can find."

"Nice fella," said Ethan.

"Word is they're waitin' on a force of five companies that will make the big push from here into the jungle for General Bell."

The pair turned toward the post hospital. Before Ethan could reply, he saw a column of wagons coming up on them from behind. The pair stepped off to the side as the parade of open wagons and mules trudged through the mud on their way to the Quartermaster's building.

"Must have just unloaded a steamer," Garcia said.

Inside the first two wagons, Ethan spotted a familiar sight, two of the brand-new Colt-Browning M1895, air-cooled machine guns, maybe even the same two his patrol had captured during the infamous patrol. The third wagon carried a much-feared but rarely seen 3.2-inch field gun. Field artillery was essentially useless in a jungle insurgency war and was just another sign of something big in the offing. The rest of the half dozen wagons were loaded with ammo and supplies, followed by a remuda of at least two dozen mules.

"They're getting ready to unleash hell in the interior," Ethan said. "I wouldn't want to be a Filipino on that island right now."

"What the hell will they do with the cannon in the jungle?" Garcia asked.

"Beats me, but it's not good news for the Filipinos. Maybe they plan to float it in on a river."

"Well, the murdering savages get no sympathy from me," Garcia added.

They stopped in front of the hospital. Ethan offered his hand and said, "This is where I get off. Glad you're okay, Garcia. Hope I see you around."

HOW MUCH DID TAFT KNOW? MORE IMPORTANTLY, WHY WOULD HE *go to so much trouble to help an accused murderer hiding out in the army?* Whatever the governor's sources and motive, his note had altered Ethan's life in an instant. It offered him a way off the wheel.

Ethan found his friend, Isaiah Feldman, sitting at the orderly sergeant's desk in the hospital. Feldman was writing a letter. "You have your own perfectly good hospital cot down the hallway. I need the desk to write my own letter anyway."

Before Feldman could even collect his materials, Ethan dropped Marty's three-page letter onto the desk in front of him, smiling. "Relax for a minute and read this. It's from Marty. I got it this morning. He's getting out, Feldman. I'm happy for him. I'll tell him you send best wishes. He's going to become an actor. Can you beat that?"

Feldman flashed a dumbfounded look and sat frozen, mouth wide open. "What the hell is wrong?" Ethan asked.

"Ethan," the corporal said softly, rising from the chair. He was holding a big envelope, bigger than what letters came in. "That's why I'm here. I asked the hospital commander if I could wait here for you. He just received a dispatch with instructions to deliver it to you. This is it. It's about Marty and he didn't want the survivors hearing it in whispers at the mess hall tonight."

They stood eye to eye with the desk between them. "Go ahead," Ethan said. "Let's have it."

"He's gone, Ethan. Marty is gone. It happened a couple nights ago out on the bay, not too far south of here."

"Just tell me, Feldman."

"He's dead."

Ethan took the envelope and sank into one of the bamboo chairs around the desk and could hear the air rushing from his lungs. "I just read his letter, Feldman. I just read it. He was getting out. What happened?"

"The boat was on its way to Manila. During the night, Marty went up to the main deck with his Krag and made his way to the stern. People heard a single shot, but when they got there, all they found was the rifle and a little blood spray. No other sign of Marty. He must have been standing outside the rail when he did it."

Ethan rose from the chair, carefully collecting Marty's letter from the desk, pages in order, and began, not to read, but to inspect the document itself, silently, like you would a dead man's kit. The thing was written on fine, letter-quality stationary, like he'd been saving it for this specific task.

Poor Marty was making fun of this whole crazy world while it was silently killing him all along. The sarcasm and laughter were his way of living with the pain, but he seemed to invite more pain every day. He even took the surname of a saint who had rejected a life of killing in favor of the priesthood.

Martin of Tours, he'd explained to Ethan, was a Roman soldier in the Seventeenth Century and a Frenchman. As Ethan recalled the story, the man had some kind of epiphany and quit the army for a life serving the poor. Marty would sometimes joke privately that if he'd joined the army and become a killer first, he might have grown into a contented old priest later in some peaceful Midwestern town. But the transformation from priest to killer required too much effort.

Marty's handwriting was fluid and even, the hand of a man at ease with himself and born to the gift of expression. The picture conveyed Marty's confidence in this collection of closing thoughts, if not in the decision to end his life, and a reliance on the written word to help create a lasting thing of beauty and value. Marty had wanted to leave some small bit of himself behind and had entrusted it to Ethan Cooper, Ethan figured.

It was the same letter he had placed there only a minute earlier but now a different thing entirely, he thought, a thing unto itself. There would be time later to think about all that, time to read endlessly between the lines in search of the dark places wherein his friend had waged his final battle and untold battles before it. He tucked the letter carefully into an old newspaper from the desk, then folded and secured the package inside his shirt.

"Ethan, Ethan, are you all right?"

"Oh…I'm fine, Feldman. Thanks for telling me about this yourself. I think I'll have a nap."

"Sure."

"By the way, Feldman, do you know what 'antithetic' means?"

"Never heard the word, Ethan. Sorry."

It was just like Marty, he thought, to have some last bit of fun with him, even from a lonely, watery grave.

CHAPTER FIFTEEN

"Sergeant Ethan Cooper?" asked the ghostly figure standing just beyond the table. The formality stood out in the ignoble, dimly lit environment of the Last Chance Saloon, a half mile from Camp Lincoln on the main trail.

In the fluttering glimmer of coal oil lamplight, the new face cast a suspicious shadow across the table. "I'm Cooper," he said, as the soldier across the table shuffled the deck for a fresh deal. Fortunately, the other five men in the game seemed not terribly bothered about the intrusion, probably because Ethan was losing. It could have been that the stranger was savvier than he looked, maybe waiting for the right moment.

The man stepped into the lamplight and removed his hat, allowing Ethan to recognize a familiar face from the governor's reception. "Charles Grayson," Ethan said, "from the Governor's reception in Manila."

"I'm afraid so," Grayson said in a peaceful, pleasant voice, "Someone on the post said I might find you here. I'd appreciate a few minutes of your time if you can spare it."

The sudden appearance of this Grayson in the middle of nowhere raised a host of interesting possibilities, none of them comforting. Ethan had taken an instant disliking to Grayson that night at the reception if only because he resented the man's trappings of privilege. He still found it annoying that a woman like Tala Espinoza would choose to be his "guest."

Grayson was far too old to be traipsing around the outer islands alone, but he was clearly not a newcomer to Asia. His clothes were English tropical, a khaki, jungle-friendly ensemble replete with pockets. The faded Australian hat and old boots marked him as a man who'd seen the jungle.

"All right," Ethan replied. "It sounds like a friendly enough invitation. If you boys don't mind, cash me out while I join this gentleman at the bar. I'm pretty much cleaned out anyway."

"Sure, Ethan," one of the poker players said. "Let us know if you need any help with the dude." A couple of them chuckled as Ethan joined Grayson at the bar.

"May I buy you a whiskey?" Grayson asked politely, signaling for the Filipina bartender.

"At least you know how to start a conversation, but the liquor quality here may not be up to your standards." Ethan said. Two young bar girls descended on the pair in a well-practiced, stalking movement. Ethan waived them off.

The two clinked glasses and downed the shot. Ethan's new friend looked to be well practiced in the ritual. Grayson signaled for another round and said to Ethan, "How are your wounds, Sergeant Cooper?"

"Word gets around like a grass fire in the Philippines. I'm pretty much healed. Thanks."

"I'm a sugar merchant, as you may know, and a bit of a sugar farmer. Been here in the Philippines most of my life. I live on Negros but I have a house over on Panay at Iloilo."

"So you said at the reception. I seem to recall you're Canadian," Ethan observed. "Maybe it's just the way you pronounced the word house. It comes out 'hoose' or something."

"Hard to believe I still do that. It comes from my parents, but the truth is, after all these years, I speak Waray and Tagalog now better than English. Only been to Canada a few times."

"Didn't know about any sugar farms." Ethan observed. The old proprietor appeared with the bottle himself and topped off the glasses.

"The farms are called *hacendas,* which kind of makes me a *hacendero*."

"So what's your business with me, Mr. Grayson?" Ethan asked.

"To come to the point, I have a proposition for you, a temporary job, one might say."

The man was already off script. "I have a job," Ethan replied. "I'm wearing my work clothes."

"Come, Mr. Cooper, I'm not a greenhorn, as you Americans say. I've maintained contacts all over the Philippines since before you learned to walk. I know who you are, what you have been through recently, and even know about certain distinguished actions for which you will never be recognized. Let's just say I'm well acclimated to this Byzantine utopia. In short, I want you for your soldiering skills and for your familiarity with the jungle on a certain island. I'm planning an excursion."

No reference to Pinkertons or Pittsburgh. Ethan threw back the shot, laid the glass carefully on the bar, and said soberly, "Yes. I know you have friends in high places, friends who know things, and something tells me our first meeting in Manila was not by chance."

"But it was, Sergeant Cooper, purely by chance. Later, I realized that our meeting was a stroke of good fortune for both of us."

This encounter triggered almost all the warning signs of disaster, but Ethan's curiosity got the better of him. "So you want to go running around insurgent territory without military escort?"

"That's a crude way of putting it," Grayson replied, "but that's roughly the idea."

"Hmm…and what is it you think you know about me that would bring you here with a suicidal offer like that?"

"I know a few things relevant to my purpose, Mr. Cooper. I know you've chosen not to return to The United States and will soon be discharged from service and unemployed for a time in a foreign land. It has occurred to me that you might have a reason to stay on here awhile. Why else would you request a discharge specifically on this island? Other Americans have stayed in Manila, but you may be the first to honor this primitive region. Whatever your reasons, I believe fate has either smiled upon us both or cast us together in the same tragic play. I will pay you five hundred dollars."

Is he being coy or does he just not know about Pittsburgh and the Fiddler? Since Ethan was staying in the Philippines to avoid a rope, he could use the money until the Quartermaster job started. Besides, this romp in the jungle could lead him to the "might-be" deserter, Alamo Jones, and maybe even to Asuncion, the woman who may have led Marty to his death. He said, "I'll hear you out. Let's have a seat."

They found a table on the porch out of general earshot. The proprietor followed shortly with fresh drinks.

Ethan said, "I'm curious to know where you get your information, Grayson." He figured leaving out the "mister" would help establish their relationship going forward, assuming it lasted beyond the next few minutes. He knew the information had come from Taft's young chief of staff but wondered just how much this stranger knew.

"Sorry, Sergeant Cooper, that has to remain my secret for now."

"Well, you may need to upgrade your sources, Grayson. See, I'll be going to work for the Quartermaster Department right here in the Philippines."

"I'm delighted to hear you confirm that information," Grayson replied, "You're very fortunate, but my understanding is that employment is still several months off. Am I mistaken?"

Ethan couldn't suppress an admiring smile, but two could play that game. "Even if I were interested, I don't know the going rate for suicide missions. I guess you also know what's about to be unleashed on that island."

"I know all about the battalion preparing to embark for this very spot with dispatch. The army has made no attempt to conceal the information, Mr. Cooper."

Grayson was well-informed, but Ethan wasn't about to show his cards to some fancy dude who strolls into a bar in the middle of nowhere offering to tick off all the boxes on Ethan's wish list. "Just why are you so determined to put your head into the cannon barrel, Grayson? You're no spring chicken, and even an experienced combat soldier has a less than even chance of coming out of there alive."

He thought about saying, *Why would anyone in his right mind leave a woman like Tala Espinoza to traipse off into a hostile jungle?* Instead, he said, "I don't get it. Why? And why now? I mean, it's more dangerous than ever. You won't be buying sugar in there. General Martinez is only one of your problems, and the Army doesn't appreciate civilians running around the Philippine jungle unescorted."

"I have my reasons," the Canadian replied. "As for the Army, that would be your department."

Don't make it too easy for him, Ethan. "Not good enough. I'd sooner go in there on foot myself with a couple of natives than throw in with you blind as a bat. You'll have to come up with something better, Grayson." Ethan shouldered his Krag and offered the Englishman a handshake. "It's bedtime for me. I'll sleep on it, and you think it over. Maybe we'll talk tomorrow."

Grayson handed him a business card. "Your commanding officer provided suitable guest accommodations for me tonight. They have a hut for friendly civilian visitors. I'll head back home after lunch tomorrow."

"I can walk back to the post with you if you like," Ethan offered.

"Thanks, but not necessary. I'll stay for a last nip or two and reflect upon our discussion. Oh, by the way, I should mention I have a modest steamboat and crew. I keep it for trips among the islands. There are over seven thousand, you know."

"So I've heard. How much of a crew do you have?" Ethan asked.

"Three, in addition to myself. You would make four."

"Are you armed, Grayson? These are uneasy days on Samar."

Grayson smiled and patted the big right pocket of his tropical tunic. "I do have a handgun. I keep it with me but not for the reasons you think."

"Whatever you say. Sounds like you have it all figured out. Maybe we'll talk again. Good night." Ethan stopped at the poker table on his way out and added, "Do me a favor, boys, and see my new friend gets back to the post in one piece with all his limbs?"

The so-called saloon on the main trail had no walls, just a thatched palm roof with the bar and a few tables set back off the trail, but it did have mosquito netting. The establishment was one of the three things that distinguished army life at Camp Lincoln from more remote, smaller places. The other two were whores and whiskey.

A right turn from here led back to the city and the outpost. Everybody turned right from here. A left turn would lead east into the jungle, then the bay, then another island, and another jungle and so on. A left turn would also at some point lead into the bowels of the particular jungle he feared most, a land primed to explode with anger, hatred and revenge, not to mention insurgent fighters, swamps, pythons, crocs, and spiders big enough to digest a finger.

For the first time in years, Ethan Cooper was a man with choices. He looked at the crude, painted sign with an arrow pointing toward the bar: Last Chance Saloon. Tonight, he turned right.

He was completely alone for the moment with the nocturnal jungle symphony, not unlike the ones he'd known around Apostol. A thousand birds played harmony for the crickets and chirping monkeys, the melody of a jungle settling down for the night. The rustling sounds of things moving in the near darkness provided an element of suspense. This jungle was far richer and more alive than the one he'd known along the bustling Manila trails. It was the lack of sounds in Manila. Monkeys, mostly. That was it. Monkeys were fewer in Manila, less chatter, no luminous eyes tracking from the treetops, no branches rustling as families glided gracefully across the canopy just before darkness cast its net across the forest.

The monkey had been a revered friend in Apostol, rarely intimate but never unfriendly, like a neighbor always meriting a mutually respectful wave or nod if not an invitation to dinner.

The clusters of nipa huts were closer together now, occupants huddled inside. He could make out soft light peeking from the huts through the vegetation as he passed. The laughter mingled with family chit chat and the clatter of humans melted into perfect harmony with the twilight forest melody. Just before dark was the worst time for mosquitos in the forest. He picked up his pace and remembered the pleasant scarcity of mosquitos so near the sea at Apostol.

He wondered why the monkeys would choose to gather in such places and not around Manila. But were they so unlike humans in their choices? Monkeys were as plentiful as people in this archipelago and smart. What humans gather knowingly in a place where they may be shot from a tree for sport, caged for human amusement or even killed by a stray bullet? Monkeys are too smart for that, Ethan thought. They gather and live and play where they choose, where they can be free, where they need not cower in terror or captivity.

He removed his hat, using it as a mosquito swatter. His discharge would be final within a week, surely, and what then? He still had no workable plan, just the job offer, the chance of a free and independent life as Ethan Cooper. But a part of him could not let the massacre alone, could not let the questions about Marty's death go unanswered, the questions about Jonesy and Asuncion. Most of all, he'd made a promise to Marty, so he would stay in the Philippines at least until he could deliver the envelope to Asuncion. Then he might have to kill her.

Maybe he'd misjudged her and maybe not, but the answer didn't affect his obligation to a dead friend. Besides, five hundred dollars was a lot of money to do something you were about to do for free.

A lone farmer, even a rich one with a decent boat and an armed, ex-infantryman, would face long odds against survival in Martinez's stronghold. There was a storm of retribution gathering somewhere, preparing to sow vengeance across the island for the atrocities inflicted on Americans. The burial expedition's account of the scene at post-battle Apostol had spread throughout the ranks with the speed of a plague. Bodies beheaded, mutilated, penises severed. The cry of "Remember 104" had become the regiment's anthem in less than two weeks.

Out of nowhere, the skies opened to unleash a tropical deluge. In an instant, he was drenched, but the jungle was also a place that counter-balanced itself against extremes. A steamy downpour always meant suppression of mosquitos until the rain stopped, and they returned more ravenous than before.

Despite the grief for his dead comrades, despite his anxiety over those still unaccounted for, a part of Ethan Cooper pitied these clueless Filipinos with names and hoped that Asuncion and her brother had the sense to disappear deep into the quiet forest with their old neighbors, the urban monkeys.

He reached the perimeter guard post just before dark. With no natural fortification available, the army had built earthen breastworks around the post on three sides to the sea and fortified them with bamboo in the wake of the disaster at X-104. It was a never-ending job to hold the vegetation at bay and maintain a free fire zone beyond the perimeter. "Cooper," he announced to the guard. "Enjoying the mosquitos?"

The private handed him the register to sign back onto the post. "Hey," the man said, "Cooper. You're the guy who brought those people back from X-104." The man smiled and offered a hand. "Proud to know you. I'm Simpson. Word is we got a big surprise on the way for them niggers. Wish I could go."

He shook the man's hand out of politeness mostly. "Is that so? Good to make your acquaintance, Simpson. I'm a little tired now but see you again maybe." All hell was coming to that island.

CHAPTER SIXTEEN

L ess than three weeks into his stay at Camp Lincoln, Ethan's morning started like virtually every morning of his military career. Reveille was like sunrise. You didn't have to see the bugle to get the message. It took a minute for the reality to hit him. As of today, it was just an obnoxious noise, a familiar tune like any other. He could dance to it or ignore it. No more uniforms. No more assembly and no more marching. No more killing on command. The never-worn civilian duds came courtesy of his new employer, and they felt surprisingly good.

He still had second thoughts about this venture with the Canadian sugar farmer, but Grayson's story had convinced him at least enough to roll the dice. Besides, Grayson's fool's errand served Ethan's own agenda perfectly.

Emmett O'Leary appeared in the doorway while Ethan was still dressing for breakfast. It took a moment to recognize the Irishman. He'd shaved off the big old red mustache. "First time I've seen your face. If you did it for me, you'll be disappointed. No goodbye kiss for you. You think I'm still good for a free breakfast?"

"I do, indeed, Master Cooper," said the big man, "as a very humble parting gift to an old soldier. I'll vouch for ye meself."

Mess kits in hand, they passed a line of wagons on the parade ground. The caravan was heading down to the port. The one carrying the three-inch artillery piece was first in line.

"Appears we got another transport ship down at the port," said Ethan.

"Complete with a battalion of infantry," O'Leary added, "and we both know where they're headed, Ethan. I just hope you know what you're doing."

"When have I ever? I think this Grayson character is on the square. He's lived most of his life in the Philippines. You know more about Canada than he does. The thing is, he's got a good reason for going in there, a really good reason."

"I hope so," O'Leary said. His face was easier to read without all the hair. He looked worried.

At the door of the mess hall, Ethan felt a hand on his shoulder followed by Feldman's voice. "Sorry, Mister. This chow is for military personnel only."

Ethan laughed, and the three entered the mess line where he had to fend off considerable teasing and shake more than a few hands.

When they were seated with their food, O'Leary said, "So tell us, why then is he so hell bent on marching into the jungle?"

"To get his daughter back," Ethan answered. "He said she ran off with some bolo brawler, one of General Martinez's mob, in the summer of 1900, when it became clear the war was entering its final phase. Luzon was close to being pacified, and insurgent fighters were plagued with increasingly short life spans. It seems she was at the university in Manila at the time and involved with the Katipunan and the insurgent forces. I guess she wasn't ready to quit the cause."

Feldman asked, "Just how does a nice Canadian girl end up running around the jungle with a band of savages?"

"That's the thing," Ethan answered. "She's only half Canadian. According to Grayson. he married a Filipina back thirty or so years ago. They had a daughter, and the wife died."

"So that's Grayson's reason for going," said O'Leary. "I'd like to hear yours."

"He gave me five hundred reasons," Ethan said. "Let's leave it there. I guess he just has a fearsome hankering to get the girl back."

O'Leary looked annoyed. He said, "Well, ye two have that in common, Ethan boy, but Grayson may learn that his feckin' precious lassie was one of the savages who murdered our friends."

Ethan hadn't thought about that, but before he could respond, a group of officers entered the mess hall, unmistakably marines, in all white uniforms with brass buttons and standard, wide-brimmed field hats. Major Glenn, the water torturer, was with them in khaki at the front with some general or other as the group made its way to the officers' mess.

"Who's the brass?" Ethan asked. The man looked old, really old, and no bigger than the average Filipino with a huge mustache drooping past his chin.

"That's General Jason Bell himself," O'Leary answered. "Fought in The War on the Union side. He's a mean one, Ethan."

153

"He's with the invasion force," said Feldman. "They're shoving off today when the heavy weapons and supplies are loaded. They say he's ordered the commander to kill every man over ten years of age capable of bearing arms against us."

"Ah, that's daft," said O'Leary.

"No," Ethan said. "Marty told me the same thing in his letter, but I can't believe anyone would do that. I mean, we've all done some pretty bad things but..."

"And just when are you shoving off with the Canadian, Ethan?" O'Leary asked.

"He's coming over in three or four days to pick me up."

"Well, I hate to be a bore," O'Leary added, "but what's your plan exactly?"

"That's not up to me," Ethan replied, "but I think he plans to shadow the task force south around the coast toward Apostol and swing inland from there. There's supposed to be an old Spanish trail that cuts off the southern part of the island east to west. That's what the force commander is after. He can't control the interior until he finds it. While he's doing that, we'll be looking for Grayson's daughter."

Feldman seemed startled by the answer, instantly grasping the potentially grim consequences. He said, "That means you'll be looking for Martinez. What you reckon to do if you find him? Maybe I should say what will he do to *you* if you find him?"

Ethan thought, *What was it Marty would have called that? A rhetorical question.*

THE CREW WAS OUTFITTED IN LONG RAIN SLICKERS AND FLOPPY hats that morning when Ethan boarded the old whaler in a steady rain. "Welcome aboard," said Grayson as he stepped onto the rail from the dock. "The crew will stow your gear. What's wrapped in the tarp? Rifles?"

"Yes," Ethan replied. "Five Krags."

"We can talk about the rifles when we have some time," Grayson said. "Take a spot in the stern under the canopy while we get underway. It will be a bit rough on the bay for a while."

Within an hour, the whaler was well on its way, keeping the coastline in sight. The weather did not improve, and Ethan heaved twice over the side.

Grayson gave the wheel to a crewman and made his way to the stern. He said to Ethan, "It should calm down soon. In a few hours we'll hit the channel. It will look more like a wide river than an ocean, completely protected and narrow." He shed the floppy rain hat and, with his sleeve, wiped the sweat from his brow. In the daylight, the man didn't look quite so old, fifty-two maybe, Ethan thought, with only hints of gray hair. In terms of height and weight, they looked identical.

"I know where we are from there," Ethan managed to say.

"When you feel better, come up and meet my crew."

The craft's sturdiness surprised Ethan as it performed well enough in the swell. It looked to be an old, 30 feet, V-hulled, modified whale boat powered by a small, single-stack, steam engine and complete with a nautical steering wheel. The open bow was rigged end to end with a canvas top across bamboo poles, the single stack protruding through the center. Along the rear half of the hull, where Ethan had taken residence on a bench, someone installed a bamboo deck over the deep hull bottom. It looked suitable for sleeping on in a pinch.

When the weather settled down a bit, he checked the oilcloth wrapping under the bench to be sure the weapons were still dry, then made his way up to the open wheelhouse. It was complete with a wind screen to shield the driver's vision in rough weather. Grayson was at the wheel as his three companions fiddled with lashings on their supplies.

"How are you enjoying civilian life, Mr. Cooper?" Grayson asked.

Seemed Grayson liked to ask dumb questions. Ethan said, "When it calms down a little more, I'd like to give you all a lesson on using the rifles. I managed to scrounge enough serviceable Krags and one pistol from the post. We may need them sooner than you think."

"May I call you Ethan?"

"I've been called worse."

"Ethan, I think you'd agree we won't be winning any engagements with a few rifles."

"I don't know," Ethan replied. "Five Krags can put up a lot of firepower, maybe enough to get us out of a jam."

"Ethan, nobody in these islands carries a Krag-Jorgensen unless the U.S. Army issued it to him, or he stole it from a dead soldier. When we encounter Martinez's men, which basket will they put us in?"

"I'd rather fight it out with them than march into that jungle unarmed," Ethan said defiantly. "Besides, like you said, there are a hundred other things in that jungle that will kill you like big snakes that don't die from one bullet."

At that moment, the boat topped a steep swell and slammed to the surface with a thud. Ethan felt the impact up his spine as sea spray drenched the mariners and blood from his mouth announced he'd bitten his tongue. The pain held off a few seconds. The others took the bouncing in stride, even seemed to anticipate it.

Grayson didn't notice Ethan's self-inflicted injury. He said, "Think about it, Ethan. We have four old single-shot Remingtons with a good supply of ammo and a half dozen handguns. It might be better to take every possible precaution and hide the Krags. They're not enough to save us, and they might get us killed."

The new Ethan opted for a change of tactics. He said, "Look. You hired me for my military experience, so let me put it this way. If the Krags don't go, I get off at the next stop, and you get your money back."

"Well, since you put it that way…"

THE SEAS SOON SETTLED TO A GENTLE ROLL AND A DETERMINED SUN banished the rain clouds. Grayson decided to anchor for an afternoon meal and short rest. The two taller crew members had shed their rain gear. Grayson said, "Ethan, you should meet our crew. The older one there is Sixto, my wife's twin brother. The pretty one next to him is Gabriel Sanders. He's a business partner of mine from England."

Grayson signaled to Sanders and the younger man smiled. "Cheers, Mate," he said. Ethan figured him for about forty years old. The Englishman was close to six feet tall and muscular but in a subtle way that conveyed an image of agility and elegance. Despite his masculine characteristics, Ethan thought, the combination of green eyes and sandy hair made him look like a stage actor. His face was bright and engaging, clean-shaven with no sad story to tell. A most privileged-looking fellow, all things considered.

Sixto was skinny with elongated features. The man looked hard and weather-bitten like he'd lived his life in the jungle and appeared considerably less jovial than Grayson. Sixto showed no interest in making new friends, but neither did he exhibit hostility. Chinese *Mestizo*, Ethan figured, somewhat disheveled, even wild-looking, but in a practiced, dignified way. He had tired eyes, amber-colored maybe, light brown but not quite golden like the lingering residue of light just after sunset. Dark, puffy circles below seemed to draw the eyes down on his face.

The man's hair was peppered gray with black, long and matted around deep wrinkles in the forehead. A drooping gray mustache with goatee framed a sad look tinged with depth and character. It was, in all respects, a sympathetic and most mysterious face despite the contradictions with few clues to his age. Clean, Western-style clothes, a simple green cotton shirt and white trousers, contrasted with the man's earthiness and only fanned the mystery.

Grayson turned to the last crewman, the short man tying off the starboard anchor. The man lifted his floppy rain hat to reveal the decidedly female face of Dr. Tala Espinosa. "I believe you have met our last crew member," Grayson announced matter-of-factly.

"Yes," was the best he could do. There wasn't much to choose between her gilded princess look from the reception and the deckhand version except the clothes, he thought, but for the shimmering black, shoulder-length hair falling straight around a finely sculpted neck. This time, outside in the natural elements, he could see how the artistically formed eyebrows showcased the same penetrating eyes. It was, he thought, a most ennobling and appropriate face for the empathetic personality wearing it, and her presence exhilarated him.

"Welcome to my uncle's yacht," she said, smiling.

Grayson said, "Sixto is Tala's father. Tala and my daughter Cristina are cousins. We are all family with the exception of Gabriel."

"So, she's your...niece? Your *actual* niece?"

Grayson laughed and said, "Is there another kind?"

Of course there was, but it didn't matter. It was hard to keep it all straight. As near as Ethan could figure, the only parent unaccounted for was Tala's mother. He thought she must have been a great beauty, beauty enough to negate the biological influence of the hairy forest dweller standing beside him.

The inclusion of Tala on their expedition made Ethan wonder if Grayson had been up front with the others, especially the girl. Ethan said, "I'd like to make sure every one of you understands that some or all of us may not survive this journey."

Satisfied with their chorus of yeses, Ethan said, "All right then. After we eat, let's go over the operation of the Krag-Jorgensen rifle."

BY SUNDOWN, THEY CRUISED JUST OFFSHORE IN SEARCH OF A SECURE inlet to spend the night. As they rounded a sharp point, Ethan spotted thick columns of smoke rising beyond the tree line, eerily morphing into all manner of ominous form against the deep orange glow of cloud fire. He turned to tell the others, but they were already working to plot the smoke on their chart.

"The place has no name on the map," Grayson said.

Ethan knew the tiny *pueblo* well enough, a sleepy little fishing village of around a hundred people just beyond the point. He'd inventoried their food and animals as part of the X-104 survey and recalled counting only two carabao and not a single grain of reserve rice stored in the entire village. "Not much there," he said. "Old people and some fishermen with their families." He pointed to a spot onshore just off the port bow. "There's a sandy, horseshoe shaped beach just over there. We'd better pull in for the night best we can and check it out in the morning. Too dangerous walking into a scene like that at night."

The whaler eased right up onto the sand, saving the crew an hour of work. They chanced a small fire to cook and keep the bugs at bay. Everyone seemed grateful for the hot meal and a few hours of sleep under a clear sky. Ethan stood the first watch.

When the other men had drifted off, Tala emerged from under the netting and settled beside Ethan within range of the fire's warmth. She grabbed a tin cup from the blanket and said, "Coffee?"

"I suppose I should," he said, "but I'm confident there's no danger out there tonight. The jungle has a way of talking to you, I mean once you learn the language."

She poured from the pot and handed him the cup. "It talks only to you or to anyone who listens?"

"Anyone," he said. "Take tonight. Dead silence since dark except for the crickets. Not so much as the rustle of a snake. We're safe for tonight. The monkeys are the first to sense danger. They tend to flee as it approaches and return when it passes. But you're a Filipina. None of this is news to you."

Leaning against a supply box, she kind of curled up her legs, wrapping her arms around them. She was as beautiful in khaki jungle wear as she'd been in golden lace. "That's one of my biggest problems," she confessed. "I don't really know what it is to be a Filipina. That's why I felt a kinship with you at the reception. Uncle Charles bought me that dress and took me as his guest, kind of a celebration for my becoming a doctor. You see, we were equally out of place that night. The difference was you didn't know."

"I don't take you for a fool, Doctor," Ethan said. "You know what I thought, but you're too kind to shame me with it. That makes me more ashamed."

"Don't be," she pleaded. "Thoughts can only hurt when we give voice to them."

"How could you possibly feel out of place in Manila? That's a strange thing to say."

"Not so strange. Before the revolution against the Spanish and the friars, I was the daughter of a successful doctor, a part of Manila high society. My mother passed away from fever before my tenth birthday. I had a tutor, a nanny, everything a girl needs, except friends."

"Sixto is a physician?" he asked.

"...and a skilled surgeon."

"But you're educated," he protested. "Surely you had school friends."

"Uncle Charles arranged for me to be educated in England. My father, Sixto, was behind it. Father was afraid I would become involved in his revolutionary activities with the Katipunan like my cousin Cristina eventually did. My six years in England as a Filipina were very lonely, so I filled them with work and study. Now, I'm home, and sometimes, I feel more like a foreigner than you. Cristina is my only friend. We were always like sisters, grew up together without mothers."

Ethan wasn't sure what to make of all that and decided he was unqualified to even comment, but he wanted the conversation to go on. He said, "I feel I owe you an explanation for my behavior that night at the reception. You know, running out on you like that after you were so kind to me."

159

She smiled and touched his forearm with elegant fingers. "I know you were in some kind of trouble," she said. "Maybe you can tell me about it one day, but in your own time." She rose from the ground gracefully without using her hands, like a dancer in a jungle ballet. Looking out onto the water, she said, "I fear I'm about to learn something about being a Filipina." Returning to her blanket, she added, "Goodnight, Ethan. Please, call me Tala."

"Goodnight, Tala."

THE SMOLDERING LITTLE *PUEBLO* IN EARLY MORNING LOOKED LIKE the shell of a surface mine. The entire beach was fouled by a layer of black soot leading up to a concentrated pool of gray ash where nipa huts had once perched from bamboo stilts in the sand. The *bankas,* a dozen or more, lay framed in ash or broken to pieces by axes and rifle butts. Dazed human figures of all sizes still wandered about beyond the beach, some carrying or pulling charred corpses or body parts. Ethan had seen this misery inflicted before, had even raised his hand in aid of the burning when so ordered, but never stayed to witness its gruesome aftermath.

Anchored in the whaler not fifty yards from shore, they breathed the soot and inhaled the stench of charred flesh until Grayson said, "We can't do anything for these people. Let's move on."

But Sixto already stood shirtless on the bulkhead, tears rolling over the course terrain of his leathery face, and pushed off headfirst into the sea, bound for the dead village. Grayson pounded angrily on the wheel and said, "Damn him. He'll get us all killed before we even find her."

Grayson reached into a compartment under the wheel and removed two pistols. Handing one to Ethan, he said, "It's loaded." Ethan made sure.

The sandy bottom around the point allowed the whaler to ease right onto the beach where the men dropped over the side and up the beach to survey the carnage.

By the time they made it to the burn site, the terrified Filipinos had scattered into the jungle, leaving only Sixto to greet them. They found him standing beside a neat line of charred or badly burned corpses. A few had suffered only fatal bullet wounds. The most badly burned, Ethan knew, had died in their own homes, being too terrified to step outside during the mayhem.

"They were getting ready to bury them," said the man called Gabriel in a funny accent, leaning over to pick up a hard piece of tree bark. "This is what they're using to dig. There's nothing left here."

"Well, we can leave them the shovels," Grayson said.

"We'll leave them some food too," said Sixto in Spanish. It was the first time Ethan had heard him speak. Without looking at Ethan, he added, "The *Americanos* will not be back here. They have killed and stolen everything. There is no more revenge to be had in this place."

SEVERAL MILES ALONG THE SHORELINE THEY CAME UPON A SIMILAR scene in the twilight at a slightly larger coastal village. The task force had leveled and burned the place, likely on their way to Apostol. From a hundred yards offshore, Ethan and his companions could observe no sign of an American presence. As they debated whether to put in and investigate, several shots rang out from the beach.

"So that's it then," said the man with the accent. "Even if we did have food to spare, the survivors are in no mood for help from white people."

"Look," said Ethan, pointing. "At two o'clock, coming around that rock outcrop. It must be the transport that took the troops to Apostol. It's an army transport. Make sure you all smile and make them feel at home when they board us." He grabbed the binoculars from their box and focused on the bow. "Yup. USS Vicksburg with a machine gun and cannon fixed to her deck."

"Right," Grayson said, "so what about the Krags, eh? Won't they want to know how we got them?"

"We'll tell them the truth. We should pass muster okay. No regulation against looking for your daughter." Looking at Gabriel, Ethan said, "You're from England, Mr...?"

"Sanders. I have shares in Mr. Grayson's company and manage his private sugar plantation." He said it like a man rehearsing a story.

"Do you have papers?"

"Of course."

During the boarding process and inspection, one of the privates watching the procedure from the Vicksburg's rail recognized Ethan and hollered out, "That's Cooper, the sergeant who brought in those survivors from the massacre."

A round of cheers followed, then a round of back-patting from the boarding crew. Sanders didn't even get a chance to show them his papers. In a minute, the Cristina Grayson rescue team was back under way, heading for a nearby protected inlet to spend the night.

All four men smiled and waved into the near darkness for effect as the lifeboat backed away toward the transport. Ethan said, "I doubt the Filipinos will be as cooperative."

As the smoke and devastation faded away off the stern, Ethan thought no one would ever know the name of that little *pueblo* now. Before you could be *wiped off the map*, you had to be on the map in the first place. He remembered how the two dozen or so nipa huts had once been clustered just behind the beach with fishing *bankas,* nets and drying racks strewn across the fine, crystalline sand. They were mostly old people. Marty had slipped away one night with Asuncion to visit her widowed aunt there with a few pilfered cans of tomatoes. What could they have possibly done to aid the *insurrectos*? Even if they had...

CHAPTER SEVENTEEN

If it wasn't for the charred stone church and steeple, Ethan would not have recognized the place. What was once a picturesque coastal village, resembled a wartime fortress and the reception committee included no fewer than a dozen Krag-Jorgensens aimed squarely at the little whaler's occupants.

The only other building standing was the municipal building now reduced to three partial, blackened walls. Tents dotted the town square with the jungle cleared and reduced to muddy swamp for a hundred yards to the north and west; river to sea. No birds, no monkeys, not so much as a cricket to be heard. A deep trench, reinforced with bamboo walls, secured what had become Fortress X-104. Wreckage of burned homes and ashes dominated the once plush jungle village named Apostol. Dead, flat, and barren. A painted wooden sign had been nailed to a mooring post. It read, *Welcome to Camp O'Brien.*

Almost immediately, Ethan recognized a few familiar faces and a swell of cheers rose from the ranks as their numbers grew, warming the group's reception. The former sergeant found the repeated hero's welcome embarrassing and unwarranted. Stepping onto the dock, he heard Grayson's voice from behind. "Now you understand what you bring to our journey."

"Enjoy it," Ethan replied, "because the real journey starts when we leave here."

THE GROUP WAS STILL COLLECTING PERSONAL BELONGINGS WHEN ETHAN heard the summons. "Cooper, Cooper, Captain Carter wants to see your whole group over at the headquarters tent now."

He was a young sergeant, a stranger with a determined face and a dutiful military bearing. "Sure enough," Ethan replied. "I guess we can pay our respects. Carter is the company commander?"

"Yup. We have a platoon-sized garrison. We'll pay them niggers back, Sarge. Kill every one of them. We got word the task force already leveled most of the villages from here to the southernmost point of the island."

"Just Cooper," said Ethan. "No more Sarge. That's at least half a dozen villages that I know of."

The sergeant laughed. "All ashes and bodies. The boys been all around this part of the coast on the gunboat. What the ship don't destroy, the troops do. Captain Carter has done a few villages himself on patrols from here."

Ethan had heard men talk like that many times before, but that almost seemed like a past life now.

CARTER COULD NOT HAVE BEEN MORE ACCOMMODATING. HE EVEN offered them food and the use of two tents until they set off into the jungle. As they began to unload supplies, two privates showed up to help, compliments of Captain Carter. They were leading a mule. The captain had apparently anticipated their logistical problem.

"Cap'n sent us down t' help you boys unload," one of the privates announced. "Says y'all can borrow the mule for your trip if you like."

Since the pack mule solved their transport problem, Ethan figured the chances of this expedition actually happening had increased to fifty-fifty.

WITH THE SUPPLIES SAFE AND DRY, THEIR BELLIES FULL AND A campfire to discourage any stray mosquitos, the group gathered around to share a drink and plot a course of action.

"Where's Sixto?" Sanders asked. "He wasn't with us at the mess tent either. The bloke must be hungry."

Grayson flung a small log into the flame from atop his makeshift chair, a supply crate. Flames crackled and sparks erupted into the humid night air, melting into the star-studded sky. He said, "Sixto's on the boat. He won't stay in the American camp."

"Why?" Sanders asked.

"Maybe because he'd just as soon see both of you with a good dose of cholera, eh?"

"He's not that bad, Uncle," Tala scolded.

"Lovely," said the Englishman.

Grayson shook his head. "Sixto and I don't always see eye to eye."

"I gathered that," Ethan said, "from your little disagreement on the boat."

"He's one of Aguinaldo's people," Grayson pointed out. "Before that it was Bonafacio and before that Jose Rizal."

164

"So, he hates all Americans?" Ethan asked.

"He doesn't hate anyone," Tala said. "He loves the Philippines."

"You're right, Tala, of course," said Grayson. "Hate is a little strong, eh? He *is* educated. Let's say he strongly disapproves of Americans, Spaniards, priests, and a number of others whom he deems averse to Philippine independence."

The fire felt good but a little warm for the jungle air. They moved their boxes back a bit from the flames, and Ethan filled all three glasses from his bottle of Jameson Irish Whiskey, a kind of thank you gift from the boys of Company M. God only knows how they'd acquired it.

Ethan nodded for Grayson to continue. "Well, Sixto is also a doctor, or *was* a doctor, a very successful one. The Spanish jailed him back in '97 for sedition and again in '98, just before the Spanish collapse. When the Americans took over, they kept him in jail. They only let him out after Aguinaldo was captured and swore allegiance to the U.S."

"Did Sixto sign the allegiance pledge too?" Sanders asked.

"I don't know how else he'd have gotten out of prison, but...he didn't say and I didn't ask."

"So, what are *your* politics in this little game of *Whose Islands are They*?" Ethan asked.

"I don't let politics dominate my life," Grayson answered, "not like Sixto, but I have opinions. Did you know we have over a hundred languages and dialects on these seven thousand islands? My wife and Sixto were born on Luzon into a system not much different from Canada or England. Their family was upper-middle-class *Mestizo*, educated, but Philippine, nonetheless. Yet we have islands in this archipelago where people still devour other people at dinner and make dried trinkets out of human heads. It's impossible to reconcile such extremes within the context of one coherent civilization. That's my belief. These islands will never be sustainably independent as one nation. Aguinaldo, the man, is another matter entirely. His ambitions infected my daughter and just may get her killed."

"Sounds like you're a reader of Kipling, Grayson," Sanders observed. "*The White Man's Burden* and all that. Isn't that why we're all here? I mean one may pity them, shower them with kindness and all that but, in the end, they're still savages until we show them the way. In time, they will learn and prosper, within their limits."

Tala stood and flashed Sanders a cold stare. "This is a good time for me to say goodnight."

Recognizing at least some measure of his ignorance, the Englishman said awkwardly, "Of course, Doctor, I was not referring to you. My apology if you misunderstood."

She silently declined to engage and disappeared into her tent.

"Of course, *old boy*," Grayson said coldly, "but please don't ever mistake me for a believer in *Manifest Destiny* or colonial barbarism. Technically, I'm a colonial subject. Britain would be an insignificant spec on the map were it not for its inclination to plunder and murder indiscriminately on a genocidal scale…Oh, and if you ever again refer to any of my family as savages, you will wake up one morning with your pecker in your back pocket."

"How do you even know she's alive?" Ethan asked.

"She left Luzon, probably to fight Americans," Grayson barked. "She didn't disown me. She sent word that she was safe."

It occurred to Ethan that Charles Grayson was growing on him. "My apology to you also," Sanders said with every indication of sincerity while rising to his feet. "Bad form that. I should go down to the ditch and drain my equipment before retiring. I'll join you gentlemen in the tent shortly."

With Sanders out of earshot, Grayson said, "He has connections in England that are useful to me. More of an employee than a business partner."

Ethan figured the time had come for some straight talk. "Grayson, why don't you cut the horseshit and tell me who this Gabriel Sanders really is? I don't like having to shovel through it to find the truth."

Grayson sighed in a gesture of defeat and said, "I should have told you before, I know, but my brother-in-law doesn't know either, and I doubt he'd appreciate it. Gabriel is an officer in Royal Navy Intelligence. They sent a man to see me. He said they knew roughly where my daughter is and who she's with. They offered to finance an expedition if I agreed to take one of their operatives along."

And just like that it all started to make sense, a little anyway. "Well, that explains how you knew so much about me. I'll bet the Brits even suggested you recruit me for this mission."

"You'd win that bet."

There was no indication yet that Grayson knew about the Pinkerton but no reason to believe he didn't. "So just what is their interest in finding your daughter?" Ethan asked.

Grayson seemed surprised by the question. "Come now, Cooper, even a sergeant can't be that naïve. They don't give a damn about my daughter, but they knew she came to this island, and they knew I would do anything to find her. A simple trade off. Her general location and the identity of her abductor in exchange for bringing their man along. They believe my situation makes me somehow protected from harm at the hands of Martinez's people, and they want to tag along to find his base of operations. Very clever, those British."

Ethan drained his tin cup of the Jameson and said, "I was just a sergeant who followed orders, and I don't claim to be educated, but I'm not stupid. The British aren't even in this war. What do they care where Martinez is?"

"The simple answer is trade. This ban on trade is supposed to help cut off supplies to the *insurrectos,* but it's hurting the British. It's hurting me as well. They can't make ships without hemp, and they depend on Philippine sugar and a dozen other crops to support their economy. The trading companies and banks are bleeding financially, losing millions and pressuring the British government. In response, they concocted their own plan to find Martinez's base. Then, the Americans can get in there and put him out of business. Anyway, that's the goal."

It made sense. The army would never find Martinez, let alone capture him, by stumbling around in the jungle. The general's security was all but impregnable, concentric rings of sentries communicating with conch drums, patrols, and lookout posts in the mountains. The only way to find his headquarters would be by invitation or by torturing someone who'd been there. Martinez would never trust that information with common townspeople, not even with local officials like Obrador. With the exact location, a plausible attack plan might be possible. The British were smart enough to see that and even smarter to find their chance in the person of Charles Grayson.

Then Ethan spotted the outline of Captain Carter through the fire's glow, a tall, smoky shadow with rigid, military bearing and moving toward the fire. "Good evening, gentlemen," Carter said.

"Captain," Ethan replied, rising to his feet. It would take time to shed long-practiced military etiquette. He forced himself not to salute.

Sanders rejoined them at the fire as the captain produced a strange looking weapon from the box he'd been carrying, a handgun, it appeared to Ethan, but with a squared, thick barrel and no rotating chamber. "I have something for you, Cooper," said Carter. "It's an experimental pistol, something entirely new. It's called the Colt Model 1900. Call it a gift from the Marine Corps. Fine weapon, semi-automatic fire, seven round magazine, fires the new .38 ACP round as fast as you can pull the trigger. I brought a hundred rounds."

Carter replaced the pistol and handed Ethan the box. Ethan said, "Thank you, Sir. I'm very grateful, but I'll need a lesson in handling this baby."

"No problem," Carter replied. "I'll show you myself in the morning before you leave. She's a real nigger killer. Be good to her and keep your eyes open, Cooper. Even if you don't find the girl, you might see or hear something that will help us find Martinez or those murdering townspeople. You might even come across the old Spanish trail everyone is looking for, the one that splits the island east to west....I mean, if any of you are fortunate enough to make it out of that jungle alive. Goodnight, Gentlemen, and good luck."

Grayson turned to Ethan, smiled, shrugged and said, "See what I mean? You're all in the same wagon. I just want my daughter back."

CHAPTER EIGHTEEN

*D*ear Marty,

  I know you will never read this letter as you are recently demised, but seeing as you asked me to write, I dutifully honor that request. Admittedly, I find comfort in the act, having drawn much pleasure from our frequent conversations. I am back out in the jungle to find Asuncion. We set out from Apostol yesterday. Oh, I'm also here for the money. I quit the army and remain confident in the wisdom of that decision. My location at present is that magnificent waterfall and pool in the hills where I let that young prisoner escape. Jonesy and I called it Chuko's Grotto. The location is truly a paradise in a world of shit, and our circumstances henceforth may be a bit inhospitable, thus preventing my taking up the pen hereafter.

  Anyway, it never came to mind that you were planning to do yourself in, but upon reflection, I do recall you were seriously bedeviled by some of the evil deeds we perpetrated and witnessed while soldiering. You're not the only one. Pop would distress over some of my actions in uniform as he served with honor in the great Union crusade to free the slaves.

  There may be answers for me in the jungle, but I cannot be certain. After the things I saw the last few days, I admit to considerable satisfaction at hanging up the uniform. I would have done it long ago, but circumstances did not allow. I will explain that whole mess to you another time, my friend. Suffice to say I am done running away.

  A kind of melancholy has taken possession of me and visits most often at night like a devil pulling my mind back to ungodly sights. Mostly I have been feeling dirty, and no amount of washing helps. Sleep doesn't help because it brings all manner of abominable visions, thus defeating its own purpose.

  What I say now might hurt you some, Marty, but I am your friend and incapable of ill intent, so hear me out. I'm not like you inside. You were wise and clever, saw the evil of this demonic crusade from the first, but you just let it wear you down. I'm not giving in to the melancholy; at least that is my plan. What we did to these people over here is wrong but lamenting about it won't fix it. It's finally clear to me. It doesn't mean I switched sides, but I'm not in the army anymore. I believe we just lost our way and allowed the evil in our nature to run loose over here. So, I have decided to stay here and live, show these folks we're not all stealers and killers and such by nature. Besides, there's nothing for me at home that I know of, wherever home is.

I'm not disrespecting you, Marty as you were likely the best friend I ever had. But I see now that you just let it all build up inside until it drove you to blow your head off. I don't know if I can forget all those things or make it right, my friend, but I promise to try and do some good things over here for both of us. My...

"IT MAY BE SOME TIME BEFORE YOU CAN POST THAT LETTER," Tala said, negotiating the rock ledge to sit beside him. The view of the river gorge below was spectacular. Her boots were sturdy and laced up the front, like his, but it amazed him to see such a tiny pair.

"Oh, it's a letter to my friend. He's...dead now, so I don't have to worry about that. Writing just clears my head." Then he laughed. "My father was the local schoolteacher back in Pennsylvania in addition to being a farmer. He made me write as a child. Anyway, I don't know how it ends yet... Be careful on these rocks. The easy way down will kill you."

"I'm not that delicate," She quipped. "Would you care to tell me what terrified you that night at the reception?"

He folded the letter and returned it carefully to his front pocket. He'd been thinking about telling her anyway, the whole story, even the parts he didn't understand. He still regretted not telling Marty, but with the Fiddler dead and a guardian angel in the governor's office, Ethan liked his odds of finding some kind of normal life— until it all started again. "It would be a long answer," he cautioned.

"I have the time," she said.

"Well, my parents had a little subsistence farm in Western Pennsylvania. The place caught fire one night right after my ninth birthday. I never knew how. It happened really fast, and I managed to get out the window of my room just in time. My baby brother was with our parents. I couldn't get back in there to save them."

"How horrible," Tala exclaimed.

"It's more than fifteen years ago. Anyway, I went to a nearby town to live on my uncle's farm. He and his wife were good to me.

I went to school and worked the farm with them. When I was nineteen, I left for Pittsburgh and kicked around awhile, ended up with a job at Winslow Steel in the smelter. Allen Winslow owned most all of the steel-making business and half of Pittsburgh. He treated the workers and their families like slaves, rented them his housing at inflated rates, even made them buy their food and clothing from the company store. When he tried to reduce our wages by a third, we decided to unionize and fight back. We went on strike."

"What happened? She asked.

"It became a war. He tried to fire us and bring in new workers. We built a fence around the plant and guarded it day and night. There were brawls every day. One day we got word Winslow had sent a huge barge upriver with three hundred armed Pinkertons to break us and tear down our fence. Hundreds of us went to the dock to meet the barge, with guns. The townspeople came with us."

A tap on the shoulder startled Ethan. "Cooper."

He turned to see the increasingly annoying Englishman. "I don't know what they do in the Royal Navy, Sanders, but out here, you don't sneak up on a man from behind if you value your life." The mule snorted behind them, thrashing his snoot into the cool, still, pool. He obviously didn't warm to the Englishman either. Ethan said, "If you'd come a little closer to the mule, you'd be at the bottom of the ravine by now. What do you need?"

"Easy, old boy," Gabriel Sanders replied. "Only wanted to extend a dinner invitation to you and the good doctor. Beans and hard tack, I believe."

"Okay, thanks," Ethan said, pretending to help Tala to her feet. She didn't need help.

Pointing out over the gorge, Sanders said, "Charles and I were wondering what are those high mountains to the north in the distance? What's up there?"

"Well, if you'd ever been to The Rockies, you wouldn't call them mountains, but folks around here do, I guess. Remote, isolated." *Wait. That's the place Obrador talked about.* He'd said something like, *When the Moros attacked the village, the people would retreat to the mountains in the north.*

The Englishman was still talking but Ethan had tuned him out entirely. Obrador unwittingly gave them a roadmap to the townspeople, he thought. That was it, but Ethan wasn't about to spill the beans to this boatless deck hand. A penchant for trusting strangers had never been among Ethan's character flaws, but reliable friends were in short supply. He didn't trust Grayson either, but at least he understood the sugar farmer's motives.

They decided Ethan and Grayson would make their way down into the river gorge and scout the area. Heavy vegetation and a constant rain made the downslope slippery and difficult to maneuver, like sliding over a cliff blind, but Ethan figured the mule would have no problem later with the group. He and Grayson reached the river within fifteen minutes. It wasn't much of a river, but that could work for them, Ethan thought, allowing them to use the bank like a trail. Thick vegetation poured over the banks on both sides.

"Seems like a fairly tame river, around here anyway," Grayson said. "Unusual to see a river flowing north, eh?"

"It's deceptive," Ethan replied. "We know the river flows north from here for a spell, not sure how far. Then it turns toward the east coast."

"So, we head north along the river?" Grayson asked.

"That was the plan," Ethan replied. "We used it before to try and find Martinez's base, but this is as far as we came. We'll be going blind from here, follow the river until it turns east or until we find a trail or run into one of his patrols. It will be rough going all the way, and I may have a better plan."

"Let's hear it," said Grayson.

Ethan pointed into the distance, then seated himself on a nearby fallen tree. "I have good reason to believe the townspeople, most of them, are hiding out at a camp in the hills on the right over there. You can see them clearly from the top."

Grayson took the spot beside him and said, "And?"

"I think it could be a day and a half through thick jungle, assuming we can make up some time using the riverbank to head north."

"Hold on, Cooper. Are those not the people who butchered some four dozen of your friends?"

Ethan had been kicking that question down this very hill. He wondered if O'Brien's Bible included a chapter explaining the appropriate measure of revenge. *Five for one? A hundred for one? How would you value crops, farm animals and people's homes in the calculation?* Sometimes, he thought, revenge just gets tiresome. He had even softened his decision to kill Asuncion if it turned out she betrayed Marty.

He decided to take a shot at an answer. "A few of them are, I'm afraid, like the police chief and some of his crowd, but the hardcore insurgents, the bolomen who mutilated the bodies and such were never townspeople. I'm convinced of it. I think they were Martinez's hard cases, *insurrectos*. The killers won't be hiding in the hills, but there may be hundreds of people up there, families, just trying to wait it out. Good chance we can pick up some useful information there without torturing or killing anyone. Someone might even know where your daughter is. Besides, neither one of us gives a shit if we never find Martinez." He did not tell Grayson what was foremost on his mind. *I might find Asuncion there.*

Grayson stood up and seemed to give the idea due consideration. "It's logical," he admitted, "but I'm not sure I understand you, Cooper. You seriously think those people will welcome us? You're off your horse, man. Let's be honest. Americans are murdering them by the hundreds this very minute, maybe by the thousands, all across this island."

Ethan moved a few feet to the riverbank and stepped in. The water was clear. He could see the bottom, gravel and rocks. They could definitely use the bank for a trail. Maybe Grayson was right, he thought, but this would be the test of his recently discovered convictions either way. Maybe it was the step Marty could never seem to take. He said, "They have no reason to be hostile to us, Grayson. Besides, my guess is we won't find fighters there, just women, children, and old people. If I'm right, we might just get a solid lead on your daughter or at least the general's location. They don't all love this Martinez. I know that for a fact. There's just one problem. It's your boy, Sanders. He could report those people in the mountains the minute we return."

Grayson looked puzzled. "So what? What are those people to you?"

"I'm still working that out," Ethan replied. "It's complicated."

That problem had plagued Ethan since the moment he put the clues together. It was pretty clear by now that, armed with the location of those civilians, the army would march right in there and probably kill them all like at Wounded Knee. It was damned hard to believe, but he'd seen it with his own eyes. It wasn't in Ethan Cooper to aid his country's enemies, but he seemed more confused about that every day. Just who were those *enemies*? "Look, I have an idea, Grayson. Let me take Sixto and go into those hills. Tell Sanders we're going to scout the area for a trail. It's a good move anyway. We can travel light, move quicker, and be back in two days, three tops."

Grayson's expression hardened. He said, "No. We all go together. If you go alone, you might be a shrunken head in two days. Besides, if they have information on my daughter, I want to be there. I don't want to put anyone in danger, but that's not my problem."

Ethan played an old hand. He reached into his front pocket and produced a money clip. He held the clip out to Grayson and said, "Here's your money. I quit. Fine with me if he gives up Martinez and his crazy bolomen, but I'm not gonna be responsible for more unnecessary killing. If Sanders goes, those people are good as dead, and I won't be a part of it. That's the end of the discussion."

Grayson made no move to take the money. "Be careful," he warned. "That won't work a third time, but I didn't know you felt that strongly about it. I don't want them dead either, so I'll go with you, and we leave Sixto here with Sanders and Tala."

"That's no good," Ethan protested. "Sixto is a doctor but, more importantly, he's a Filipino. We'll get nowhere as two white men walking into that camp alone."

Grayson seemed to know he'd been outflanked. His posture relaxed. "Fine," he said grudgingly. "Gabriel and I will stay here with Tala. We can use the grotto as a base and scout the area for trails. Three days and no more, then we follow. Let's go tell them."

The rain had stopped while they were talking. Ethan lit two cigarettes from his pocket and handed one to Grayson. He said, "Now I got a question for you, Grayson, something that's been bothering me. What if the British lied to you?"

"What do you mean?" Grayson asked defensively.

"Come on. You must have thought about it. The British. What if they just made up the story about knowing where your daughter is to get your cooperation? Maybe they just wanted some patsy with a good story. You, know, someone who speaks the languages, knows his way around, actually does have a daughter with the Katipunan, someone to open doors for them."

Ethan could see he had touched a nerve. It was clear Grayson was harboring his own doubts. The Canadian leapt to his feet. "They didn't do that. Their information was too specific. Believe me."

"How specific? What's the guy's name? He can't be just some barefoot boloman from the mountains. If she met him in those Manila revolutionary circles and he fought with Aguinaldo, he's a commander of some kind. Who is he?"

"His name's not important and not relevant to you. Trust that they gave it to me, and you will know it when you need to."

"But what if I'm right? What if the whole thing is a lie?"

Grayson's temper subsided, and the look of resignation enveloped him. He settled back onto the tree trunk, took a drag from the cigarette, and said, "Then Gabriel needs to kill me before I kill him."

It occurred to Ethan that some of the most honest and revealing conversations of his life had transpired on top of a dead log.

CHAPTER NINETEEN

Despite his advanced age, Sixto was plenty tough. Four hours of navigating over slippery rocks while fighting off mosquitoes had not slowed him down. Even along this widening river, the canopy nearly converged completely in places to block out the sky.

As the river turned eastward, Ethan spotted a huge Rosewood tree rising from the north bank and leaning over the water, through and beyond the canopy. He pointed to the tree and said to Sixto in halting Spanish, "I'm going up with the compass to have a look."

Sixto nodded and answered in perfect English, "I'm not an idiot. My niece once had a pet monkey with better Spanish than you. Let's just speak in your language if we must converse."

The former doctor was full of surprises, Ethan thought. He handed his Krag to Sixto, balanced himself atop the mule and mounted the old Rosewood like a horse. It took fifteen minutes to scoot and crawl up to the top of the canopy. The sunlight blinded him for a minute. The river had taken them a bit too far west, but it was time to get a heading and make for the hills. Then, to the right a hundred yards or so, he spotted a line of thinned-out vegetation, meandering but leading roughly where they wanted to go. Clear sign of a trail. With any sort of trail, they might make the hills before dark. And there was more…He scurried down the tree, nearly losing his grip still fifty feet over the river.

He dropped the last six feet and grabbed his rifle from Sixto's outstretched hand. "Quick," he said. "A big boar is napping on the bank just around that bend. They might need some meat up there. At least it will help our reception."

They secured the mule and started creeping upriver. "We're downwind," said Sixto. "If he's still there, we'll have a chance."

Ethan spotted the beast lying on its side along the muddy bank, hind legs just into the water, its huge, black torso heaving rhythmically up and down like a working bellows. The nose might have been transplanted from an elephant's trunk, a short, six-inch version that moved and twisted and grabbed in like manner at the tip of a pointed head. The creature was using it to drink.

The beast was ugly enough to stop horseshit in mid-air, Ethan thought, right down to the long gray hair along its back. Small twin tusks, curved and powerful, protruding from the lower jaw, gave the thing a justifiably terrifying appearance. Such tusks were known to help the animal inflict gruesome death upon unwary travelers across the islands, before consuming the entire corpse. On those rare occasions when the pig could be safely harvested, the Filipinos were known to make use of every hair and hoof, not to mention the boar's coveted dark meat.

Crouching low behind a branch, Sixto whispered, "He may be wounded."

"I doubt it," Ethan replied. "Maybe just lazy but we better take him from here. I make it about eighty yards. Let me know when you're ready. I'll fire first in case we need a third shot."

"Good," said Sixto.

Almost in one motion, Ethan fired then chambered a backup round as Sixto's bullet echoed his own, but a third shot was not required. Just like that, the big pig was dinner for eighty.

Both rounds had found the animal's left ear, more or less, and neither had exited. The scene was surprisingly bloodless. Standing toward the pig's back side, Ethan poked the belly a few times with his rifle to be safe. These Warty Pigs were even more dangerous when wounded, he reminded himself. "I guess they have pretty thick skulls," he said.

Sixto sat in the familiar, Filipino crouch position ten feet away covering Ethan with his revolver and back to the jungle, when Ethan glanced rustling foliage from the corner of his eye. Almost simultaneously, a black and gray blur erupted from the vegetation, head down and charging on the unsuspecting Sixto like an angry Rhino. A chilling crescendo of grunts and squeals announced the attack too late for Sixto to react. The first blow from behind launched the helpless victim into the air and likely saved his life as he landed squarely on the back of the beast, circling like a wounded bull in the arena.

Ethan had moved inside the death circle now, his new colt pistol in hand, chambered and poised to fire at point blank range as the massive boar pivoted to deliver the *fait accompli*. Instinct alone guided Ethan's hand in the moment and delivered a blistering succession of shots until an empty chamber rendered the trigger rigid and useless.

By some miracle, he had avoided hitting Sixto while dropping the boar literally on the man's lap. Struggling to free himself from the animal's weight, Sixto said, "You told me that new pistol held seven rounds. I heard more."

"It held enough," Ethan replied. "Good thing. Your calf is bleeding. Did I shoot you?"

"You didn't. The boar got a tusk into my leg on the first pass, but I'll live. It didn't hit an artery. Not many people survive something like this."

"I let my guard down," Ethan confessed. "I should have been expecting another one, probably the mother. Look how much bigger it is."

"We both should have, but I'm still here, thanks to you."

Ethan noticed the boar's trail back to the jungle was strewn with blood. "That's odd," he said. "I didn't shoot the thing until after he'd attacked you. Why would there be so much blood?"

"Look," said Sixto, pointing at the animal's bullet-ravaged head. "Someone's lopped his left ear off with a bolo."

Ethan retrieved the mule and returned holding a length of utility rope. He cut a couple of feet with his bayonet and took a knee beside Sixto. "We better stop that bleeding right now."

Sixto pulled up the blood-soaked trouser leg and pointed to a spot on his inner thigh. "Tie it off tight here if you would. You'll have to help me find something to dress it with."

"I have a clean towel, even bandaging right here," Ethan said.

"Tighter," Sixto said, grimacing. "I have those things also, along with sewing thread. I mean we must find the right plants in the forest, something with healing qualities. We have many in the jungle."

They followed the boar's bloody tracks into the jungle when Sixto singled out a nondescript, two-foot plant growing from the jungle floor. "Katakataka," he said. "This is the one we want. It has excellent healing properties and helps fight infection."

As they began to harvest the stiff, four-inch, sawtooth leaves, they heard a sobbing, human voice just ahead. It seemed to come from the trees. As they both moved cautiously toward the sound, Sixto called out in Waray, "Where are you?"

"Buligi, buligi," the weak, sobbing voice replied.

Sixto pointed. "There, up in the tree."

They were right below him in the dim light of the forest, maybe twenty feet, and standing in a pool of his dripping blood. A bloodied bolo lay beside the foot of the tree.

It was a boy, fifteen or sixteen, and he seemed to be losing consciousness on the branch supporting his weight. Sixto spoke with him in Waray as he began climbing the tree.

The youth was unconscious by the time Sixto lowered him to the ground. Ethan could see he'd been gored viciously in the left buttock around the hip and had lost a lot of blood. Sixto handed Ethan a towel and said, "Here, press on it hard as you can while I try to tie it off. If we stop it, the boy has a chance."

With all his strength focused through outstretched palms, Ethan managed to halt the flow as Sixto worked to tie off the vessels. "What did he say to you?" Ethan asked.

"You were right about the camp. That's where he came from. He asked if we shot the pigs. Said we have to bring them back because the people are starving. That's all I got from him."

"The kid looks like he hasn't eaten in a month," Ethan said.

"I think there are a lot more like that where he came from."

Ethan nodded and said, "That's a safe bet, but we'll have to spend the night on the riverbank and lick our wounds."

Sixto looked up from their blood-soaked patient and said, "Let's get him back there. I'll collect some plants and you make a fire."

"Why the fire?"

"We'll need it to soften these leaves. It liquifies and releases the healing elements inside. The boy will need a few other things. They're all around here. I might be able to travel tomorrow, but we'll need to rig a stretcher for the boy."

"What are the kid's chances, Doc?"

"Too early to tell. We might have to take the leg at some point—but only if he survives the night."

Ethan leaned over in the scant light to lift the boy in his arms. He pushed the long hair out of the boy's eyes, wiped the dirt from his face with a wet towel, and calmly declared, "Well, if that don't take the cake."

"What do you mean?" Sixto asked. "Do you know him?"

"I guess you could say that," Ethan admitted. "I knew his sister in Apostol."

The doctor had dressed his own wound and was still sewing up Pollito, Asuncion's brother, when Ethan appeared with the gutted and quartered boar mounted across the mule. He beat nightfall by only minutes. There was no English word to accurately describe darkness in the jungle, he thought. The camp was a quarter mile back from where they'd killed the second predator, and Ethan was exhausted.

As Ethan approached the small fire, Sixto looked at him and said through the white Fu Manchu mustache, "You look pretty bad."

Ethan looked at Pollito lying on a blanket near the fire and replied, "He looks worse. How is he?"

"Alive. Have you thought about how we get that boar meat and our supplies up into the hills while carrying this boy?"

Ethan found a suitable stick and rammed it through a big cut of pig shoulder. He assembled a spit with the aid of a few rocks and set the pig to flame. "I was thinking maybe we head back to the grotto with this kid, then back to Camp O'Brien, or whatever they call it now."

"He wouldn't make it that far," Sixto declared. "He's better off if we keep going. If the boy is still alive in the morning, he might recover. Besides, he was very clear about getting back to camp with that meat. I can peel a half section of tree bark to use as a stretcher, but the mule can't pull the boy and carry the boar as well."

"He can carry two sides and we'll each carry one," Ethan replied. "We'll all make it. What do you figure happened here? You think he was alone?"

Sixto broke a dead branch over his knee, tossing both pieces carefully on the embers and said, "Unlikely. Probably two of them from the encampment, out scavenging for food and got surprised like we did. Maybe they were dumb enough or desperate enough to stalk the boar. Who knows? But this boy managed to enrage the mother by slicing her ear off."

"Let's hope you're right and the other one got away."

"We'll have all our answers tomorrow," Sixto said, placing his palm open across Ethan's forehead. "You have a fever. I don't like it. Were you vaccinated for smallpox?"

"Yes," Ethan answered.

"Ever had Malaria?"

"Got it in on Luzon right after I got over here. They told me it might flare up every year or two."

"Drink plenty of water after you eat and try to get some sleep. You'll need it."

Even with aid of a recently traveled "trail," every step forward in the low forest challenged Ethan's resolve and inner strength. Incessant rain dragged them ever deeper into the swampy mud where the scant trail completely disappeared at one point for close to half a mile. He had to carry Pollito in his arms. Mosquitos, ravenous and unrelenting, proved more than a match for the old netting fixed to their wide-brimmed hats. Without the mule for support, he thought, they would all disappear any moment into this miserable swamp.

They were out of choices, Ethan decided. The mule was starting to falter, and the crushing weight in his arms and on his back drove him ever lower into the mud. Dizziness dulled his senses.

"Got to cut all the boar loose," Ethan said to Sixto while reaching for his bayonet. The mule bucked, swinging its head into Ethan's arm, and his bayonet disappeared into the soupy jungle.

The Filipino, with half a boar still on his back, clung to the mule's tail. "Go," he pleaded with Ethan, waving his free arm. "Leave the mule. You can make it. I see the upslope just ahead. A trail. It's hard ground."

"It's no use," Ethan said, no longer trying to hide his despair. "I'm done for. Stuck."

But Sixto had already clawed his way to Ethan's position in front. He sliced the rope across Ethan's back and the slab of boar, wrapped in a tarp, dropped into the murky brew. "Get to that high ground with the boy," Sixto said, pushing and pulling on Ethan's legs. "Get your breath and come back for us. I'll tie the mule to this tree. We can still do this."

Free of the crippling load of meat, Ethan willed himself out of the mud and forward, one torturous step, then another, never loosening his hold of Pollito. Just another few yards, but his limbs finally refused commands. He could see the dry ground, almost close enough to touch, then it faded away. A kind of peacefulness descended on him through the dense, jungle mist, painless but crippling his senses as the swamp began to swallow him, to swallow

Pollito. He did not know the voices and did not recognize the words echoing from somewhere in the next world…

CHAPTER TWENTY

Consciousness ambushed Ethan like Lazurus in the tomb. Now you're dead; now you're not. Every detail of the swamp adventure – the pain, the exhaustion, the fear – assaulted his senses like it was all still happening. Only a square of light across the room penetrated the darkness. He reached down for his pistol under the abaca sheet only to discover nakedness—and no weapon. As he reached frantically to escape the netting, a familiar voice said in accented English, "Lie back and relax, Ethan. Doctor's orders. You are all right. It's Sixto."

It was a crude hut of some kind, he could tell, the only light source an opening in the room, a doorway perhaps. Sixto sat on the dirt floor beside him, back against the wall. As equilibrium returned, Ethan managed to say, "Did anyone ever mention that you look the same clean or dirty?"

"You're the first and I'm clean," Sixto replied. "You are as well."

"Give me the details. How is Pollito? Where the hell are we?"

"Pollito is dead," Sixto replied. "He was likely dead before they pulled us from the swamp. Sorry. We're at the camp, the one we were looking for."

"Sorry to hear that. How long I been out?"

Sixto pulled back the netting and handed him a cup of water. "Drink this," he said. "If you feel like it, we'll sit you up and talk a bit."

Ethan was lying on a mat under a mosquito net between two lengths of cloth, not only naked but clean as a whistle and smelling like soap. Someone had even washed his hair and shaved him.

"You've been out two days," Sixto said. "Fever. Probably a Malaria recurrence, but the fever broke last night. You know, one of these Malaria attacks could kill you someday."

"Not a big priority right now. So, we're with the people?"

"We are, what's left of them. It's a mess here. Pollito's companion made it back here for help. The rescue party found us in the swamp and pulled us out just in time. I'm not sure who was in worse condition, them or us."

"Please tell me you didn't give me the bath." Ethan said.

"It was a young lady," Sixto answered. "Asuncion. Pollito was her younger brother or nephew, but I think you already know that."

Ethan swung his feet to the side of the mat, pulling back the netting, and tried to rise. Sixto stopped him with a hand on the shoulder and said, "Easy, you're not there yet, *Amigo*. Just lie back against the wall for a few minutes. Then we'll get you up slowly."

"How is the woman?" Ethan asked.

"She looks alright to me. Could use some more vegetables and fruit like the rest of these poor devils, but she's one of the strongest."

"Are they hostile?" Ethan asked. "Any of Martinez's men here?"

Sixto shook his head. "No sign of hostility or *insurrectos*," he said. "Just a lot of hungry, sick people."

"How is Asuncion taking her loss?" Ethan asked.

Sixto got up from the floor and said, "Like you might expect, I think. Come on. Let's get you up and walking outside a bit. Put that sheet around your waist."

It looked to be late afternoon from the sun's position, and the vegetation dripped from a recent afternoon shower. Ethan felt surprisingly well, all things considered. As they walked slowly around the area of the hut, Sixto said, "There's something you should know before we go on with this search."

"Something tells me I'm not gonna like this," Ethan said.

"You're not," Sixto replied. "Three days ago, I didn't care if you lived or died. I think you may be growing on me. The *insurrecto* Cristina ran off with isn't just any *insurrecto*. I'm fairly certain you know of him. Charles thought you would never have come along if you knew the truth. Cristina ran off a year ago with David Fagen, the infamous American deserter. Charles wasn't going to tell you until the last minute. They are on this island together. That's all I know. Charles didn't tell me how he found out, but I had my suspicions."

Ethan stopped and shook his head. "Well, if that don't beat a rug. I'd say your 'Charles' has pretty good sources. Makes perfect sense and I should have figured it out already. David Fagen, the mad dog of the 24th."

"What is Fagen to you?" Sixto asked. "Have you met?"

"Let's just say I did something he wouldn't appreciate, but he wouldn't know my face. Now, I'm starting to wonder if your brother-in-law was getting ready to trade me to Fagen for his daughter. Fagen must have come over here with the girl to help Martinez when things went south on Luzon."

Sixto frowned and said, "There is no telling what Charles is capable of. If that changes your decision to see this out, I understand. You think about it. In the meantime, I'll get you a can of tomatoes and some beans. You need plenty of nourishment and clean water, but you'll be alright."

"This means your niece has joined the *insurrectos*. It means she's out there fighting for Martinez."

"Maybe," Sixto replied.

They reentered the hut to avoid the dripping rain. "Fagen changes nothing," Ethan said. "What can he and his bunch do? Kill me? Get me some clothes so I can get out of here and hand me my pistol."

Sixto reached into his belt, along his back, retrieved the funny looking pistol, and handed it to Ethan. He started for the tiny doorway, then stopped and turned back to Ethan. He said, "And I suppose you should know you had the chills last night, and Asuncion slept beside you, naked, to keep you warm. She has hardly left your side."

HE THOUGHT SIXTO HAD RETURNED WITH HIS FOOD, BUT THERE she stood, hovering in the murky light from the doorway, a pile of his clothes in her arms. She was no longer full-figured, appearing weak and frail, but no less beautiful, and his excited reaction to seeing her was unexpected. The once smooth skin was sun-scorched and slightly weathered, more the color of toast than the gentile honey he remembered. But those penetrating hazel eyes still dominated and softened the hollow face. Her wraparound skirt and plain white top were patched and stained but freshly washed in a sign of determination, he thought, maybe even defiance. Asuncion was inside there all right. This was a woman beaten up, but by no means beaten, a different Asuncion, or maybe just the real one as she was meant to be seen, as Marty saw her. He knew he was never going to kill her.

She dropped the clothes onto the mat and said in Spanish, "You look ridiculous in that sheet, like a flat-chested woman. Put some clothes on. If you're going to shoot me, please do it quickly."

Ethan knew there was no book, no training, no manual or map to help chart the course of this reunion. Surprisingly, he did not sense awkwardness in that moment from either of them. Then he remembered her brother and said, "I'm sorry about Pollito. I liked him."

No trace of tears. Ignoring him, she said, "Even your hat smelled. The pigs let you live because they could not endure the foul odor. I would rather bathe a gorilla than repeat the experience with you. It took hours just to remove the leeches and ticks. Put your clothes on."

"I said I'm sorry about your brother. I did everything I could."

Asuncion lowered her head. "I know you did," she said softly. "Now dress yourself."

She turned her back while he dressed. The woman had even darned his socks. He said, "I'm sorry, Asuncion, but I have more bad news for you."

She turned back to face him. "Martin is dead," she said.

"Yes." Somehow, she'd been anticipating the news.

"Don't tell me how he died. Did you know he was a priest?"

"He told me, yes. He used to be a priest." Then he remembered the envelope and reached for his knapsack. "Oh, he left something for you."

She took the envelope, staring at the thing as Ethan had stared at Marty's letter. "No," she said. "He was a priest until he died. It is not like the army, Ethan. No one quits God. Martin strayed from the priesthood, and every day that fact tortured him. He simply could not function without faith. I gave him what comfort I was able. I know priests maybe better than anyone. He called me, 'the woman who sleeps with priests.'" Then, she smiled wistfully and added, "Only Martin *could* say that. Before him, I had never spoken of my shame to anyone. To him, it was simply a fact of my life, a step on my journey. He tried to make me see humor in it. Eventually, we even laughed about it." She could no longer hold back the tears.

"That was Marty," he said.

"He was the most non-judgmental person I have ever known. I lived my entire adult life knowing only pity from the people of our village. Often, I would find myself at church or at the well, praying for something else in their eyes, anything else: scorn or anger, even hatred. In Martin's eyes, I saw only love and understanding."

186

This woman knew Martin Tours better than Ethan did, maybe better than Martin had known himself. He said, "I know you tried to get him away before the attack."

She was about to say something when Sixto walked back into the hut. Ethan was relieved, for the doctor's appearance had granted them both desperately needed time and space to prepare for whatever would come next.

Sixto handed Ethan a mess plate containing canned tomatoes and another of cold beans. "Eat," he ordered. "When you finish, Asuncion and I will take you around this wretched place, and we'll talk. Oh, we managed to get all the boar meat back here. It was badly needed."

"And the mule?" Ethan asked.

"He's fine," Sixto said. "The animal has heart. We should give him a name, I think."

THE SO-CALLED CAMP WAS A RELATIVELY OPEN AREA OF HIGH, sparsely vegetated jungle, a little, sloping valley along a hillside. A shallow mountain stream meandered through the valley bottom and dissected the encampment roughly down the middle. Crude, bamboo lean-tos dotted both sides of the stream on gently rising slopes, some free-standing, others wedged against trees.

"The shelters are called *Longkashaws,*" Asuncion said. "They don't even keep out the rain."

The group walked down what passed as the main street, the lean-tos scattered on either side and people doing absolutely nothing, a good portion on their backs. The sun had already disappeared behind the next hill to the west, and a burnt orange horizon announced the coming darkness. Any blue canopy was a rare sight in this jungle, but the full, all-encompassing sky was another thing entirely, he thought. Beauty like that only mocked the cruel reality of this place. Everywhere, lay scrawny, emaciated people in tattered clothing, many prostrate under trees in various states of distress.

"Dysentery, Yellow Fever, Scurvy, Malaria," Sixto said. "Take your pick."

Ethan turned to Asuncion and said, "How many people are here?"

"Five-hundred and fewer every day," she answered, pointing to a small hill across the valley. "We bury them over there."

Asuncion stopped in front of an old, tribal hut, recently reinforced and repaired with fresh grass and bamboo. "The mayor and his wife live here," she said. "He could have gone with other well-connected people and *Principalia* to relatives or friends. He sent his children, but he and his wife came with us. He helps keep a sense of order and tries to maintain a ray of hope among the people. They let me stay with them."

"I remember him," Ethan said. "The little guy with the staff and Napoleon hat."

"I've spoken to the mayor," Sixto said to Ethan. "As of today, seventy-eight people, including children, have died of disease. There is no doctor here. I've been doing what I can."

"What about Obrador?" Ethan asked. Obrador might be the one man he could kill on sight. Ethan could hear some of the police chief's final words to him, spoken not ten days before the attack. *We Waray are a peaceful people...*

"No one seems to know," Asuncion answered.

Ethan looked at Sixto and said, "Have you told her why we're here?"

"I thought it better to wait for you," he replied. "I had plenty of work to keep me busy here while you slept."

"Yes, I see that." Ethan confessed. Addressing Asuncion, he said, "I have something for you. We also came for your help. Let's go back and talk."

On the way back to their temporary hut, Ethan spotted a group of children playing in the stream on the edge of some trees and stopped. "Look," he said. "Two of them are having a pissing contest upstream."

"The second-best way I know to spread disease," Sixto added.

"What about food?" Ethan asked Sixto. "This is the jungle. There's life everywhere. I even saw you find plants in the jungle that can save lives. There must be plants to eat."

Asuncion intercepted the question. "Yes, there are plants to eat, but they are not food. These people need Coconuts, bananas, fish, rice. We have none of those things here."

Sixto explained. "The interior jungle is not the bountiful food source Westerners believe. No camotes. No coconuts or bananas.

No way to grow rice. Humans can't survive long on plants. These people need fruits and vegetables, sanitation, herbal medicine, supplies. They are not primitive tribes."

"We catch what fish we can in the river," Asuncion added. "We hunt rodents and the occasional *Bugsok*, but you see the result."

"*Bugsok* is a deer," Sixto said in English.

To his left, Ethan spotted three young men staring defiantly at the group from in front of one of the lean-tos. They were all nearly naked and all carrying menacing-looking bolos.

Asuncion spoke first. "We should move on."

She led the group back up the far slope toward the place where Asuncion had left three women to guard their supplies and mule. "Who are the tough guys?" Ethan asked.

"Just local ruffians," she replied. "Too old to play in the stream and too young to be of use to Martinez. That may change soon. They're from the *pueblo*. One or two of them might even have played baseball with you in the square. It's not good if they recognized you, Ethan."

"What about Martinez?" Sixto asked. "He won't help all these people?"

"The great general is only worried about his war," Asuncion replied. "He doesn't have enough food for his fighters and considers us acceptable casualties of war. He has taken what he could from us and has no further interest in our welfare. He has only lip service to give."

Not far from their hut, they passed a group of twenty or so women overseeing wild boar preparation and cooking. Each of the four huge slabs had been wrapped carefully in huge, textured leaves from the forest and placed directly into its own pit on hot coals. They covered the pit with branches. The crowd, enticed by the aroma, was gathering strength from all directions.

"Come and eat with us tonight," Asuncion said. "Everyone will have a share, and you shall be honored guests—but don't let your guard down. I don't know what God has in mind for all of us, but he is testing our faith in ways I never imagined. You're not safe here for long."

God? Ethan wondered. He marveled at how these ordinary people, driven to the brink of starvation just to avoid slaughter, could cling to a faith that had failed them, even oppressed them, for three hundred years. It wasn't through an ignorance of history. Even in the village, he had encountered educated, bright people who knew their history, yet enthusiastically embraced the Catholic teachings. These were complicated people, he thought, ripe with contradictions, a fiercely loyal and generous people and downright dangerous when bullied or threatened from outside. *But God?*

They were back at the ramshackle nipa hut when Sixto finally asked the question Ethan had been expecting. "What about my daughter and brother-in-law? They've been sitting at the grotto for three days."

Ethan wanted to tell Sixto he didn't give a hog's holler about what came of Charles Grayson, but Tala's presence on the expedition had complicated the situation. Ethan and Sixto had become friends through a difficult common experience. Ethan liked the man and trusted him. He would take Sixto's concerns into account, but he didn't need to sound happy about it. "In a way," he said, "that grotto changed my life. I can't think of a better place for 'Charles' to sit and reflect for a while. Besides, Tala is safer there."

"What do you mean, *reflect?*" Sixto asked.

Ethan put a hand on Sixto's shoulder in a friendly gesture and said, "If Sanders learns the location of this camp, most of these people will be dead within a couple of weeks. I suppose it's time to tell you how Grayson got all his information, especially about me and David Fagen."

"So, my brother-in-laws's been lying to me as well?" Sixto asked.

"Let's take a tree stump over there, all three of us," Ethan replied. "There are a few things you need to know about Grayson and his *dog*. Sanders is not who you think he is. Yes, he lied to you. This involves you too now, Asuncion. We're going to ask for your help, and it won't compromise your people in any way. We're looking for a certain young Filipina…"

THE BOAR GATHERING HAD BEEN ANYTHING BUT A *FIESTA*, MORE like a food handout on the Indian reservation, but more than four hundred starving people managed to get a fair portion from their two-hundred pounds of wild boar meat. Ethan's obligatory meeting with the mayor had been tense but cordial. He thanked Ethan and Sixto for the boar and for trying to save Pollito's life, extending the hospitality of the camp, such as it was.

They did not discuss the bloody battle in Apostol. The mayor offered to post guards outside their shack overnight, but Ethan declined politely. He and Sixto would share guard duty, an arrangement that would generate far less stress. The pair would set off in the morning, guided by Asuncion, for Martinez's base in the hills, wherever the hell that was. It was enough for Ethan that Asuncion knew the way. It was also a confirmation of her deep involvement in this entire mess.

Weakness and exhaustion still plagued Ethan's body and mind as he peeled back the netting and flopped naked onto the mat. He and Sixto would split three-hour shifts for twelve hours, ensuring them both a full night's rest. He would be stronger tomorrow, he thought, and ready for what was becoming another routinely perilous journey. This one, however, would not include Charles Grayson and the Englishman. Sixto had no issue with that and was likely relieved that his daughter, Tala, would also miss this leg of the journey.

Asuncion was on board with their plan straightaway. Clearly, she knew where Martinez was, but by her reaction to their story, the name David Fagen meant nothing to her. Nor did she know anyone named Cristina Grayson but seemed genuinely eager for the opportunity to help. Surprisingly, she betrayed no apprehension about walking into the lion's den with an American. All curious observations, Ethan thought. *Why?*

As Ethan began to drift off, he heard breathing and felt the sheet move. He made room for her, but she did not speak and made no attempt to embrace him. She lay beside him on her back, almost but not quite touching. He could see her naked form only in his mind.

Her warmth and rhythmic breathing comforted him. He could feel her calmness and strength working to heal his body and soul. They lay like that, side by side together, yet so far apart, and he yearned to know her thoughts in that moment.

Ethan knew that if this woman were captured by General Jason Bell's mob, she would be brutally tortured, then killed. Stories about her already circulated around the outposts and campfires. He could never allow that. He felt in that moment he was reborn, and his transformation was complete. He had traveled all this way for answers and solutions only to find they do not exist. She was complicit in the surprise attack and slaughter of more than four dozen soldiers, many his friends, Marty, mostly decent people, a few with homes and families, yet this woman was not his enemy. Her name was Asuncion. She was a good and decent human being, and Martin Tours had loved her.

Asuncion lay beside him, revealed not through her beauty or her words but through the actions of a woman willingly bearing the burden of an entire people, not by choice, but by the commands of her very nature with only their interest at heart. What she did, she did without malice, and despite all the death and the pain and the loss on both sides, this woman had not passed a hangman's judgment on Ethan Cooper. What saint of Marty's faith could be more righteous or noble?

He longed to read her thoughts, now, along the invisible wall running between them in the dark. She'd watched him burn crops, slaughter animals, and torch homes with her own eyes. He'd done so much worse. *Why doesn't she curse me? She doesn't condemn me for my barbaric deeds.* He thought maybe she wanted Ethan's blessing or forgiveness for her actions, neither of which were his to give, but understanding was another matter. Even now, he could sense the conflict within this woman and feel her stricken conscience. She truly loved Martin Tours even as she had helped plan his demise.

A single finger brushed his thigh and did not retreat. One touch from one slender finger, yet all-embracing with the heat of a blazing fire. Silently, he offered his fingers to hers. Nothing more. Just a small breach in the wall but she seized upon it with her hand. The very idea of touching her in that way filled him with shame, but at the same time, excitement and hope and connection—even lust.

They would never be together, no matter how much they both might want to. He sensed they both knew that. They were the only two people Marty loved, and it was right to mourn him like this, together. Maybe there is no right and wrong, he thought, only truth and honor and the rest be damned. If only for a moment in time, this was what Marty would have wished for them both. Ethan's body and his mind battled to prevail in the hopeless carnal dilemma. He would let her decide. Yes, she would make the decision tonight—for both of them...

"Ethan, Ethan," he heard, rousing from a sound slumber. It was Sixto waking him for guard duty. Asuncion had slipped away in the night.

"What time is it?" Ethan asked. "Seems like I've been sleeping all night."

"It's about 3:00 a.m. I let you go for six hours but not sure how much you slept."

Ethan was into his trousers already and lacing up the new high-top boots he'd purchased for the trip. "Thanks. I'll let you sleep as long as I can in the morning."

Sixto rested the Krag against the wall and dropped his hat onto his sleeping mat. "There's something I want to tell you." he said. "It's about Cristina."

"I got the time, but maybe we should sit outside. I didn't like the looks of those wild-eyed kids with bolos tonight."

Sixto had kept the fire going just enough to give them a field of fire for twenty or so yards. Total blackness negated the advantage of a firearm. As Ethan had learned the hard way, there was no beating a bolo in close. They sat opposite each other on stumps. Sixto lit two smokes. Handing one to Ethan, he said, "Charles Grayson is Cristina's biological father, but he was never her real father."

"How do you mean?"

"My wife and I raised her on Luzon from the time her mother, Jasmine, died. Cristina was young. Charles was too busy getting rich to raise a child alone. He would visit from time to time and sent money regularly. He paid for her education. He's not a bad man. Quite the contrary, despite his proclivity for deception. He paid for Tala's entire education in England and watched over her. I didn't want Tala around Manila when the revolution started."

"Seems like he traveled a lot. You know, England, Canada. Did he ever take Cristina?"

"Not once," Sixto replied. "It's a terrible thing to say, but I've always believed it's because she looks Filipina. Such things can be a problem in England and Canada."

"Well, it's a shame but it's not unusual," Ethan replied. "I guarantee it would be worse in the States."

"Charles barely knows his daughter. I can't express what a beautiful person she is in every way. It's his loss. Without her, our lives would have been so much less. It's my fault she's out there."

"How is it your fault?" Ethan asked.

"I encouraged her fascination with Rizal and Bonafacio and the Katipunan. I wanted her to be a doctor, like Tala, but…"

"Not a revolutionary running around the jungle killing people," Ethan said, completing Sixto's thought. "I get it, but what happened to Grayson's wife, Jasmine? I mean how did she die?"

"I don't know for certain," Sixto replied. "I was in Manila. Charles and my sister Jasmine were living on Panay. It was a fever of some kind, Charles said, very sudden. Charles cabled us. My wife and I got there a few days later for the funeral. That's when he asked us to take Cristina. That's about it. Charles was devastated. I don't doubt he loves the child."

Ethan picked up their last thick branch and snapped it in two with his knee. He dropped the pieces carefully onto the dying fire, then pulled the semi-automatic pistol from his waist. Holding it out to Sixto, he said, "Take this. I'm good with the Krag, but it's hard to sleep with a rifle."

"Thanks, but I've got mine here," Sixto replied, patting his pocket.

"Not like this. Go on. Just flip the safety if you need it. There's one in the chamber. Get some sleep."

Sixto took the handgun and held out a hand in friendship. "Goodnight, Mr. Ethan Cooper," he said.

Just as Sixto reached the doorway, Ethan said, "Just one thing I don't understand. Why would Grayson give a hoot in hell who the girl ran off with seein' that he never had time for her all these years?"

"Who can be certain what someone else is thinking?" Sixto asked rhetorically. "As I said, the child didn't fit in with his lifestyle. He was away from home routinely from the beginning, sometimes for weeks at a time. Jasmine was lonely at first, but only until Cristina was born. He never took either of them on one of his trips abroad, and it always bothered me."

"So, Cristina sees you as her father and not Grayson," Ethan declared. "I get it."

"You could say that. I'm her father in every meaningful way."

"Well," Ethan said. "Grayson won't be happy about us cuttin' him loose like this, especially if she won't come back. Goodnight, Sixto."

CHAPTER TWENTY-ONE

B y the end of the first day, the group came out of the mountain through a narrow pass to a river. There was no place to rest as the vegetation poured right over the bank. Asuncion said, "There's a spot to cross just upriver and a rocky clearing along the far bank. We pick up the trail right there. It's a good place to spend the night."

Ethan slogged along behind her in the water, as close to the bank as possible, followed by their three young bearers: Clara, Candida, and Belinda, three sisters, friends of Asuncion from her Spanish class. Sixto trailed with the mule.

"How far is it to this General Martinez?" Ethan asked, swatting some hanging vines from his face.

"Maybe another day," she replied. "Watch for snakes. They're everywhere around here."

"Snakes. That's great. So, tell me." He said, hacking away at a low-hanging tree branch. "Have you been here before? I mean to Martinez's base camp?"

She kept forging on without turning around. "Yes," she replied. "You may as well know now. The general summoned me two weeks ago. He sent fighters to collect me, so I had no choice. He gave me a ridiculous medal. He's trying to make me into a hero. It serves his purpose somehow."

It sounded confusing to Ethan. She didn't like Martinez. That much had been clear even before the natives' attack. Yet, they say she was actually present during the battle and helped evacuate women from the town. *Tread carefully*. He said, "Well, I'm not sure what to make of that, but it was obvious you're a hero to the local people."

She didn't stop or even slow down but said, "I want freedom and self-determination for all Filipinos but it's not a fight for freedom if we oppress our own people to achieve it. That was not Rizal's or Bonafacio's dream. The only things this Tagalog General Martinez ever saw in our *pueblo* were potential fighters and supplies. Our peaceful home on the bay was only a resource to him.

"The Americans are our enemies. They burned our food and our homes and jailed our men. They are murdering people all across the island. To choose between a user and an abuser is not a difficult thing, Ethan, and sometimes necessary for survival. We chose the lesser of two evils and did what was necessary. Had the Americans treated us with respect, things might have been different. I am not proud of my part but would do it again, if necessary."

Her cards were all on the table now. It was a clear and precise defense of her actions and beliefs, Ethan thought, delivered with confidence and not a hint of guilt or emotion. *This is a remarkable woman*, he thought. Marty had seen it on day one.

She stopped and pointed across the river. "There's the clearing ahead, and we can cross the river right here. It's shallow enough to walk."

He signaled Sixto and the others, then said to Sixto, "Tell the ladies to hang onto the mule in case it gets too deep. I'll cross last."

Mules were excellent swimmers, but Ethan doubted the creature, proven though he was, could carry his load and pull the three women across the river at the same time, but the crossing was without incident. The river tried to swallow up the shortest of the three bearers halfway across, but she held fast to the mane and required no rescue.

The travelers hung their wet clothes on branches near the fire, claiming spots near as possible to the flames, thus avoiding mosquitoes. Ethan strolled over to the riverbank, filling his hat with cool water. He said, "I think our four-legged friend deserves a name."

The mule foraged lazily nearby on a long lead but headed directly for the fresh drink in Ethan's hat, burying his nose in the water. Patting the animal's neck firmly, Ethan said, "You're a good, old mule. We'll call you Pop from now on."

They all laughed as Ethan returned to the fire. "I never saw anyone scarf down army beans and jerky like those women did," Ethan said.

"They may have come just to get some food," Sixto observed.

Asuncion unrolled her mat between Ethan and Sixto and was the last to settle in for the night. She said, "Of course they did. What would they do with money anyway?"

"At least the rain is holding off so far," Ethan said.

"If it stays like this and the trail is good, we can make it in a day, a day and a half maybe," she said. "Unless we find a *banca*, we'll have to make a raft to get in close. The jungle is just too thick in there, and there are rivers everywhere beneath the cliffs."

"That means finding a place to secure the mule for a day or two." Sixto added.

THE TRAILHEAD WAS LITERALLY BESIDE THEIR CAMPSITE, SO THERE would be no hacking blindly, inch by inch, through thick jungle. It was wide and looked like an old Spanish road used to transport goods and materials, probably abandoned by the Spaniards for a hundred years. The vegetation along the trail was young and thin, nothing like hacking through virgin jungle. Asuncion and Ethan took the point of the little column and progress was unhindered most of the morning.

"Mountain people still use this trail sometimes," Asuncion said, hacking away with her bolo, "not to mention *insurrectos.*"

Ethan couldn't help but laugh. He said, "Well, then at least we're on the right trail."

Without warning, Asuncion froze, raising her arm as a signal. Everyone stopped dead.

"What is it?" Ethan whispered.

She pointed to a spot ahead on the trail. "It's a tarsier. I think his leg is hurt."

"A what?"

She crept forward at a snail's pace with Ethan in tow. He still couldn't see anything. Then, she stopped and pointed again. "Right there," she said. "It's a little monkey, five or six inches long. A tarsier. They're very rare, and I think you only find them on this island. He must have fallen out of a tree and hurt his leg."

Sixto had joined them now as the little guy just stared up at them with big, sad eyes, as big as a six-inch monkey can have anyway, Ethan thought. He said, "Cute but we're not in any position to stop and care for a little monkey. I'm sure his mother will find him."

"She's not a he," Sixto said, "and she probably *is* someone's mother. It's a mature female."

By that time, Asuncion had the thing in the palm of her hand. Ethan shook his head and said, "Now what?"

Asuncion held out her palm while Sixto did a quick examination of the tiny monkey and announced, "It's not broken. I think I can fix her up."

Enough was enough, Ethan decided. "Hold on. Even if you fix it with a splint, she can't climb trees or jump. How long do you think a midget monkey will last limping around the jungle floor with pythons and cats and God knows what else? I think we should put her out of her misery out of kindness."

"Tell me, Ethan, how do you propose to kill her?" Asuncion snapped. "A bullet? Crush her in your hand perhaps? We will take her with us and care for her until she is mended."

Sixto smiled and said, "I think you lose this argument, Mr. Cooper. I will make a little contraption to keep weight off the leg while she heals."

Ethan thought, *This from the Heroine of Apostol, the Slayer of American Soldiers.*

Sixto put up his arms and shrugged. He said to Asuncion, "For now, I'll make her a little cage and you can carry her around your neck. We will treat her tonight."

Asuncion smiled. "She will be my new *anting-anting*," she said.

"What are you going to feed it?" Ethan asked.

"That's not a problem," Sixto replied. "It eats almost any kind of insect or spider. No shortage of those around here."

They were preparing to resume their push to the river when Ethan noticed a small abnormality ahead on the jungle floor in the center of the trail, just a five-foot square section where the ground cover did not match. It began only inches from where Asuncion had seen the monkey and not five feet from Ethan in that moment. The patch looked greener than the rest and seemed randomly placed, as if dropped by hand. It was one of the signs he had learned during training in Manila.

Calmly, he said, "Nobody move. Tell the ladies. Not one step."

Carefully, he moved to the edge of the jungle and hacked off a five-foot length of bamboo, roughly the thickness of his fist. Trimming the end to a point, he stepped to the edge of the patch and hurled the makeshift spear at the middle. At impact, the entire five-foot square, a thin, bamboo, brush-covered frame, collapsed into a deep pit.

Ethan held the others back and moved warily to the edge of the pit. It looked to be about ten feet deep with pointed bamboo spikes anchored into the ground. He held up his palm and said, "Everyone stay put."

198

"Is there poison on the stakes?" Sixto asked.

"It doesn't matter," Ethan replied. "The stakes would kill you on their own."

Ethan scouted the trail ahead for about fifty yards, finding no signs of trouble and returned to his anxious companions. "It looks clear ahead," he announced. "They usually post some kind of warning sign for their own people, but we missed it. We'll go around the pit but keep an eye out for unusual markings on trees or something man-made hanging on a tree. If you see something, stop and give a holler. Keep to the edge of the trail."

They all nodded, but no one spoke.

Then Asuncion said, "What do you think of my *Nenita* now?"

Ethan removed his hat, wiping his brow with the other sleeve. He said, "My Spanish isn't that good."

"It's the name of my new friend. It means *little monkey.*"

He laughed and said, "I think we'll stop right here until *Nenita* is comfortable, fed and ready to travel. I'm not moving without that little monkey. She's good luck. Tell her to keep those big eyes wide open for trouble."

THEY REACHED THE RIVER MID-AFTERNOON OF THE SECOND DAY without further incident, having dropped the mule and hidden the reserve supplies in a small canyon with a freshwater spring a half mile from the river valley. Clara, Cadida, and Belinda seemed quite content camping with Pop and babysitting their new mascot, *Nenita.*

"This is it," said Asuncion, dropping her knapsack near the bank. "From here, we have to go in by raft. We'll go north. This river turns a half circle a few hours ahead. Martinez's base is only an hour or two straight west of here, but even the *insurrectos* can't cross this jungle. Too many high cliffs and too much impassable forest."

"I don't think we'll need a raft," Ethan said calmly.

"Why not?" Sixto asked.

Putting his knapsack down slowly, Ethan said, "Because I'm guessing these fellas have a boat, maybe two."

Ethan counted half a dozen men, all armed, at least two with rifles and forming a semi-circle around the riverbank. The men were barefoot and dressed in faded white abaca shirts and trousers, typical military dress for *insurrectos*. They did not appear to be friendly.

"Don't do anything lethal." Sixto pleaded. "Even if you kill them, our mission is over."

Asuncion was ahead of them both. Dropping her bolo, she raised her hands into the air and said, "Do you speak Waray or Spanish?"

"We speak Waray," said one of the riflemen. He was taller than the rest and sporting a thick, black mustache. "Tell the others to put their weapons on the ground."

Ethan didn't need a translation, and Sixto followed his lead.

Mustachio appeared to be the leader. On his order, the others collected their weapons and tied their hands with vines. Waving his rifle, *Mustachio* ordered them to sit. While Ethan and Sixto sat silently captive, Asuncion engaged the man in animated conversation.

Five minutes or so into the conversation *Mustachio* began pointing at Asuncion and carrying on in Waray. The only words Ethan could make out were, "*Mujer Guerrera?...Mujer Guerrera?*" He figured her answer was a long "yes" because the man pulled out his knife and cut the vine binding her hands. He immediately handed back her bolo. Ethan figured he didn't need to understand Waray to know *Mustachio* was groveling. Her performance was most impressive and much appreciated, Ethan thought.

They promptly cut Ethan and Sixto loose but kept their weapons as Asuncion explained their ever-changing situation. "They have two *bancas* just around the bend and will take us to General Martinez. You will not be harmed. Please let me do all the talking from this point unless the general addresses you directly. Pick up your packs. They will take us to the boats now."

THEY PADDLED NORTH, DOWNSTREAM, FOR A COUPLE OF HOURS, Ethan and Sixto paddling the trailing boat. This was an indication to Ethan that at some point soon the river would turn west and then south to resume its natural flow as Asuncion had predicted. The weather was pristine, hot but just enough cloud cover to blunt the burning sun with a gentle breeze along the water.

The landscape was like nothing else on earth, Ethan thought. Nothing near the scale of the Grand Canyon, but alive, lush and imposing. Towering cliffs on both sides rose straight up from the crystal-clear water, some smothered in thick, Emerald green vegetation and others pure rock erupting straight up from the river, all glimmering under the sun. Birds of all shapes and sizes, by the thousands, smothered the trees, stifling the natural spread of their branches with life as crocodiles lurked stealthily along the banks for their next careless meal to stop for a drink.

In the afternoon, as the sun announced their swing south, small tributaries and inlets began to appear, sometimes indistinguishable from the main channel, like a maze, itself a formidable deterrent to would-be invaders, Ethan thought.

TOWARDS LATE AFTERNOON, THE RIVER NARROWED, REVEALING Martinez's great surprise, an impregnable cliff-wall of stone, perhaps two hundred feet high on the west bank. The wall was honeycombed with dozens of cave-like openings nearly to the top and connected to the ground with a system of portable rope ladders. One way in; one way out.

As the boats neared the beehive-like complex, Sixto said, "Look, up at the top of the cliff."

A series of rope nets hung from over the cliff, anchored to the top and each filled with dozens of huge rocks. Ethan said, "Those rocks would sink any boat assaulting this compound. They could pick off the survivors easily from those caves. Ingenious."

The headquarters complex came complete with a landing beach and an area of cleared jungle, roughly the size of a baseball field, between the cliff and the water. Ethan could see dozens of men populating the sea-level area amid a dozen or so crude nipa huts, others in the caves, and even a few on top of the cliffs, but not in the numbers he would have expected.

The presence of the strangers attracted immediate attention from the *insurrecto* soldiers, and they seemed to drift toward the two boats out of curiosity. Ethan noticed that the men generally appeared weak, maybe even malnourished, and not in the least menacing. They had arrived at the lion's den where, for the time being at least, the lion was still king.

CHAPTER TWENTY-TWO

*M*ustachio instructed the group to wait in a lean-to on the beach where they sat under guard on U.S. Army supply boxes, mostly empty, while awaiting their fate. Considering the *insurrectos'* treatment of Asuncion, Ethan was feeling cautiously optimistic.

Within a few minutes, *Mustachio* returned and exchanged some words with Asuncion in Waray. Asuncion rose and announced, "The General wishes to greet us personally. We are requested to follow this gentleman."

They didn't have far to go. They followed *Mustachio* to the hut farthest from the water, literally backed up to the rock cliff. "We are to wait here for the General," Asuncion said.

Ethan said, "While we wait, might you explain to us what *Mujer Guerrera* means?"

"It is a nickname given to me years ago by my cousin, Mariano Obrador, the police chief. I was the only woman to attend the Katipunan meetings during the days of my schooling. *Mujer Guerrera* is the Katipunan nickname he gave me. It means "female warrior" in Spanish."

"I think I'll just stick with Asuncion," Ethan said. "Is Obrador here now? Did you see him when you were here?"

"There is so much you don't understand, Ethan. Obrador is no friend of this general. Obrador was forced to act to avoid the wrath of General Martinez. He is no more a friend of Martinez than he is yours."

"Then where is he?" Ethan asked.

Before she could answer, two men entered the hut and promptly turned Ethan Cooper's world upside down. Ethan hardly noticed the general because the taller man standing beside him was Ethan's old friend, Captain O'Brien's translator, Renaldo, complete with his trademark blue U.S. Army shirt.

The man had lost weight, Ethan noted, and his blue army blouse had seen better days, but there was no mistaking the baby face. Ethan's mind struggled to remain in the moment. *Renaldo?* Had he been a spy all along? Why was he here?

All three "guests" stood for the General, and he addressed them as a group. "Good evening," he said in Spanish. He was unusually short with a long black mustache and a chubby face below a high forehead. Maybe it was just a receding hairline. In all other respects, it was an ordinary face. "It is an honor to welcome *Mujer Guerrera* once again to our camp. As for your associates, I confess some disappointment that you would bring unannounced visitors to our encampment, *Mujer Guerrera*, especially a foreigner."

"I vouch for them both personally with my life, General. And as for the 'foreigner,' are you not from Luzon? You are a long way from home. You speak of foreigners, yet you yourself do not speak our language."

Ethan winced and Martinez visibly seethed at her last remark but held his temper. "Gentlemen, I am General Vicente Martinez. This is my Chief of Staff, Captain Renaldo Torres."

Chief of Staff?

Renaldo interrupted. "Sir, I believe I can introduce the American as we are well acquainted."

"Please do," Martinez replied, obviously surprised.

"General, may I present Mr. Ethan Cooper, formerly a sergeant in the American Army."

Martinez bristled, snapping at Asuncion. "You would bring an American soldier here?"

"A former soldier," she corrected.

Renaldo chose that moment to intervene again. "Sir," he said, "Perhaps we could discuss that question alone after we learn what brings *Mujer Guerrera* here with her two companions. As for the American, I can only say that I know him well, and I know him to be a man of honor and good character. Lieutenant Jones will also vouch for him, Sir. From my perspective, Sir, Cooper is not our enemy."

Lieutenant Jones? Ethan thought. *So Jonesy did defect. Had he been working with Renaldo before the Apostol slaughter? Did Jonesy know about the attack in advance? Did he participate?* Ethan wanted to say, *You're wrong. I am your enemy.*

"Very well. We will discuss it later then," Martinez declared. "And the other one?"

"Dr. Sixto Espinosa," Asuncion replied. "He…"

203

"Of the Katipunan?" Martinez asked. "You were locked up by the Spanish on Luzon. Were you not?"

"And then by the Americans, *Señor* General," Sixto replied.

Looking at Ethan, Martinez said, "And you trust this American?"

"I do," Sixto declared.

Martinez seemed to relax a bit and spoke directly to Asuncion. "I am curious to learn your business," he said. "Captain Torres will see to your needs. You need to wash and rest. You will all join me for dinner, and we will speak further."

Ethan spoke up, against Asuncion's advice. "Sir, would it be possible for Lieutenant Jones to join us? We are old friends."

Martinez nodded. "I see no harm. I will extend the invitation, and the lieutenant can choose for himself." With that, the General turned and left the hut.

By this point, Ethan was so thoroughly confused that he thought it wise to hold his tongue completely. Renaldo maintained a strictly military demeanor while escorting the three to a small cave at ground level. A lean-to extended from the cave mouth, affording some additional protection from the rain.

"Make yourselves comfortable," Renaldo said. "There is a private spot just around the bend for the lady to bathe. Watch out for snakes. I will collect you in two hours for dinner. If you have any additional requests, simply ask the guard."

Before leaving, Renaldo turned to face Ethan and offered his hand. He said, "It is good to see you again, my friend. I know this is a shock to you, Ethan, but we are all bound to our duty. You have done yours honorably and I mine."

At first glance, the outstretched hand evoked transparent emotions like hate and revenge as memories of severed heads and limbs flooded Ethan's brain. But relationships with Marty and Asuncion and the utter madness of this war had by now revealed a new, opaque reality, a labyrinthine world where righteousness never lingered in one place and sometimes even chose to cohabitate with evil without a hint of conflict. Other times, one could barely distinguish between the two. In such a world, truth had become the most valued commodity, not to mention the scarcest, and honor the only reliable guide through the labyrinth.

Despite the facts, Ethan saw truth and honor in the outstretched hand, recalling stories of Renaldo's heroism, his almost inexplicable lifesaving deeds on the chaotic, seagoing retreat from the carnage. During the battle itself, Ethan thought, it must have been Renaldo who managed to spare the lives of the two men in the convent. How many more were there? Ethan accepted the hand in friendship, deciding that words were neither appropriate nor necessary.

The *guests* dined in the same hut where they had first met Martinez. The table was set for five, not six. The General appeared in his full white uniform, complete with sword and was seated last, at the head of a table newly placed for the event. Captain Renaldo Torres was the fifth guest. Only two coal oil lamps on the table illuminated the hut. Ethan was surprised when one of the servers began to fill their cups from a decanter of wine.

"We will eat first," said the general, "and then discuss your business. Lieutenant Jones respectfully declined the invitation but sends his regards."

"May I see him later, General?" Ethan asked.

Martinez seemed to consider the request, then said, "Yes. I think it in his best interest to give you the chance. He is assigned to our training section. You should know that he has not engaged with American troops since joining us and played no role in the recent battle. He is a good soldier, but, as you know, not particularly bright. Corporal Garcia here will escort you to his cave later. I hope you can climb a rope ladder...Oh, Mr. Cooper, I think you should also know that we identified six men as having mutilated the bodies of your American dead at the *pueblo*. Obrador was quite emphatic about identifying them. They have all been executed. It is not the way we conduct warfare."

EACH PLATE CONTAINED A FULL FISH, GUTTED AND COOKED ON AN open fire complete with head. The side dish looked and tasted like plantain, mashed and maybe flavored with sugar. No rice or camotes or coconut or fruit of any kind. Still, the best meal Ethan had tasted in some time.

"If you want more, I will have them bring you another one," Said the general. "The fish is *Gatan*, abundant in our freshwater rivers here."

Perhaps not so abundant as you would have us believe, Ethan wanted to say. The general's faint was too obvious, Ethan thought. *He wants us to believe all those emaciated bodies in the camp are by choice and this part of the jungle teems with tropical foods.*

The wine, likely once destined for some American general's table, was very red and very good. It kept coming after dinner when the small talk and braggadocio gave way to the business at hand. *Patience,* Ethan told himself. They were in the lion's den. He didn't have long to wait.

The general raised his glass. "I give you a toast," he said. "To our *Mujer Guerrera,* Asuncion, the Heroine of the Philippine people."

"To *Mujer Guerrera,*" they all said. Only the general and his Chief of Staff clinked glasses.

Then the general said, "So you have all come to ask my help in finding Captain David Fagen. No?"

No one responded. The evening was not going to finish as smoothly as it had started, Ethan thought. *How much does he know? How? Who?*

Asuncion tried to rescue them. She and the general spoke Spanish. "*Señor* General, we have no lies to tell you. All three of us are here looking for a woman named Cristina Grayson. She is the wife or lover of David Fagen. We have learned that Fagan came to this island when the last Luzon forces surrendered because he would not be given amnesty. We think the woman is with him. Doctor Sixto Espinosa is her uncle. This is a personal family matter. If Fagen is here on the island, you would know."

"And the American?" asked Martinez.

"Hired to help find Cristina," Asuncion replied.

The general slammed his palm on the table and howled, "Hired by whom?"

"Charles Grayson, Cristina's father," Ethan announced.

Martinez snapped his fingers, and the two guards sprang to attention. "Now," he said.

Within seconds, a guard walked into the hut with three crude chairs followed by Charles Grayson, Gabriel Sanders, and Tala Espinosa. The Englishman was hardly recognizable. Swollen eyes, blood-stained clothing, and a severe limp all combined to present the portrait of a broken man, recently tortured, and successfully.

"By chance do you know these people, Mr. Cooper? One of them also claims to be *Doctor Espinosa*. My men captured them in the jungle. They tell a story remarkably similar to yours but much more interesting and detailed."

He must know everything, Ethan concluded. Most likely, Grayson gave up the Englishman to avoid torture. He'd always figured Grayson wasn't the type to take one for the team.

The general said calmly, "I know exactly why you are here, but let us not waste time. *Mujer Guerrera*, you are beyond reproach. I ask you one question." Then he pointed directly at Sanders and asked, "Who is this man?"

"I do not know this man, General. I have never seen him before this moment.

Ethan could not stay silent. "She has no clue who he is."

The general clenched his teeth, clearly holding back rage, and said quietly, "I believe her, but you, Sergeant Cooper, would bring a spy to my camp under the guise of a mission of mercy?"

Ethan thought about standing up, but his words and reactions in the next minute would likely decide his fate. *Tread carefully.* He looked Martinez squarely in the eye without moving and said, "I did *not* bring him to your camp, General, and my friend, Dr. Espinosa, did not bring him to your camp. *You* brought him here. We left them both, *intentionally*, at a little pond with a waterfall in the high country. I'm guessing that's where you captured them."

"It's true," Sixto added. "We did not want the Englishman and Grayson to know the location of the townspeople or your encampment. Doctor Tala Espinosa is my daughter."

Martinez waved his hand, and the guard escorted Grayson and Sanders from the hut. Then he spoke to the server in Tagalog as Tala was seated at the table. The server refilled the wine cups. "Very well," Martinez declared. "Now we will finish our talk. My people will escort you to Captain Fagen. The woman you seek is with him. Make your petition directly to the captain. Thereafter, your fate will be in his hands. I can do no more. Your daughter has spent three days, nearly without sleep, treating my sick people. She is not my prisoner."

"Thank you, *Señor* General," Sixto said.

"One last thing," Martinez added. "Mr. Cooper, I must ask for your word that you will not disclose anything you have seen here, not to anyone, especially the location of this camp."

"You have it," Ethan said.

"*Señor* General," Sixto said, "Charles Grayson is my brother-in-law, as you must already know. May I ask what you intend to do with him and with the Englishman?"

Martinez seemed to reflect for a minute, then leaned back in his chair and said, "I no longer question your motives, Doctor, nor those of Mr. Cooper. Those I trust most believe you are both honorable men and that is enough for me, so I find no reason to withhold the truth.

"Things are going badly for my army here, worse every day since General Aguinaldo's capture and surrender on Luzon. This is no secret to the Americans. We are short of supplies and food and being hunted everywhere by American troops. They burn the *pueblos*, destroy the crops, kill civilians. We cannot maintain the fight much longer, and they will soon find this place on their own. I need leverage for the coming negotiation. Therefore, I will not kill Grayson or the Englishman. You doctors may both treat the Englishman before you leave. I will not harm them, but they will remain my prisoners pending the result of amnesty negotiations. The young doctor will remain here as my guest to treat my men."

"No," Sixto cried out. "She must be allowed to leave with us."

"It's all right, Father," Tala said. "The general has already agreed to let me treat the townspeople as well."

The general, being a general, proposed a solution that Ethan suspected had been on his mind all along. "Very well then, Doctor Sixto. If you agree to stay with us willingly as my physician, your daughter may go with the others." And so, it was decided.

The general rose to indicate the dinner had ended, but Ethan had one last agenda item. "General," he said, "what happens to Lieutenant Jones when you have your amnesty? You know my country will never agree to amnesty for a deserter."

"We see the lieutenant as a defector to our noble cause," Martinez replied, "but your point is well taken, and I have considered it. David Fagen is a great hero of our struggle. I will give you a letter for Captain Fagen. He may have a solution. Goodnight, Gentlemen. Goodnight, *Mujer Guerrera*, and may God be with you."

"Goodnight, *Señor* General," she said.

CHAPTER TWENTY-THREE

"We'll have to blindfold you now, Ethan," said Renaldo in English, "and the doctor as well. They'll come off when we get to Fagen. If the captain doesn't kill you, we'll escort you back to that waterfall where you let Chuko escape."

Chuko? These boys are still keeping secrets. Renaldo might know about the incident itself at the grotto, but nobody knew that boy's name except for you. Nobody, not even Jonesy. "Wait a minute. How did you know about Chuko?"

Renaldo smiled. "Jonesy confirmed the story, but the boy, Chuko, told me himself. Don't you recognize him?"

Ethan turned to face the other three Filipinos in the escort detail. They were all young, but the one in the middle looked like a baby. When their eyes met, the boy broke into a wide grin, revealing the prominent, empty space between his teeth. Ethan walked over and greeted the kid with a hearty handshake. "Well, I'll be a monkey's uncle," he said. "Good to see you, boy."

"We found him alone on the river, and he told us the story," Renaldo said. "He's one of us now. The people your soldiers killed were his father and brother. He fights for revenge."

They left the area early morning by *banca*. The blindfolds rendered Ethan and Tala dead weight passengers, leaving the paddling for Chuko and his comrades. Renaldo rode in the lead *banca* with Ethan and two guards. The only thing Ethan knew was that they had started out traveling north three hours ago in a solid rain that continued to pelt them, at first from the east, and now it had to be from the south, he figured.

Renaldo manned the stern paddle, just behind Ethan. The last thing Ethan wanted was to engage with the former infiltrator, but he had to know more about Alamo Jones. Ethan's conversation with Jonesy last night hadn't gone well. In a way, Ethan wished he'd never forced the confrontation. He said, "Renaldo, is it true Jonesy was not involved in the attack?"

Renaldo didn't hesitate to answer. "Like the general said, he knew nothing about it until it was over. I mean nothing. He'd been considering defecting ever since we left Manila."

Suddenly, it was all clear to Ethan. Jonesy wouldn't talk about it last night, but his decision to desert was not made on a whim. "The VIP prisoner," he said. "I know it was Aguinaldo. Jonesy told me after he was beaten. The warm greeting, the books, the walks in the garden. Jonesy was constantly switching assignments with people to guard him. Aguinaldo had been working on Jonesy all along—and you likely helped."

"It's not for me to admit or deny," Renaldo replied, "but the general could see how the other Americans treated Jones as an outsider, a 'nigger lover.' Jones was a lost soul, a gentle halfwit who only wanted to belong and be accepted. There is no cruelty or duplicity in Alamo Jones. The prisoner counseled him through books and long conversations. I think they had a genuine friendship. Jonesy finally made the decision when his own men tried to kill him. I made contact with Jonesy when he left the infirmary and disclosed my real identity."

"Mark Twain," Ethan mumbled.

"What?" Renaldo asked.

Just like that, the rain stopped, and Ethan felt the morning sun warming his right cheek. *Heading north or northeast now, maybe.* The river was wide enough at this point to welcome blue sky and sunshine. "Nothing."

Renaldo repeated himself. "What did you say about Mark or…"

"Never mind…Did you use Jonesy for information? Did he spy? Even unwittingly?"

Renaldo laughed and said, "Ethan, I worked directly for Captain O'Brien, the company commander. What could a lowly private know that I didn't? Jonesy just liked the idea of being a lieutenant. He wanted respect, and he has it. Is it so difficult to believe that General Aguinaldo simply saw Alamo Jones as a person worthy of respect and attention?"

Having spent time with the general himself, Ethan had to admit that was possible, but there was more to it. His meeting with Jonesy last night had left Ethan with a sense of sadness. Jonesy was lonely. Worse than lonely. He was a man-child filled with regret for a choice he could never undo, like someone who had given up on himself. The Jonesy he spoke with last night was a stranger, a pitiful soul playing out his last hand with no interest whatsoever in the game.

He wanted Renaldo's opinion and said, "How does he seem to you now?"

"Hard to say," Renaldo replied, "but I'm not his mother. He hasn't adjusted well, but it's understandable. No one adjusts well to short rations. He keeps busy. I sent him with two men early this morning to get your three women at the trailhead. He knows where to bring them, so don't worry. I always liked Jonesy. But to answer your question, some men will always be lost."

Surprisingly, Ethan felt no hatred or bitterness toward Renaldo now despite the man's deceptions. He kept remembering Brock's miraculous escape from death by bolo in the church annex and figured he would just ask Renaldo directly. "Do you mind if I ask one question about the attack?"

"It depends upon the question," Renaldo answered.

"Back there in the church annex, the bolomen ran right past two of my men to get to the officers. Brock said you were with them. Did they survive by chance, or did you spare them?"

Renaldo smiled and said, "I leave you to wonder about that, but I will tell you the doctor was not supposed to die. That was a terrible mistake, and both Obrador and I regret it very much. O'Brien was a fool without compassion. He was the target of our raid on the convent. The bearded man I did not know." The reference confirmed the fortuitous demise of the Fiddler.

The second day was slow going on foot all the way with Ethan and Tala free of the blindfolds, helping to portage the two small boats along what seemed to be a decent jungle trail through thick vegetation. Tala's endurance and strength surprised Ethan. Asuncion's did not. The entire day was rain free, allowing travel on solid ground, but the mosquito netting on Ethan's hat remained under constant assault. With no hint of light or sun for hours, Ethan had no clue of the group's direction of travel. He and Tala were well and truly lost.

They reached another river where Renaldo decided to make camp, and the insurgents thoroughly enjoyed their dinner of U.S Army canned beans, tomatoes, and jerky.

Ethan bedded down in the center of the small clearing between Asuncion and Tala with the insurgents encircling the three. One remained on guard. From his bedroll looking up, Ethan could make out a thin strip of sky through a space in the canopy, dotted with hundreds of tiny stars.

He tried to put the danger of tomorrow out of his mind and was thinking of the two women when he heard Tala whisper in English, "I haven't had a chance to tell you, either of you, but when I treated Gabriel's wounds the other night, I had a long conversation with my uncle Charles. I told him Martinez's intentions. He was very open with me for the first time. It turns out Charles is dying of cancer. The surgeons tried to cut it out, but the disease had spread throughout his body. He doesn't have much time and wanted to make things right with Cristina before..."

"Too bad," Ethan said, "but that explains a lot."

A brief silence followed, after which Asuncion asked the question Ethan had been trying to put out of his mind. "Ethan, what do you think this Fagen is up to here on the island?"

There was no getting away from it, Ethan thought. "I suppose he's doing what he did on Luzon, killing Americans. There's no organized Filipino army on Luzon anymore, so he just brought the fight here most likely, along with his woman. He's probably commanding a unit of insurgents for Martinez, a kind of last stand to the death."

"Fagen won't be in a hurry to give up when Martinez surrenders," Tala said.

"You catch on quickly," Ethan replied. "Fagen's even worse off than Alamo Jones when it comes to surrender. At least Jonesy has a chance for a long prison sentence. They will execute Fagen without ever bringing him back to the U.S. General Funston still has a six-hundred-dollar reward on him."

"Definitely sounds like a last stand to me," Tala said. "Suicide by war. I know why I'm here, but I'm still not sure why you are, Ethan."

Ethan was beginning to doubt his own rationale for hooking up with Grayson's mad journey. He'd signed on primarily to find Asuncion and give her the envelope—or kill her, a noble farce that ended up only exposing his own bad judgment and lack of compassion. The woman was rock solid by every standard of measurement, and Marty had trumped him again in death, if good naturedly.

He'd found Jonesy and couldn't do a damn thing to help the boy. Now, he couldn't even make up an excuse for walking into David Fagen's hands voluntarily. Come to think of it, Asuncion had no reason to put herself at risk either. That *Mujer Guerrera* stuff might not carry so much weight with the Mad Dog of the 24th.

Maybe he was doing it for Tala and her father. Sixto and Ethan had pulled the curtain back on each other over the course of this trip and come to rely on each other like the left foot does the right. Sixto was his friend. Tala was…well, he didn't know yet. For the life of him, he couldn't manufacture a convincing reason. But he knew clearly that what happened between him and Asuncion that night, as powerful as it had been, was really about Marty. He decided none of it mattered because, at this moment, he was in the right company by his own choice at the right time in his life. Everything else would either work out or not.

Nature took pity on the weary travelers that night, holding the nocturnal showers at bay and sweeping away the dampness with a gentle north breeze. The narrow band of bright stars above them followed the river north. Beside the fire, looking straight up from his back at the display, Ethan recalled his nights in the Allegheny Mountains. The star-studded canopy in its infinite breadth had never once surrendered its sense of possibility or its determination to inspire. For the seasoned infantryman, dreams of redemption had long since faded into a reality of snakes and scorpions and overbearing swelter. But the sense of involuntary confinement had mostly fueled his recent discontent. It was good to be facing a life of choices again.

On their fishing trips to the mountains, Pop would say that no matter where you were in the world, the sky was always the same sky, even if revealing only a small slice of itself. It was a place to store dreams, a place a man could count on to guide him if he gets lost and kick him in the ass if he gets too big for his britches.

Everything in Ethan's life seemed a mess now. Asuncion, Fagen, Jonesy, even where he would live or what he would do with his life. Despite all of it, he felt free for the first time in years. He was still the same person as that boy in Pennsylvania, but more, and these folks whose lives were now so intertwined with his were just like any other folks anywhere. He only needed to keep following the path forward, and it might all work out.

Around mid-day on the third day, they landed the boats and left them hidden in the jungle to proceed on foot. Even blindfolded, Ethan could tell the new trail headed uphill, but God only knew in what direction.

He heard Renaldo say, "This is it. Let's go."

"This is what?" Ethan asked.

"You wanted David Fagen. Right? He lives here," Renaldo said, pointing to the house on the ridge in the distance.

There were no guards, no warriors, no defenses of any kind, just a large, open field recently reclaimed from the forest and two men in the distance continuing the work. The house was torn from the pages of Swiss Family Robinson, Ethan thought, the children's adventure book his mother would read from at bedtime. Built around a huge Rosewood tree near the edge of a cliff, the structure touted multi-levels with porches all around against a panoramic backdrop of crystal blue sea and matching sky. With the sun setting at his back, Ethan's best guess on their location was somewhere on the remote northeastern coast of the island. Three bamboo sheds and an animal pen rounded out the structures and housed a carabao, a couple of pigs, and some chickens.

"Welcome, y'all," Ethan heard someone yell. He saw a man in the banana grove on the right, waving. "Ova' hea, y'all." He was a big, powerful Negro, muscled and black as coal in the ground, bare-chested with his shirt lying across a branch. The man pointed to the big treehouse and started moving that way. He wore a pistol on his side but implied no threat to employ it.

Renaldo said, "He wants us at the house. Let's move. He knows we're coming. The general sent word yesterday."

"What do you mean, 'sent word?'" Ethan asked.

"We have our little communication system, Ethan."

As the group started across the clearing, a young woman appeared on the second porch up. Ethan figured her for Cristina Grayson. He could see the baby bulge from just that far away. The woman was tiny and bronzed with short hair and Asian facial characteristics. They all kind of reached the front of the house at the same time. The big black man was wearing his shirt.

Tala ran ahead. She and Cristina and embraced. Cristina cried. They chattered on in Tagalog, then embraced again. Cristina took

214

Tala by the hand and said in English, "Tala, I want you to meet my husband, David Fagen."

Fagen removed his army issue hat in a gesture of respect, not submission, and said shyly, "Right proud t' make yo' acquaintance, Docta Espinosa. Heard lotta nice things 'bout you."

They hugged and Tala said, "You are my cousin now."

This is David Fagen? Ethan asked himself. *The Mad Dog of the 24th?*

Fagen covered the three steps over to Asuncion, hat still in hand, and said, "And this here I 'spect is *Mujer Guerrera.*"

Asuncion smiled, extending her hand. In Spanish she said, "Thank you, Captain Fagen."

Wearing his hat again, Fagen turned immediately to Ethan with a sober look and said, "You'd be the sergeant from the village."

"Former sergeant," Ethan corrected. "I'm a civilian now."

Fagen shook his head and said, "That make two of us then but don't make no matta'. Les' you n' me git us a understandin' right here n' now. Ain't no niggas here 'ceptin' da' niggas in yo' head. You understand me, Sergeant?"

Ethan nodded. "I understand you fine," he said. "Didn't come here for trouble."

"Then you won't find none. Now, y'all come on into my house, and we chew the fat a bit while ma' wife find us a refreshment. I'm learnin' me how to make banana wine but m' recipe ain't perfected yet. Anyways, I let you pass judgment on ma' wine but not m' woman." Fagen laughed.

The last thing Ethan had been expecting was a happy family reunion. Aside from two Krag-Jorgensen rifles and Fagen's personal pistol, the house and grounds revealed no hint of a military presence. Nailed above the front door was a sign carved into a decorative piece of driftwood echoing his warning. It read, *The only niggers in this house are the niggers in your head. Leave them on the doorstep.*

"Cristina made that sign for me," Fagen announced proudly.

After cleaning up, they sat at a table on the second story porch overlooking the sea on store-bought chairs with Chuko and the other insurgent guards napping on the porch. Ethan could see a pristine beach below. The banana wine wasn't half bad, he thought, certainly a step up from the tuba they'd been forced to drink in Apostol. It was almost like being on leave. The conversation was surprisingly light and easy at first, in a back-and-forth mixture of

Tagalog, Spanish, and English. Fagen immediately demonstrated a mastery of Tagalog.

The black man was far from the cowering, starving rat Ethan had expected. The deserter seemed genuinely fit and happy—and proud to entertain *guests* on *his* little farm as Cristina and Tala laughed and reminisced like they had never been apart.

Sixto's niece, Cristina, was handsome, if not beautiful, full-figured with intense brown eyes and a smile that could warm your morning coffee if she chose to flash it. Even Asuncion seemed swept up in the unexpectedly light, storybook atmosphere, surprisingly partaking in the banana wine and laughter. Ethan had the clear sense they were all celebrating Fagen's retirement from soldiering. How could Fagen think such a thing possible? He had to know this war was nearly over, and the Filipinos were losing. His prospects for a future were non-existent.

Despite the jovial mood, it didn't take Cristina long to ask about her father. Somehow, she already knew Martinez was holding him captive. The insurgents' communication network was remarkable, Ethan thought, but she didn't know everything.

Cristina and Tala had been speaking to each other mostly in Tagalog but, for whatever reason, Christina switched to English. "What is the state of my father's health?" she asked.

"He is completely unharmed." Tala answered, and Ethan wondered if the duplicity was temporary.

"I told Cristina her daddy be fine," Fagen said. "General Martinez finna hold him nice n' safe til dis' all git sorted out."

The mention of Martinez immediately drew Renaldo into the conversation. "Cristina, I hope you understand that the general required the services of a physician, but David is correct. He will not be harmed, I assure you, on behalf of General Martinez."

Cristina nodded. "Yes, of course, Renaldo," she said.

Fagen reached across the table with the jug of wine to fill Ethan's glass. He smiled mischievously, and his wide, pancake nose seemed to stretch ear to ear. "Ethan Cooper, it sho' nuff a pleasure to finally meet you, seein' as you da' man most likely lost us dis' here war."

That one caught Ethan completely off guard. He said, "I'm not sure what you mean." But he looked over at Renaldo, and the guilty look on the man's face confirmed his suspicion.

"Well," Fagen began, "iffn' we'da' bin able to blow up Mr. Taft and Gen'ral McArthur back in Manila, dis' war be ova now."

The subject of the attempted assassination brought Renaldo back into the conversation. He said, "Captain Fagen's not exaggerating. We believed at the time that the assassinations would turn the American people decidedly against this oppressive war and cause them to demand their troops abandon the effort. It was a profound loss for us when you thwarted Captain Fagen's operation."

Ethan leaned back in the chair and, looking at Fagen, said, "So it *was* you."

"Yup," Fagen replied. "Worked on it fo' six months. You wiped it out in one night. I would sho' hate to meet ma' maker without knowing how you found us out. I always b'lieved one ma' own peoples gave us up."

Ethan could see no harm in giving Fagen an honest answer, so he told him about the patrol, and the group of young street vendors who gave them up because Fagen's men had cheated the kids of their just payment.

Fagen laughed openly, a gregarious belly laugh. "Ain't dat'da' way o' the world?" he bellowed. "Whooped by our own cruelty and human vices, seems like. Likely Jesus hisself had a good laugh that day."

Ethan reached for the wine jug. He was feeling much better by that point. "Wasn't sure how you'd take it if you found out."

Fagen slapped the table—hard and said, "Hellfire and brimstone, white man, it ain't 'bout you n' me. I's drinkin' wit'choo. Ain't I? It ain't personal 'tween us. We two men drinkin' t'getha like equals.

"I was fightin' on Luzon t' give these little bruthas they freedom. That's all. Good feelin' too. Ol' Roosevelt had me killin' Spaniards in Cuba, then McArthur had me killin' deez lil' brown bruthas on Luzon by the hundreds, all for da' white man who just'z soon see me swingin' from a tree. These folks ova here neva' hurt me. D'em the ones been shit on by da' white man, just like me. I ain't no nigga ova here, Ethan Cooper. Got me respect, got ma' freedom, got me ma' own house and a beautiful wife. Now how long you think da' Klan let me last back in Tampa da' way I is now?" He laughed again. "Every white soldier I kilt in this war had it comin,' but it weren't never personal. Felt good fightin' fo' a cause, but 'dem days ova' now. I's retired now. Finna raise me a family."

Ethan looked him squarely in the eye and said, "This war won't last too much longer, David. You know that. The Philippine Islands will be U.S. territory, every last one of them, and they will hunt you down."

Renaldo couldn't seem to keep from injecting himself into the discussion. He said, "I only hope I meet Major Glenn before that happens."

Fagen drained his glass, then said, "Don't matter. We be just fine right here. Did you know dis' place a gift? It's ma' pension from General Aguinaldo n' his whole staff. General Martinez sent twenty men here t' he'p me built dis' house, even give me da' animals. Ain't nobody in fifty mile o' here finna give me up. We all bruthas and sistas. As far as the white man know, Mad Dog David Fagen still on Luzon. You'll see. I's a retired soldier finna raise ma' family peaceable like, right here and die a old man in dis' here house."

Ethan had almost forgotten about the letter from General Martinez. He retrieved it from his pocket and held it out to Fagen. "Oh, General Martinez asked me to give you this letter. It's in English."

Renaldo instantly grabbed the letter from Ethan's hand. "I'll read it for you, Captain Fagen. The general has terrible handwriting."

He can't read, Ethan said to himself. *Renaldo knows it and Martinez doesn't.*

Renaldo read the letter aloud:

> *"Dear friend, if you are reading this letter, Mujer Guerrera and her companions have reached your home. As you know, Filipinos will always remember your great courage and contribution to our cause of freedom. You and I both know we cannot hold out forever against the Americans. My men and I will eventually return to our lives at least temporarily defeated, but safe and alive, all but one. The American defector, Lieutenant Alamo Jones, has served us faithfully and would likely face execution by the Americans. I ask you, in a final act of support, to provide a haven for him where you presently reside. I will send him to you when the time demands. Thank you, my friend, and good luck to you and your family. We shall see better days. Vicente Martinez.*

Fagen laughed again and said, "I sho' hope dat' boy know sumpn' bout farming."

"You'll take him?" Ethan asked.

Fagen laughed again. "C'ourse I will, long as he know who da' boss. I could use da hep' 'round here."

Following a much-needed dinner of fish, camotes, and more banana wine and coconut, Ethan rose from the table and said, "Is there an easy way down to the beach, David? Since I'm not a prisoner, I thought Tala might join me for a walk."

Asuncion forced a smile, and Ethan could see her conflict, but they both understood that what had brought them together was what would always keep them apart.

Fagen was anything but dumb. He flashed a coy grin and said, "No trouble t'all. Ma' man, *Jose,* show you the trail down." Then he winked. "Take a lamp and a couple o' blankets. Gits a mite chilly down there nights. Jug o' banana wine hep' keep you extra warm too. Oh, y'all can have your weapons back whenever you like."

CHAPTER TWENTY-FOUR

They emerged from the downhill trail into the soft light of a full moon, gigantic, bright, and suspended low off the horizon. Ethan placed the lamp in the sand to mark the trail. A dead calm sea just below the moon made the night quiver in silver tones. Ethan could see at least half a mile down the beach. Holding hands, they walked slowly along the edge of the water.

"At home, they call this a Beaver Moon," he said.

"Why?"

He laughed. "I don't know why. Nobody ever told me. I just know when the moon is full and big like this and low on the horizon, it's called a Beaver Moon. You need to know the *why* of everything. It's one of the things that makes you different."

She squeezed his hand. "I'm a doctor. I've lived most of my life in books. I would rather have grown up with my own people, but I don't resent my father for it. He made the best decisions he could in a difficult world."

"I like your father, but I'm glad you're different. As a rule, he doesn't think much of Americans."

"As a rule, who does?" She plopped down on the sand and started unlacing her boots. He sat down beside her. "As a nation, he deplores America. But my father judges people individually. You should know that by now. As for me, I never had time to think of politics or existential issues like independence and colonialism. I see that Americans have brought science and medicine to the Philippines. I see that Americans are building huge infrastructure here for health and education. Rizal was also a doctor, but he was very unusual. Most of us have time only for medicine. If we change the world, it will be through our medicine."

"Why didn't you tell Cristina her father is dying?"

"You ask difficult questions," she replied. "I suppose it's because I'm still my father's daughter. That's not up to me. It's my uncle's decision, but I agree with it now. Let her be happy as long as she can. A day, a week, a month…

"I'm a bit confused," she announced, changing the subject. "Why are we here together?"

"There's something I need to tell you about Asuncion," he confided. It was time she knew everything.

She dropped down into the sand, facing the water. "I know you made love. She told me. She told me everything."

"It doesn't change your opinion of me?" He asked, sitting down beside her.

"Of course not," she declared, dismissively. "I don't judge people. Life is complicated for everyone. But she does love you, Ethan."

Ethan had to consider that for a minute. It wasn't an accusation, just a clinical observation from a doctor. He smiled and said, "In a way, she might, I guess, but not how you think. Tell me, can you accurately diagnose a disease from one symptom? Say a fever and nothing else?"

"Of course not. It's more complicated than that. I see your point."

To his surprise, Tala reached into his carry bag for the banana wine, downing a healthy swig right from the jug. He joined her. She said, "What is your real name?"

He laughed and sprang to his feet, minus shoes. He found a flat pebble and handed it to her. "You have a lot of questions. Tell you what," he said. "Try to skip this stone on the water. I'll give you one question just for landing it in the water and another one for every time the stone skips."

He knew before the stone left her hand that she would never play baseball. Her form was pitiful, and the stone barely breached the surf before sinking. "One question," he said. "One only."

"She didn't hesitate. "Will you tell me the rest of your story?" was her choice. "You were at the dock near the coal plant with the crowd and a barge of *picket* men with guns coming to attack you."

"Pinkertons," he corrected her. "They are a kind of private police force for hire. Tensions were high as the barge prepared to dock. Everyone was armed. One of the strike leaders picked out me and another man to rush the dock with him and cut the bow line with a hatchet. As we started hacking away, someone fired a shot, and it was all out war. We were exposed and a group of Pinkertons started firing on us from point blank range on the dock. We fired back and killed three of them."

"It doesn't sound like murder," she said.

"Not in a perfect world, but Allen Winslow, is one of the world's most influential men. He flashed his money to the newspapers and mustered his troops. Before we knew it, public opinion had turned against the strikers and in favor of Winslow. It wasn't long after that we were all indicted for murder. I'm the only one who got away."

"That has something to do with you rushing from the reception. Doesn't it?"

"Yup. One of the Pinkertons has been on my trail for a long time. It was quite a shock when I saw him in Manila, but he was killed in the attack on Apostol."

They turned around, heading back toward the lamplight. "Then what's your real name?" She asked.

Ethan considered giving her a bonus answer. He wasn't going back to Pennsylvania or anywhere else in North America. He didn't mind being Ethan Cooper, not anymore. Ethan Cooper was the man who had finally opened his eyes, with help from Marty and Asuncion, allowing him to see beyond the visions and prejudices and motives of people with power over whole countries. He would never change the cruelty of politics, he knew, but liked seeing things and people more clearly for what and who they really were. Yes, he liked Ethan Cooper a lot right about now, so he smiled and said, "That's another question for another day. The man you know is named Ethan Cooper."

Tala was quiet for a minute, then said, "I'm going back with Renaldo in the morning."

He never saw that pitch coming. "Why?" he asked. "You made it out of there. You're safe."

"We should go back now."

He took her arm, stepping in front to face her. "First, tell me why. Hell is coming to that place. You could be killed. Worse!"

She resumed her stride. "My father is there. I know him. He will take it upon himself to be their physician. He will feel a responsibility to help the people as well. Two doctors are better than one. Besides, my Uncle Charles is there and terminally ill. What else would I do?"

He searched aimlessly for words, like a child. "I thought...well..."

"No, Ethan. That will never be. I told you before, my own people are virtually a race of strangers. I am not at that point in my life where I would even think about…"

He thought of his old friend, Jimmy Jeffries. *You have good in you, Boy…If you manage to live long enough, listen to it and let it guide you over time; it will show you who you are.* He had feelings for this woman. More than that, he respected and admired her, all of which made her dismissal of his affections more hurtful. But he understood her dilemma and her determination perhaps because he had survived the same journey on which Tala had only just embarked.

With unrepentant tears, Ethan took her gently into his arms, kissing her lips there on the silvery beach, under the Beaver Moon. "A part of me will be with you," he whispered.

EPILOGUE

Six months later, on Panay Island

The Quartermaster job had worked out well for Ethan Cooper. He was even hoping it might develop into a permanent thing. Turned out he had a head for numbers, just like his mother had claimed when he was seven or eight. He'd breezed through the training to become a full-fledged buyer for the U.S. Army. Sugar, lumber, nails, clothing, whatever appeared on his ten-page monthly shopping list and conformed to his authorized specifications and regulations.

The rules were simple. Wait for a good quality, suitable item and buy it as cheaply as possible. Then ship it to places that needed it. No killing, no burning, and no more hacking through miles of virgin jungle and no more severed heads rolling on tables. The nightmares? Well, maybe in time…

With the leftover money from Grayson and the Canadian's good word to a local banker, he'd bought some pallets of real lumber and a little piece of coastal land on the edge of town from a local farmer. *Casa Cooper* was finally under construction by some grateful local laborers.

Life had settled down for Ethan Cooper and the new, *Americanized* Philippine Islands pulsated with commerce and trade for some people at least, while the insurgency had been reduced to a few roving gangs of bandits on the smaller islands. Everyone had amnesty, and it was said the population of Apostol, X-104, what was left of it, had returned to rebuild its town. One of the officers over at Camp Lincoln had even told Ethan that Mariano Obrador, leader of the attack, had cashed in and was the town's new mayor. He'd heard nothing of Asuncion, and neither he nor Grayson knew the whereabouts of Tala and her father.

Ethan was doing paperwork by lamplight near dinner time in his temporary home, a small nipa hut beside the new construction, when he heard the buggy creaking its way up the trail toward the hut. From the door, he could make out a man and a woman in the seat. It looked like she was holding a baby. He filled a bucket from his well and went over to tend the horse and welcome his visitors. They were his first.

"Hello, Ethan," said Sixto, jumping down from the rig.

Ethan didn't bother taking the doctor's hand. He embraced the man in a bear hug and said, "Good to see you, my friend."

Sixto pointed to the woman and said, "I brought Cristina and my little niece, Asuncion Fagen. We're hoping you might make room for some weary travelers tonight."

Sixto took the baby as Ethan helped Cristina down from the buggy and embraced her warmly. He said, "Asuncion?"

Sixto held up the baby girl and pulled the blanket from her face. He said, "Yes. Asuncion, meet your Uncle Ethan. Thank the saints above that she has her mother's looks."

Cristina chided him playfully, "Uncle Sixto."

"We brought some things from town to eat," Sixto said, "even found a bottle of whiskey. Oh, I almost forgot. We brought another visitor."

From the tiny rear seat of the buggy, emerged the diminutive figure of Doctor Tala Espinosa. Tala smiled, extending her hand as was her habit. Ethan simply ignored the gesture, taking her into a full embrace. "Well," he muttered, "I'm speechless. This is a wonderful surprise." Turning to the others, he said, "Come on in," waving them to the hut. "It's not much now, but the house will be very nice. I'll take care of the horse."

AFTER THEY HAD ALL SETTLED IN AND EATEN, CRISTINA PUT THE baby down for the night in her blanket on a soft mat. Ethan poured the whiskey. He said to Sixto, "It's hard to believe you brought the baby through all that jungle."

Sixto laughed and said, "Good Lord, no. I hired a real boat, an old launch with a sheltered cabin, or Charles did. We sailed across to pick them up right at their farm. David sent word how to get there by boat. He sends his greetings."

Ethan could barely hide his excitement over having guests. He refilled the empty glasses on his crude table and said to Tala, "So you and your father were with the general until the end?"

"Back and forth between there and the camp in the mountains. Hundreds more people died, but we were able to help many others.

Several months ago, we went back with them to help rebuild the town."

"Was Asuncion with you?" Ethan asked. "Is she all right?"

"She's in good health," Tala said. "We worked closely together and became very good friends. She told me all about Martin Tours. You should know that the envelope you gave her included money to help rebuild the church. The work is already underway. That money was everything he had."

With the baby settled down and asleep, Cristina walked over to Ethan at the table. Bending down, she gave him a warm hug. "Thank you for sending word about my father," she said. "I wanted to see him. I wanted him to see my baby and to know that I'm happy. We want you to come with us to visit him."

"It's not far. I'd be honored," Ethan said. "I've been there many times." With that, he walked over to the corner of the hut and started rummaging through a pile of boxes looking for the clipping. By chance, he also came across the unfinished letter to Marty Tours and, for whatever reason, slipped it into his shirt pocket. He said, "I have something for Cristina as well, something that will also amuse David Fagen. Ah, here it is."

Unfolding a New York newspaper article from a few months back, he handed it to Cristina. "Read it," he said, smiling. "David will get a kick out of it too. Tell him I underestimated him."

Reliable sources have reported that on December 5, 1901, a Tagalog hunter on Luzon delivered a severed head to American authorities, claiming it to be the head of the notorious deserter, David Fagen, a highly skilled Negro infantry soldier. Fagen defected to the Philippine Forces in 1899 and wreaked havoc on U.S. Forces across Luzon for more than a year, most infamously capturing a steamboat on the Pampanga River, inflicting multiple U.S fatalities. The native hunter also delivered the West Point ring of Lieutenant Frederick W. Alstaetter, an American officer captured by Fagen in one of the actions. The lieutenant remains missing. While U.S. Army Headquarters, Philippines, declined to confirm the report of Fagen's death, the office issued a brief statement indicating that the head 'appears' to be that of the notorious deserter and the $600 reward for the death or capture of Fagen was withdrawn on December 12 and paid."

"This will please David very much," Cristina said. "David makes light of it, but the prospect of being hunted down by the Americans has weighed heavily on him. He still sleeps with a pistol and suffers horrible nightmares."

Ethan chuckled. "Well, he's not the only one with nightmares, but being a Negro works in his favor this time. They assume he's stupid, and they couldn't be more wrong. That trick with the ring was brilliant, and the Army will never admit he fooled them. Just make sure he keeps a low profile. He does like to have fun."

Ethan grabbed an oil lamp from the table and said, "Come on. I want to introduce you to my new friend."

"I'd better not leave the baby," Cristina said.

"It's all right. The corral is just outside. You can hear the baby if she wakes."

Sixto started to laugh before they all reached the corral. "How in the world did you end up with Pop?" The old mule with the gray hair just kept grazing like he was deaf or bored. He had his own little area of the corral.

"Renaldo came to see me about a month ago," Ethan replied, "after the amnesty. He brought me Pop as a gift from Vicente Martinez. Pop will have a good life here."

"He's earned it," Sixto declared.

Cristina had to stand on the bottom rail to get a good look. Sixto's old buggy horse looked content enough near the trough but Ethan's new horse, a beautiful, chestnut-red mare, trotted the perimeter nervously. A wide, white strip ran from the top of her head to her nose.

"They call the stripe a 'blaze,'" he said. "Her name is Esmeralda. She's temperamental. This is her territory. It's been a while since she's had to deal with other horses. I got her at the army auction over at Camp Lincoln. She's eight years old, close to retirement age, and she's only known one soldier. They trusted each other and were best friends. He was wounded on Luzon about a year ago and decorated for bravery, can never ride again, so they transferred him to Fort DeSoto in Florida.

"The horse had trouble dealing with the loss, couldn't seem to adjust to another rider, so they auctioned her with the older horses. We're trying to get to know each other, and I think it will be okay eventually. Pop helps. Esmeralda and I have plenty of time. I think she's getting to trust me."

"It's kind of a sad story," Sixto said. "Is that why you picked her?"

"Partly, I guess. Esmeralda and I have a lot in common. Hers is a normal reaction to loss, I think. I don't know the fancy words, but I think Esmeralda just wanted to quit, saw things in simple terms, couldn't see she had a whole life ahead of her and a lot to offer even without her friend. I think about Marty a lot and the way he died. Esmeralda and I just kind of make each other feel better, I think."

Ethan tapped on the fence and made a clicking sound, calling the horse's name. "Esmeralda, come on over, girl." Esmeralda stopped in her tracks, swinging her majestic head back toward the sounds, frozen for a minute, like she was trying to decide. Then she moseyed over to the fence, head bobbing up and down, and planted her big, wet nose on Ethan's ear.

Sixto reached over the top rail and started to pat Esmeralda on the cheek. Ethan said, "She likes it when you scratch hard behind her ears."

Esmeralda sneezed, blowing Sixto back off the fencing, and everyone laughed. Then Cristina said, "David reminded me to tell you that Alamo Jones has still not shown up at our place, and David hasn't heard a word about him."

"He won't be coming," Ethan replied. "The Makabebe Scouts captured Jonesy about three months ago right before Martinez surrendered and took the oath. The Army court-martialed him in Manila last month and sentenced him to life in prison. Executing him would have been kinder."

"I'm sorry," Sixto said.

They started heading back for the hut, and Ethan said, "I think it's time Esmeralda and I took a ride together. I'll saddle her up in the morning, and we'll all head for Grayson's place early."

THE WHOLE GRAYSON HOUSE REEKED OF DEATH. IT WAS ETHAN'S second visit to the old Spanish-style urban villa in Iloilo this month. He had been helping Grayson with books of account.

Grayson had been spiraling downhill since he was released in the prisoner exchange around three months ago. He'd greeted Ethan with genuine warmth, even apologized for his multiple deceptions, and the two had become real friends.

Grayson hadn't seen Cristina since their adventure in the jungle, so on this visit, Ethan opted to wait in the parlor while the Filipina housekeeper escorted the others into the first-floor room where Charles Grayson awaited his appointment with the Angel of Death.

The housekeeper served Ethan refreshments, and he waited patiently until Sixto came into the parlor an hour or so later. "Charles would like to see you," Sixto announced.

A blind man could see Grayson was on his last leg, but Ethan had seen worse, like First Sergeant Flood's severed head staring at him upside down from a plate of beans. Grayson managed to lift his palm in a "hi" sign and wave Ethan in closer. Using all his effort, he held out an envelope for Ethan and whispered, "Take this to my lawyer. You can trust him. Sixto will go with you. All the information is in there. Cristina and the baby get everything: the farms, my business, this house. This is a power of attorney. Protect her. Manage everything for her and see they are cared for. Do this for me. I trust you."

Ethan felt Tala touching his arm. "Of course, I will," he said.

GRAYSON DIED THAT VERY DAY BEFORE DINNER, AND CRISTINA buried him with a full Catholic mass and service the following Saturday. He must have been less duplicitous in his business life, Ethan figured, because the church service teemed with mourners from all classes of people: farmers, sharecroppers and businessmen from Negros, Panay, and even two bankers who made the trip from Manila. Word had gotten out about Ethan's new responsibilities, and he was literally pelted with business cards, cigars, and offers of lunch at the "club." Ethan knew he had a lot to learn and had been reassured by Grayson that he could count on the lawyer for honest and straightforward counsel.

A FEW DAYS LATER, ETHAN AND ESMERALDA RODE TO THE ILOILO docks to see Cristina and little Asuncion board their vessel for the trip back to the place that never existed. Sixto had arranged for himself and Tala to accompany them safely back home before heading back to Manila. There was no sign of Tala on the dock.

"Where's Tala?" Ethan asked.

"She decided to stay on to take care of Charles' house until we get things settled," Sixto replied. "She asked me to extend you an invitation to dine with her tonight." The news tickled him down to the toe of his left boot, but he thought it best not to speculate on her motives.

Ethan promised to visit the Fagen family before the next rainy season. In the meantime, the co-conspirators had worked out a foolproof system of communication by written correspondence to keep Cristina advised on matters of business and finance. The departure was uncomfortably emotional, Ethan thought, but a nudge from Esmeralda immersed him enthusiastically into the hug festival. There were also tears.

Cristina kissed him on the cheek. "Be well, Ethan Cooper," she said through the tears. "You are a good man." It was the third time Ethan had heard that and, by now, he was starting to believe it might be true.

CONVENIENTLY, ETHAN'S OFFICE FOR THE QUARTERMASTER Department was located less than a quarter mile from the docks, and he arrived at work nearly on time. His boss was on business in Manila, and their secretary was not due for another hour.

He took a seat at his desk, back to the window, withdrew the letter from his pocket, the unfinished letter to Marty, and unfolded it onto the desk. So much had changed in the months since he'd last seen it. He read the letter again, silently.

With a strong morning sun at his back, he picked up the pen from the inkwell and resumed:

(resumed May, 1902)...I'm back to finish this letter, Marty, as best I am able, and to share a few details you may find of interest. Many things have changed here in the intervening six months since I set page one to paper, including myself, but they have changed so rapidly I have only now reached any conclusions about their meaning.

Since beginning to craft this correspondence, I have managed to do some good over here. I am reticent to divulge details for fear of beating my own drum like a damned braggard or such. My circle contains many friends here now, including an old cavalry horse named Esmeralda and a Negro deserter named David Fagen. Yes, that David Fagen. I should also mention that Renaldo works for me now and has proven to be a most effective administrator with a gift for organization.

While the melancholy seldom visits these days, I am not without problems. That brings me to the important matter weighing on my mind at present, Doctor Tala Espinosa, the young woman in the golden lace dress from the reception. She is a handsome woman, as you may recall, with fine Asian features and a fearsome intellect. Yours truly has for some time harbored an interest in becoming better acquainted, and my belief is that Tala may no longer be entirely opposed to the idea. She has even invited me to dine with her this evening.

You will be pleased to know that Tala and Asuncion became close friends in the months leading up to the peace agreement and general amnesty. My friend, you were always correct in your lofty opinion of Asuncion's character. In doubting her, I doubted you, and for that I apologize.

Tala informs me that the people of Apostol, mainly Asuncion, were thrilled with your gift of four hundred American dollars for renovation of the village church. You should know the church when complete will include a statue to St. Martin of Tours, Patron Saint of Soldiers. I may never visit the church as the trip may unavoidably include a confrontation with that police chief Obrador. I still believe him to be a shifty character and worthy of the knife. But I digress...

My current problem or problems, as you will by now suspect, are these damned naked sisters on my arms, Nona and Mona. Until today, I have been successful in covering up the girls while in Tala's presence, but that could change. Success in love inevitably means the girls will make their presence known, exposing me as a person of ill repute or even a follower of Satan. I am neither of those as you know.

Iloilo is loaded to the barrelhead with high class people. Some new friends of mine here regularly eat lunch in restaurants and "clubs" with cloth napkins and silver forks and such.

Anyway, I don't know what will happen with Tala, but time will tell. Thanks for listening to me ramble on, old friend. I think my Pop might finally be proud if he could see me now in the light of my recent conduct and dealings and such. I am also going to write old Jimmy Jeffries, the old Negro who so kindly helped me escape from Pittsburgh. Writing to you now and again seems to help focus my thoughts and make sense of things, so look for another correspondence down the road.

Oh, and one more thing, Marty. My travels and experiences over this past year obligate me to declare that the Pope in Rome never deserved the service of a man such as Martin Tours or whatever the hell your Polish name is. You were the best priest he ever had…and a better one than you or he ever knew.

Your friend always,
Ethan Cooper, Esquire
Manager, Grayson Enterprises

ETHAN COULDN'T REMEMBER A MORE ENJOYABLE DINNER, COMPLETE with silver, tablecloth, and candles. In addition to free room and board, Tala had inherited the services of Grayson's housekeeper, a local woman with excellent cooking skills. She served them dinner as if they were in a fine restaurant, in courses one by one. The main dish was something called Chicken Adobo. The bird, served in boneless strips, was perfectly cooked with some kind of sauce, but the spices would take some getting used to, he thought. Not surprising, since most everything he'd eaten from the Philippines so far was out of a can, pulled straight from a tree or yanked from the dirt.

They kept the conversation mostly light during dinner, his jobs, her future plans, even Grayson's house, a fine city house squeezed into Iloilo's most fashionable street. In contrast to their previous conversations, Tala now seemed uncertain about her future and more at ease with herself as a Filipina than she was back in the jungle. He'd expected as much, maybe even hoped for it. Six months in that jungle with hundreds of poor, sick souls had surely tested her metal.

Tala had mentored under the perfect teacher as well. Asuncion was, if nothing else, the quintessential *Filipina* in every respect: strong, compassionate, loyal, and brave almost beyond her own capacity. The change gave Ethan hope.

The housekeeper announced she would serve dessert in the sitting room forthwith, and the couple followed her in where coffee was waiting. Ethan was adjusting nicely to these strange customs of society but stressed by the weight of his imminent confession.

With the dessert served and the housekeeper gone, Ethan assumed a somber tone. "Tala, I don't know what will happen in the future," he began, "but if we decide to keep seeing each other, there is something about me you need to know now."

Tala looked up from her upholstered chair, incredulous and said, "Well, it seems to me we've already decided that, so you'd best tell me."

Using a hand gesture for emphasis, he said, "Of course, of course we have." He didn't, of course, actually know until that moment. Then he swallowed hard and rolled up both sleeves. "I've lived somewhat of a coarse life," he declared. Then, holding out his forearms, exposing Nona and Mona in all their naked splendor to the woman he loved, he said, "I'm not proud of these, but it seems I'm stuck with them."

Tala gasped. "Oh, good heavens," she declared, then burst into a fit of laughter, covering the small mouth with her left hand. "Yes," she added. "We will need to address the ladies going forward. Tell me, Ethan, is there a story that goes with these girls? After all, if we develop a relationship, they will be permanent parts of it."

It was the most supremely embarrassing moment of his life, but Ethan was determined not to hold back. "Yes," he confessed. "There is a story, and I will tell you now, if you like."

She held up her palm in an emphatic *stop* signal. "I don't think it's necessary to tell me the story. Oh, maybe someday when we know each other better but not now. Just meeting the girls for the first time is enough for tonight. All right?"

"That's all right with me," Ethan said, and it most certainly was.

"I think you're making too much of it," she said, obviously trying to relieve his embarrassment. "I'm told those tattoo artists around the army post at Camp Lincoln are very talented. Perhaps, one of them could ink some proper clothing onto the girls. I'm thinking a nice hat as well, something modest but fashionable. Then we could introduce them as your nieces."

She'd learned a lot in the jungle from Asuncion. "You're making fun of me," he said.

"Yes. I was," she replied, "but only to let you know I don't care about the girls. Well, maybe you *could* put something on them later, but I don't care what girls you have known or what sins you have committed. I see you through my own eyes and through the eyes of the many people who know and love you. That's enough. I will figure out how to live with the girls if we stay friends. Now, if there is nothing else you need to shock me with, let's eat our desert. I heard how you love bananas."

As the evening was about to end, Ethan was keenly aware he had not addressed the central issue on his mind. *Should I tell her?*

Not two months ago, Ethan had gotten ahold of a Pittsburgh newspaper on a business trip to Manila. It was right there on page one: *Governor Grants Full Pardons to Steel Plant Killers.* The story went on to detail how, on the eve of execution, two death row inmates were pardoned by the new governor as was the third man charged in the case, currently a fugitive.

The article went on to explain how evolution of public opinion in favor of the labor movement had combined with growing acceptance of labor unionization by industries to shed new attention on the case, leading to the generally accepted position that the killings were obviously in self-defense and the prosecutions politically motivated. In addition to the pardon, the company under a separate settlement agreement offered all three men full employment and back pay.

The pardon was a complete vindication for Ethan. He could go back whenever he wanted, to anywhere in the United States that tickled his fancy, with money in his pocket. He could have his name back.

What would she think if he told her the whole truth now? The truth was he had decided two months ago not to go back, not to claim the money. His freedom was all he ever wanted, freedom to choose what to do and where to live and even whom to be. He had made that choice before Tala ever stepped from the buggy that night, but she wouldn't believe that for a minute, not yet anyway.

If he told her now, she would think he was doing it for her, doing it under pressure. He could lose her before their life together even started, all out of some useless gesture of nobility. He wanted to live the rest of his life here among the people who taught him about love and pain and living. He would tell her in time, tell her everything. But first he needed her to understand all those reasons he would never go back. He needed Tala to see the Philippines through his eyes. Then, he would tell her.

He felt her tapping his shoulder. "Ethan, Ethan, wake up. Your mind is elsewhere. Your dessert is melting."

"Johan Glattfelder," he blurted out.

"What?" She asked.

"My old name," he said, "Johan Glattfelder. That's who I used to be. It's Pennsylvania Dutch."

"Oh, Lord," Tala exclaimed. "I like Ethan Cooper much better."

"So do I," he said, smiling. "So do I."

ABOUT THE AUTHOR

Bob was raised in Chicago, enlisting in the Air Force in 1968. Following four years of service as a Russian Linguist in the Security Service Command, a branch of the NSA, Bob attended DePaul University and the John Marshall Law School. With over thirty years of experience as a criminal defense lawyer in Chicago, Bob brings a lifetime of understanding and experience to his novels. His Running with Cannibals is the Grand Prize winner of the CIBA 2022 Hemingway Award for best 20th-century wartime fiction.

The author lives in the Chicago area.

http://www.robertsmithbooks.com

Also by Robert W. Smith

A Long Way from Clare
https://mybook.to/smithalwfclare

To Pledge Allegiance
https://mybook.to/smithtpa

A Gamble on Liberty
https://mybook.to/smithgambleonliberty

The Sakhalin Collection
https://mybook.to/smithsakhalin

Made in the USA
Monee, IL
09 December 2025

37979800R00142